Childhood in a
Sri Lankan Village

The Rutgers Series in Childhood Studies

The Rutgers Series in Childhood Studies is dedicated to increasing our understanding of children and childhoods, past and present, throughout the world. Children's voices and experiences are central. Authors come from a variety of fields, including anthropology, criminal justice, history, literature, psychology, religion, and sociology. The books in this series are intended for students, scholars, practitioners, and those who formulate policies that affect children's everyday lives and futures.

Edited by Myra Bluebond-Langner, Board of Governors Professor of Anthropology, Rutgers University and True Colours Chair in Palliative Care for Children and Young People, University College London, Institute of Child Health.

Advisory Board

Perri Klass, New York University
Jill Korbin, Case Western Reserve University
Bambi Schieffelin, New York University
Enid Schildkraut, American Museum of Natural History and Museum for
   African Art

Childhood in a Sri Lankan Village

Shaping Hierarchy and Desire

BAMBI L. CHAPIN

RUTGERS UNIVERSITY PRESS

NEW BRUNSWICK, NEW JERSEY, AND LONDON

LIBRARY OF CONGRESS CATALOGING-IN-PUBLICATION DATA

Chapin, Bambi L.

Childhood in a Sri Lankan village : shaping hierarchy and desire / Bambi L. Chapin.

  pages cm.—(Rutgers series in childhood studies)

Includes bibliographical references and index.

ISBN 978-0-8135-6166-0 (hardcover : alk. paper)—ISBN 978-0-8135-6165-3 (pbk. : alk. paper)—ISBN 978-0-8135-6167-7 (e-book)

  1. Children—Sri Lanka—Social conditions. 2. Children—Family relationships—Sri Lanka. 3. Child development—Sri Lanka. 4. Child psychology—Sri Lanka. 5. Parenting—Sri Lanka. 6. Sri Lanka—Social life and customs. I. Title.

HQ792.S72C53 2014

305.23095493—dc23

2013037737

A British Cataloging-in-Publication record for this
book is available from the British Library.

Visit our website: http://rutgerspress.rutgers.edu

Manufactured in the United States of America

For Tucker Wentworth Chapin,
who has grown up alongside this book

CONTENTS

ACKNOWLEDGMENTS

This book illustrates the ways that children are shaped by those around them, those who care for them, and those they feel strongly about. Likewise, this project and my own development have been shaped by many others—more than I could possibly list in this short space.

The central role in this project was played by the people in Sri Lanka who shared their lives, their homes, their help, and their friendship with me—and it is to them that I owe my biggest debt. Without their generosity, patience, and insight, this book would not have been possible and my research would not have been nearly so enriching. In order to protect the privacy of people in the place I have called Viligama, I have used pseudonyms and changed identifying information throughout the book, so I cannot name those who helped me the most. I hope they have some idea of how grateful I am to them. In addition, I am grateful to those who helped my family and me get settled into Sri Lanka and supported us while we were there: Loku Menike, Kush and Nandana, Velu, the Rajapaksa family, the Egodage family, and the teachers and families at Araliya Montessori School.

My work in Sri Lanka brought me into contact with fellow scholars and researchers who have shaped and supported my work in ways that I deeply appreciate. I am especially grateful to my research assistant, Inoka Baththanage, for her friendship as well as her assistance and insight. I am also grateful to the many others who helped me by tracking down information, transcribing and translating interviews, conducting surveys, and sharing their own research. This includes the village administrator (the Grama Niladhari), Kanthi at International Center for Ethnic Studies in Kandy, Tilak Jayatilake, sociology students from Peradeniya University, and my Sinhala teacher, Indika Ratnayake. I am grateful for the guidance of Professor Kalinga Tudor Silva, my supervisor at the University of Peradeniya, as well as advice from Professors Gerald Peiris, Indrasena Mendis, Sunil Goonasekera, and Gananath Obeyesekere. At Cornell's summer language program, during which I was supported by a Foreign Language and Area Studies scholarship, Professor W. S. Karunatillake, his wife Kamalavithi, and John Paolillo gave me a solid start on Sinhala before I ever got to Sri Lanka. Friendships and conversations with other researchers I met in that class and in Sri Lanka continue to shape my work, as do conversations with fellow members of the American Institute of Sri Lankan Studies (AISLS). In addition, the staff at the U.S.–Sri Lanka Fulbright office in Colombo made the early stage of my research possible, and the friendship of fellow students and scholars whom I met through that office and through the Intercollegiate Sri Lanka Education (ISLE) program in Kandy were also much appreciated.

The U.S.–Sri Lanka Fulbright Commission was the primary supporter of my initial field research, along with the University of California, San Diego's Department of Anthropology and Friends of the International Center. Funding for the two subsequent field trips as well as a portion of the analysis and writing was supported by the National Institute of Mental Health through a Postdoctoral Training Grant at the University of Chicago's Department of Comparative Human Development under the leadership of Rick Shweder. Since joining the faculty of the University of Maryland, Baltimore County, I have been fortunate to receive time off from teaching and summer support to allow me to concentrate on this book, as well as travel grants to present preliminary pieces at national conferences. I am also grateful to the Lemelson/SPA Conference Fund, which supported a conference on attachment that challenged me to think through this material in new ways, and to the AISLS, which supported my participation in a workshop for new books about South Asia. All of the research presented in this book was conducted with the approval of an Internal Review Board, either at the University of California, San Diego or the University of Chicago.

As I have developed this book over the past decade, I have presented pieces of it along the way. It has benefited from feedback at many workshops and conferences, including national conferences held by the American Anthropology Association, the Society for Psychological Anthropology, and the Annual Conference on South Asia hosted by the University of Wisconsin–Madison, as well as more intimate groups: UCSD's "Psychodynamic Seminar"; the University of Chicago's "Culture, Life Course, and Mental Health Workshop," "Personhood and Psyche in South Asia" group, and "Clinical Ethnography Workshop"; and UCLA's "Mind, Medicine, and Culture" workgroup. Portions of this book have also appeared in earlier published forms within *Countries and Their Cultures* (Chapin and Silva 2001), a special issue of *Ethos* (Chapin 2010b), and Quinn and Mageo's *Attachment Reconsidered: Cultural Perspectives on a Western Theory* (Chapin 2013), as well as in my dissertation (Chapin 2003). I learned much from the editors, reviewers, and co-authors as I worked on each of these pieces, especially Tudor Silva, Kathleen Barlow, and Janet Keller.

Many people helped directly and indirectly with the preparation of this manuscript. I am especially indebted to Jack Friedman, Naomi Quinn, Christine El Ouardani, and John Chapin, who read multiple drafts, talked through arguments with me, and shared their insights and encouragement. Marlie Wasserman, my editor at Rutgers, as well as Margaret Case and two anonymous reviewers, provided astute and speedy comments, for which the book is stronger. Uvindu Chandrasiri provided the cover photo. I am also indebted to countless colleagues, friends, and mentors who offered their comments and support during this project. I particularly want to thank Jeanne Marecek, Cindy Caron, Jeff Samuels, Mark Whitaker, Deborah Winslow, Susan Seymour, Sandya Hewamanne, Jenny Huberman, Jocelyn Marrow, Mike Kaufman, Hallie Kushner, April Leininger, Allen Johnson, Cate Knorr, Heather Rae-Espinoza, Julie Monteleone, Susan McDonough, Seth Messinger, and my students at the University of Chicago and UMBC. I also want to thank my teachers: Chris Crocker, Susan McKinnon, George Mentore, Cindy Lamm, Steve Parish, Mel Spiro, and especially Roy D'Andrade and Tanya Luhrmann; they have shaped my work and my mind more deeply than I can say.

Finally, I want to thank my friends and family for their patience and encouragement. Most important, I want to thank John and Tucker. Without their help, openness, humor, and companionship at every step of the way, I could not have done this research or written this book.

NOTE ON TRANSLATION
AND TRANSLITERATION

I have written this book with general readers in mind, rather than for specialists in Sinhala or others interested in close linguistic analysis. Accordingly, I have avoided diacritics and special characters, selecting spellings for Sinhala words that I felt best reflected local pronunciation, the Sinhala characters in the written words, and commonly used English transliterations, taking cues from other ethnographers of Sinhala speakers. For clarity, I sometimes pluralize Sinhala nouns by adding an "s," in keeping with common English practice.

The statements I have quoted from people in Viligama are generally drawn from tape-recorded interviews. I typically conducted these interviews in Sinhala, unless otherwise noted. The Sinhala statements have been translated as closely to the Sinhala as possible without losing the meaning. In both the Sinhala and English transcripts, I have changed identifiers and smoothed out minor infelicities for the purpose of clarity, for instance adding pronouns that are typically omitted in colloquial Sinhala.

Childhood in a
Sri Lankan Village

1

Introduction

In the Sri Lankan village where I conducted ethnographic fieldwork, little children are given whatever they demand. Yet, somehow, they turn into undemanding, well-behaved ten-year-olds. This surprised me. Like many in the United States, I believed that giving in to children's selfish and rudely articulated demands would reinforce that behavior, teaching children to expect that they will always get their way if they scream loudly enough. However, in the Sri Lankan village I call Viligama, this did not seem to be the case.

Other things surprised me, too. A two-year-old girl whose mother gave in to her temper tantrum demanding ice cream would, at other times, sit quietly on her mother's lap while her mother popped little balls of rice and curry into the girl's open mouth. As she fed the girl, the mother did not ask which bits of curry she wanted next or whether she was full. Instead, the mother confidently gave the child what the mother deemed suitable, as she did with the girl's eight-year-old brother. This surprised me because of the contrast between the two styles in which the girl was given things—one in which she demanded her own way and the other in which she passively accepted whatever she was given. But it also surprised me because of the contrast between the way this mother fed her children and how I fed my own son. Like many mothers in the United States, I had encouraged my son to feed himself from his own plate sitting in his own chair, beginning almost as early as he could eat solid food. By the time he was four and we were living in Viligama, mealtimes were sometimes a struggle, as I tried to get him to try unfamiliar foods, not expecting that he would just happily eat whatever I gave him.

Further, the style of interaction in Viligama in which children accepted what their caretakers provided, without a discussion of preferences or choices, did not stop at age six or at ten or even at eighteen. When it came time for young people to marry, ideally it was their parents or other senior relatives who would begin looking for a spouse for them. Ultimately, the consent of the young person was required, but their specific preferences were not something parents and children typically discussed with each other. For young people in this village, maturity was marked by a greater sensitivity to hierarchy and a deference the wisdom of elders, rather than the kinds of self-assertion, choice-making, and independence that typically mark growing up in the United States.

What is more, this type of interaction between parents and their children in Viligama struck me as similar to interactions between superiors and sub-ordinates that I observed in other settings in Sri Lanka. Students repeated the lessons teachers taught but did not ask questions or contribute their own ideas. Bakery counter workers did not correct the manager when he misinterpreted a customer's problem, even though they had been working to solve it before he arrived. When I asked people what should be done about the civil war going on at the time in the north of the country, my neighbors said that the politicians should solve it. Senior people should provide what they judged junior people to need, without consulting those juniors directly. The juniors, in turn, held their tongues, accepting what they were given—although they might leave a relation-ship or otherwise act out their displeasure if they were not being taken care of satisfactorily.

These kinds of observations prompted many questions for me—questions about people's relationships, about their wishes and desires, and about how these developed. My own cultural understandings about people and relation-ships were not very helpful in answering such questions. These understandings that I carried with me, formed by my own experiences growing up and living in the United States, included a firm—if not uncritical—grounding in the ideas of human psychology and healthy personhood that circulated widely there. In trying to work out these initially puzzling observations, I learned not only about life in this Sri Lankan village, but about the limits of my own cultural understandings.

This, of course, is how anthropological fieldwork works. What is initially strange becomes familiar, and what were taken-for-granted truths are recog-nized as products of one's own cultural context. Through my participation in and observation of daily life in this village, through my interviews and casual conversations with those who lived there, I arrived at a clearer view of the life worlds of the people I came to know in Sri Lanka, a better understanding of the cultural models they used to act and interpret action, and a better grasp of the kinds of relationships and selves they valued. I also gained a clearer understanding of how people developed within this particular context, how they felt, and what they cared about. This, in turn, gave me a clearer view of the limits of my own cultural theories of personhood and suggested approaches to crafting ones that might apply more universally. My observations of life in rural Sri Lanka and my efforts to make sense of them also suggested a model for thinking about what culture is and how it is transmitted, taken up, used, and transformed through everyday interactions. This book is the result of those efforts.

The Book

At its core, this book is about relationships, why people participate in them as they do, and what they learn through them. It is both an effort to describe the ways that people relate in a Sinhala village in central Sri Lanka and an argument about how such interactions form and are formed by the participants. This book describes ways that Sinhala children in rural Sri Lanka grow up to understand, participate in, and care about relationships with others and how they come to understand and experience themselves. Through early and ongoing everyday interactions with others, children build sets of understandings, habits of action, and orientations of desire. From the beginnings of their lives, people come to know and feel about themselves and their world through interaction with vitally important others. Although this process begins in childhood and has its most foundational effects then, it continues throughout the life course. In their moment-by-moment interactions with each other, people continually bring themselves and the systems in which they live into being. I argue that it is through emotionally charged relationships, as enacted in everyday moments, that people acquire and mobilize culture; to understand those relationships is to understand that process.

In this book, I describe some of those everyday moments that I observed in Viligama and elsewhere in Sri Lanka. I collected these observations and the commentary on them from people I knew over several field visits to Sri Lanka, the first and longest of which was for two years beginning in 1999. During these visits, which I will describe in more detail later in this chapter, I primarily interacted with the women and children who lived in this Sinhala-speaking village in the Central Province of the island. There, I collected extensive ethnographic material through participant observation, person-centered interviews, and community surveys. This set of observations focused on desires and relationships—how they are experienced, shaped, and enacted in a variety of contexts at different points over a life course—provides the material for this book.

I present this material with two main goals in mind. The first is to describe and document these intimate interactions, particularly those that involve children, in order to contribute to the scant ethnographic record on Sinhala families and child rearing. The second is to provide an illustration of and support for my claim that culture is learned, used, and transmitted through emotionally

laden relationships as they are enacted in the course of everyday life. Along
the way, I describe how my own cultural assumptions and those embedded
in the psychological literature on child development were shaken up—and I
present these in the hope of unsettling some of this "common sense" my readers
might share.

In what is to follow, I will describe how this project developed and something about the village and the island I came to know. I will then begin with a
closely focused analysis of family interactions around one particular two-year-
old girl. As the book progresses, the view widens, focusing progressively on a
range of children and their families, interaction outside of the home, adult
patterns of social interaction in different contexts, and, finally, efforts at social
change. Throughout, I will introduce initially puzzling observations that led me
to further investigation and eventually to greater clarity, both about the cultural world that the people of Viligama inhabit and about the processes through
which culture is enacted, conveyed, taken up, and altered. In the conclusion, I
will return to the discussion opened in this introductory chapter, summarizing
my findings and the contributions I aim to make.

In the remainder of this opening chapter, I will summarize the field research
I conducted that led to this book and introduce key theoretical perspectives
with which it engages. In Chapter 2, I present an overview of Sri Lanka, its history, and its people. In the following two chapters, I examine cultural lessons
and ways of being that children are internalizing through early interaction with
important others, taking up the puzzles involving desires and ways of relating that opened this book. Chapter 3 investigates how two-year-old children
who are given everything they demand turn into undemanding ten-year-olds.
Through this examination, I argue that the combination of continuous indulgence with disappointing social, material, and emotional results leads children
to disavow their own desires by middle childhood. I argue that this is linked
in complex ways to Buddhist and other cultural doctrines about desire, suffering, and destruction. Chapter 4 examines a very different pattern of interaction
between children and their caretakers, a pattern reflected in the ways that children are fed by hand mentioned earlier. In these types of interactions, children
wait passively, rather than asserting their desires, accepting the actions, gifts,
and decisions of their superiors. I argue that in these experiences children
learn and imbue with feeling a cultural model of hierarchical relationships and
a way of being that they will bring with them into other domains. I use this
analysis of how children learn to participate in hierarchies to contribute to a
more culturally informed theory of the development of attachment.

The second part of the book examines how these cultural lessons learned
at home are combined, mobilized, and made more complex as children grow up
and move into a wider society. Chapter 5 explores how several teen-aged girls

and the people around them draw on the lessons about desire and relationships described in the earlier chapters to understand their conflicts and emotions. This chapter also explores the limits of those cultural understandings in helping to sort out complex feelings and relationships. Chapter 6 examines how the lessons learned in intimate relationships emerge in and are potentially changed by participation in other types of relationships and institutions, focusing in particular on an education system responding to globally circulating ideas.

The understandings about desire and hierarchy that this book describes are central and interrelated cultural themes in Viligama, especially as they relate to children. I am not arguing, however, that these are the only themes, cultural models, or experiences that matter in the lives of the people who live there. Nor am I claiming that these patterns I describe are static or shared evenly by all people in Viligama, let alone by the whole nation. Rather, I present these sets of observations and my exegeses of them in order to offer a clearer understanding of how culture is transmitted by one person and reassembled by another during the daily interactions through which people make their lives. I use it to demonstrate how people make use of culture actively, if not always consciously. I also use it to demonstrate the importance of looking at interaction and relationships rather than considering individuals in isolation from one another.

In the final chapter, I summarize my description of these important, though not all-inclusive, aspects of child socialization and cultural lessons in a Sri Lankan village, emphasizing how they fit together, overlap, and contradict one another, offering an array of possibilities that people use to act, feel, and interpret. I return to the discussion begun here about what this analysis of Sinhala relationships suggests for a more general model of enculturation, elaborating the argument I am making about the ways that people learn, transmit, transfer, and transform culture through emotionally charged everyday interactions with others, who are themselves involved in the same process.

In each chapter, I raise descriptive and theoretical issues that extend beyond this particular ethnographic setting. I discuss the variability and patterning of child rearing and child development across cultures. I examine the relationship between explicit cultural doctrines and individual psychology, advocating the view that everyday interactions shape both. I introduce and draw on cognitive anthropology and psychodynamic theories, as well as theoretical perspectives on the role of practice, demonstrating their usefulness in understanding how culture is internalized.

Throughout, I emphasize that it is not "the culture" doing things, but people doing things—individual actors, including children, making interpretations and choices in a field of possibilities shaped by culture and social structure, as well as historical, political, and economic contingencies. At the same time, this field of possibilities is continually being reshaped by the interpretations, feelings, actions, and choices of fellow actors. By attending to the dynamic processes between and within people as well as the sociocultural medium in which they occur, I provide a model of and for thinking about how everyday practices lead children to develop culturally patterned thoughts, behaviors, and feelings, preparing them to find subsequently encountered cultural material and social interaction meaningful in ways consonant with those around them.

Fieldwork

In October of 1999, I moved to Sri Lanka with my husband, John, and our three-and-a-half-year-old son, Tucker. I had come to conduct my doctoral fieldwork, while John worked on several writing projects of his own. We landed outside of the principal city of Colombo and headed to Kandy, the provincial capital of the area that would be the site of my research and our home for the next two years. My initial research began with eight months living in the town of Kandy, after which we moved to the village I call Viligama, which is the focus of this book.[1] While living in Viligama for the next sixteen months, I employed participant observation and person-centered interviewing, along with other data collection methods. In 2004 and again in 2006, I returned to Viligama for month-long visits to collect additional material. In Chapter 2, I will give a more comprehensive overview of Sri Lanka. Here I introduce Kandy, Viligama, and the research I conducted there.

Kandy

Lush and temperate, Mahanuwara, Kandy's Sinhala name, is a city of about 100,000 people nestled in the central hills of Sri Lanka, the island nation located just south of India.[2] Predominantly Sinhala speaking and Theravada Buddhist, this city is in some ways the symbolic capital of the nation as it is imagined by the island's Sinhala majority. It was the last stronghold of the Sinhala kings until it fell to the British in 1815. It is the site of the Dalada Maligawa, the Sacred Temple of the Tooth that houses a tooth relic of the Buddha, from which the state derives religious authority. Today, Kandy is a bustling commercial center with shops, banks, Internet cafes, and offices, as well as street vendors and produce markets. It is home to many schools, including several of the island's most elite, and on its outskirts is one of the premier public universities.

During the first eight months of my initial two-year field stay in Sri Lanka, my family and I rented a dusty, colonial-era house in Kandy. One of the first things we did after moving in was to look for a housekeeper to come a few days a week. With a stroke of good fortune, we were introduced to Loku Menike. A widow from a village in the hills above town, she had not been a professional housekeeper before. This and the fact that she was an exceptional cook were both unexpected and unmitigated blessings. Since she had never been a servant and I had never had a servant, we negotiated a relationship of our own, one that was partly servant-madam, partly mother-daughter. Because she claimed to speak no English, she was my best Sinhala teacher, as she was my teacher and guide in so many things.

During those first few months, we also met others who would continue to be a part of our lives and my research effort. Indika Ratnayake, a young single woman from a middle-class family who spoke English as well as Sinhala, became my official language tutor and translator, helping with consent forms and assessment tools, initial interviews, and transcript translation. Throughout my stay in Sri Lanka, I made regular visits to the University of Peradeniya, under the auspices of which my visas and funding were approved. The best part of these visits was the chance to talk with Dr. Kalinga Tudor Silva, the sociology professor who had been assigned as my advisor by the Fulbright Commission, which funded my initial research. During one of these early visits, he suggested I meet one of his former undergraduate students, Inoka Baththanage, a young woman from a rural, Sinhala-speaking family not far from the university.

With Inoka, I had what I think of as an "arranged friendship." Professor Silva thought that she and I could help each other. Both of us needed to practice our language skills if we were to advance in our studies. I needed to practice Sinhala, and Inoka needed to practice English. So, at Professor Silva's direction, we began to meet regularly to talk, half in English and half in Sinhala. At first it was awkward, sometimes frustrating, and occasionally dull. Neither of us had yet mastered complicated grammatical forms or much useful vocabulary, so our conversations were restricted to talking about who was in our families, what we liked and did not like, and when we would meet next. Out of obligation to our mutual teacher, we continued to meet. Little by little, not only did our language skills improve but our conversations also became richer and more intimate. Our interest in, admiration of, and affection for each other was growing as well. Within a short time, she had become my best friend. I could not wait until the next time we would meet, saving up questions to ask her and coming to count on her insights. A year later, she joined me in an official capacity as my research assistant. The fieldwork and analysis presented here bear the stamp of her energy, empathy, and insight.

My son, Tucker, was also developing friendships that brought us deeper into the fabric of social relationships. When we first moved into the Kandy house, we discovered that right next door was an English-medium "Montessori school," as preschools in Sri Lanka are generally called regardless of their adherence to the Montessori method. Relying on the connections of the well-to-do woman whose compound we shared, we arranged to send our son to this little school. It turned out that "English-medium" meant, in this case, that the teachers were young women from elite, English-speaking families who primarily spoke English to the children at the school, but that most of the children spoke no English at home. The parents of the students were mostly upwardly aspiring professionals who sent their children to this school in order that they learn English and prepare for competitive admission to Kandy's better schools.

It was through Tucker's friends at this school that our family forged some of our most important social relationships on the island. When I participated with the other mothers—waiting for the children, attending pageants, going on fieldtrips, visiting each others' homes—I did so not as a researcher but as a fellow mother. Through these friendships, we were also invited on some of our more interesting journeys in Sri Lanka. The father of one of Tucker's best friends managed a tea estate, and we spent several weekends there. Another friend's father invited us to accompany his family and the army training group he led on a pilgrimage to Sri Pada, a sacred temple-topped mountain. The openness of these and other friends we made while living in Kandy provided us intimate access to many aspects of life on the island, as well as much appreciated friendship and support.

Viligama

After eight months in Kandy, my family and I moved to a house in Viligama, the village that would be the primary setting for my study of family life and child rearing in Sri Lanka. In this small community, I hoped to see how people's experiences interacting with each other over time shaped who they were, what they thought, and how they felt. I was particularly interested in seeing how these interactions over time shaped people's interaction with their own children, in turn shaping those children. In order to do this, I wanted to be in a place where people interacted with each other on a daily basis, where there were multiple ties between neighbors, and where relationships had been playing out over a long period of time. Viligama was such a place.

Viligama is about a twenty minute bus ride from Kandy, in the warmer, drier region just to its north. The house we rented there was at the intersection of the two main roads that ran through the village. These narrow roads were partly paved, rutted by the rain and the large public buses that came to and from the village twice a day, as well as by traffic from the more frequent private buses, the hired school vans and three-wheeled taxies, and the few motorcycles and bicycles that people owned. We found this house through a contact at the university whose wife worked at the Viligama school and knew a family who might want to rent out their house. This house was one of the nicer ones in the village, with brick and plaster walls in the front, mud ones in the back, a tile roof, and poured cement floors. There were three bedrooms in the front part of the house, arranged around a large living space with two sitting areas, a dining table, and an upright piano that was the prized possession of our landlord. In the back was a kitchen, a storage room, and a small Western-style toilet, as well as an in-ground toilet outside. The house had electricity and piping from the municipal water system, although the water only came sporadically while we were there, and there were regular cuts to the electricity. Around the house were mango, avocado, and coconut trees, which kept the house cool much of the day, along with banana, guava, and coffee plants.

Some of the other houses in the village were similar, with a few that boasted of second stories or tile floors. Many were simpler, with walls of cinderblock or wattle and daub, roofs of asbestos or corrugated metal, and dung floors. Some of the houses had been there for generations, but many were newer. It was not uncommon to see homes in partial states of construction, rebar sticking up where second stories were aspired to, plastic sheeting hanging in windows while a family saved up for the glass. Some houses had wells, which meant they had water when those who used the public taps or piped water did not. Most people cooked over wood fireplaces in their kitchen areas, a cooking method that produced tastier if more time-consuming curries than did gas cooking. Few people had refrigerators, but the majority of the houses had electricity, and in the evenings when the power was on, the sounds of the popular teledramas spilled out of open windows.

Our Kandy neighbors thought we were a little bit crazy or terribly naïve when we told them we were moving to what they considered a poor, low-caste area with residents of questionable moral habits. The moral habits of those in town, of course, were likewise questionable to those in the village. But Viligama did have its economic troubles, and many struggled to make ends meet. Although some families had an income from rice paddy fields and supplementary crops like peppercorn or fruits, many worked as laborers. Some of the men were employed in transportation, in construction, or in the military. Some women and men worked in nearby factories making matches, garments, or chocolate. Others worked in offices in Kandy, in stores, or in other business ventures. Still others found employment away from home, in other cities or abroad. Over half of the adults had completed at least the ninth grade of school, with many of them finishing their ordinary-level exams (11th grade) or even advanced-level exams (13th grade).[3]

However, this is not a study of Viligama. As Geertz has pointed out, "Anthropologists don't study villages (tribes, towns, neighborhoods . . .); they study *in* villages" (1973: 22, emphasis and ellipsis in the original)—and, of course, often they don't study in villages at all. Rather, this is a study of the ways that children in Viligama are shaped through their experiences with others, and how that shaping relates to adult social life and cultural understandings.

In order to do this study, I had to get to know, observe, and talk with people in this village. However, making an entry into people's lives was not easy or quick. During the first month in Viligama, my family and I alternated between making forays into the public spaces of the village, where we were gawked at from a distance, and hiding in our house, where we struggled to deal with what seemed to us the difficulties of life in this small village: disease-bearing mosquitoes; deadly vipers; huge scorpions; a frequent lack of water, electricity, and telephone; and full dependence on capricious bus service as our only transportation. I had envisioned that the neighbors would introduce themselves to me and that I would get to know them that way. I knew they were interested in us. I could hear them talking about us in the street outside my window. After a few weeks of this, I decided to take a more active approach. I took to calling on my neighbors, one each morning, bearing pineapples as gifts. After a while, the women I met began to respond to my greetings in the street or at the *kaday,* the tiny general stores scattered along the principal roads of the village. By the time my mother visited a month later, we had begun to forge the connections that would make my fieldwork possible. Invited to a wedding by a well-respected man in the village, my mother and I found ourselves included in the group of women who spent much of the long afternoon vaguely watching the children, with whom my son was playing, and complaining about the men who were drinking alcohol and delaying the lunch, my husband among them.

Participant Observation

This integration into village life enabled me to do what ethnographers do: participant observation. During the year and a half I lived in Viligama and during each return visit, I spent countless hours hanging out with women in their kitchens, drinking tea and chatting with them as they went about their daily tasks. I watched as they interacted with their children, with other family members, and with each other. I talked with people at kaddees and bus stops. I joined in village festivals, pulling for the winning team in a new year's tug-of-war. I visited with teachers at the village school and monks at the nearby temples. I got to know a group of teenaged girls who were in their final years of schooling, accompanying them on outings and sharing cool drinks in their bedrooms. I paid close attention to the ways that younger children went about their day and how they related to others. I watched how babies were held and listened to what people said to and about them.

By participating in everyday activities of the village, I came to know people—some very well and others at a distance. I came to see patterns in interactions, as well as divergences. Most important, this ongoing participant observation raised questions and suggested possible answers. Most of these questions were best investigated through qualitative methods: why did people do the things they did, what was being communicated, how did they feel about what had happened, and why did others respond as they did? These were questions I raised in everyday conversations and more formal interviews. However, some of the questions required more quantitative investigation: what did household composition look like throughout Viligama, what percentage of marriages were arranged matches, where and when did people sleep, eat, and bathe, and with whom? To answer these types of questions, I arranged a survey of seventy-one households in the village by pairs of sociology students and Viligama residents, as well as looked to published census data and records shared with me by the Grama Niladhari, the local government administrator. These surveys, while not a primary part of my research or this book, help establish a context for the more qualitative data.

Participant observation also helped me recognize some of my own cultural assumptions and consider alternative perspectives. By trying to figure out and follow the usual ways of interacting in Viligama, by getting it wrong time after time and being alerted to that, by figuring out what I had done wrong and working to correct it, I came to understand more about how life was lived in this village. Through this interactive, self-correcting process, I was not only learning a new set of cultural schemas, rules, and ways of being; I was learning something about how the process of being socialized happens.

Person-Centered Interviews with Women

In order to better understand what I was observing and to see how people in Viligama made sense of their own and each other's actions, I needed to talk with people. Accordingly, each phase of my research involved extensive interviewing along with more casual daily conversations. The interviews that I have relied on most heavily in this book are the multiple person-centered interviews I conducted with a core set of thirteen women in Viligama, ranging in age from nineteen to fifty-five. Each audio-recorded session typically lasted between one and two hours, with an average of six interviews with each woman over the course of the initial fieldwork period, plus follow-up interviews during my return visits. These interviews were open-ended, covering a wide range of topics, from childhood recollections, current relationships, and dreams for the future to patient explanations of the many things that puzzled me about life in Viligama.[4]

These women acted both as "informants" about sociocultural beliefs and practices and as "respondents" to my questions asking them to reflect on their own particular experiences, feelings, and relationships.[5] The interviews were in part modeled on the work of those who developed person-centered ethnography, which takes the individual as the unit of analysis through which the operation of social, cultural, and psychological factors are examined.[6] This methodological approach offers access to the lived experience of people and a glimpse into their psychodynamic processes. These person-centered interviews allowed me to see how people in Viligama thought about their interactions with others (their children in particular), how they worked their way through these interactions, and how they felt about themselves and others.[7]

My first recruit for these interviews was Sii Devi, my neighbor and first friend in Viligama, the one person I knew there who spoke English fluently. After a little while, others heard about my research and offered to participate. Sii Devi suggested that I interview several of her friends, to whom she introduced the idea. With a research assistant to help with my Sinhala, I began interviewing these women as well as one of their sisters and another of their daughters.[8] I also started interviewing a young woman finishing her A-level exams at the village school. Through her, I met and began interviewing one of her friends and the friend's mother. I asked the mother of one of the early volunteers if she would allow me to interview her, but she was too busy and so recommended another family in which the father was temporarily out of work, so she figured they would have time. I interviewed that whole family together at first, then focused on the mother and the daughter.

Recruiting people within a nexus of social ties was not only convenient; it afforded me a fuller understanding of the social context in which each person lived and a better sense of how relationships worked. It did, however, also mean that I was occasionally pulled in different directions by my obligations to different participants while I was in Viligama. It also presents some difficulties in writing about this research, making it harder to protect participants' privacy, as their relationships may reveal who they are and how they felt about each other.

When I returned to Sri Lanka in 2004, it was with the express purpose of conducting follow-up interviews with these women and their families. I was able to meet with ten of the women from the initial set of thirteen respondents, one having died and two having moved away. In what were sometimes formal interviews and sometimes more casual conversations, I was able to explore some of what had changed for these women since I had left in 2001. In addition, I was able to discuss with them new observations about children and child rearing in Sri Lanka that I was making while staying with families during that visit. During my next visit in 2006, which was primarily focused on the village school, I had the opportunity to follow up with many of these original respondents, and I continue to stay in contact with them from a distance.

Before I left at the end of my initial fieldwork period, I asked each woman to reflect on the interviewing experience. One woman put it this way,

> I had a longing, actually, to talk with you . . . to get to know you, to talk and get to know you. I thought that would be good. You said that you are writing a book. After that, little by little I talked it over with my husband, too. I thought, they are coming to do something, so we will help them as much as we can. They are asking for information from us because they

don't know, no? They want to learn, no? For education, no? So we will do what we can.

This interest in talking and listening, in helping those who ask, and the respect for learning and education embedded in this statement were reflected by all of the interview participants, and indeed are key parts of Sinhala culture.

Interviews with Men

When I first arrived in Viligama, people assumed that, since I was doing research into Sinhala culture, it would be senior men who would be in the best position to tell me about it. I had the feeling, however, that if I wanted women to talk to me, I could not spend much time with the men. Much of social life in Viligama was separated by gender—not by rule, at least for married people, so much as by preference. It seemed to me that if I wanted to be part of women's conversation, I would have to refrain from entering the men's. This strategy proved effective; after enough time demurring in the face of men's attempts at conversation and deferring to my own husband, women began to include me in their circles, inviting me into their kitchens rather than leaving me in the more prestigious front rooms with the men.

In the later stages of my research, I began to wish I had a better sense of how men felt about their relationships and themselves. I did not feel that I could embark on a series of long-term, private interviews with men without jeopardizing my relationships with women or my standing as a respectable woman myself. However, I might reasonably do a few one-time interviews focused on parenting issues. I brought up this idea with a few women whose families I knew well by then and arranged private interviews with two of the older fathers. Both men talked deeply and reflectively about their relationships with their children. Although more such interviews would be ideal, these few allowed me to fill out the picture a bit.

Working with Children

This book is centrally about children. It is about what children make of the lessons they encounter, as much as it is about what lessons the adults think they are presenting. But the evidence needed to think about this is much harder to get at than it is for adults.

My initial research design placed a heavy emphasis on developing a child-centered ethnography. Although I had carefully considered the ways I would tailor the formats and activities from the adult-centered interviews to better suit children's developmental level, I had not appreciated the extent to which that development was shaped by cultural context. Further, I had not anticipated the difficulty I would have establishing rapport with children in Viligama. Much more than adults, children found my accent and grammar mistakes impenetrable. A system that fosters shyness around respected persons meant that my attempts to draw children into conversation were initially met with giggles and avoidance, if not outright fear. Almost insurmountable for me was my habitual reliance on what I have come to think of as "preference talk" to draw children out. This is a style of interaction so common in the United States in which adults ask children about their favorite colors, what they like to do, and other preferences they have been encouraged to develop and to articulate as a matter of establishing their own identity. These kind of ice-breaker questions about favorite teachers and colors elicited wide-eyed confusion from children in the village, even when my translations into Sinhala were technically correct. Before coming to Sri Lanka, I had had extensive experience interviewing and teaching children in the United States. My initial difficulty connecting with children in Viligama made me realize how culturally framed my relations with children were. I became aware of what had until then seemed a natural strategy of asking children what they liked to do and what they thought of school, gradually leading to soliciting more revealing preferences and opinions. American children are well schooled in this kind of talk and are generally flattered by it. The children in Viligama, by contrast, had little practice or facility articulating their opinions and preference, especially not to a high-status foreign adult, something I will develop in later chapters.

Although I had set aside my plans to interview children soon after arriving in Viligama, toward the end of my first stay I was ready to try again. This time, equipped with a roofless miniature of a typical Sinhala house, lots of dolls, drawing supplies, and a better command of Sinhala, my meetings with village children were more productive, if still less so than I had hoped. In this second attempt, I was able to interview six children, three boys and three girls ranging in age from four to fourteen. The interviews with the younger children were more like playing and those with the older ones were more like conversations. As with the interviews with the fathers, these helped me round out the picture of these families. However, these meetings with children told me more about the cultural models children had learned than about the processes through which they learned them.

What I needed in order to understand how children made sense of their culturally patterned experiences was to see this in action, not to ask children to tell me about it. And this I had been getting all along. All the time I had been spending with women and their families, I had been seeing children encountering culturally patterned material and making sense of it as part of their everyday lives. The observations were giving me the kind of data I needed to understand much about these processes. When I returned in 2004 and 2006, I had further opportunities to see this, staying with families on my own during those visits.[9]

This book is largely the result of such observations, a child-in-relationship-centered ethnography more than a child-centered one.

Explorations of Health and Education

Although my primary attention was focused on family life and interpersonal relationships in Viligama, I needed to situate what I was finding there within other domains of life and related institutions. Health and education were two areas that became especially important to this project.

Health, both physical and mental, was of general interest to me and seemed deeply related to child rearing. Not surprisingly, it was a topic that was also of great interest to my neighbors. Accordingly, the person-centered interviews I conducted included discussions about health concerns such as injuries and illnesses, menstruation, pregnancy and childbirth, bathing, and nutrition.

In order to understand more about these beliefs and practices, as well as to learn more generally about the health care system and options available, I visited several different kinds of clinics and interviewed health care providers. Included were visits to an ayurvedic hospital, an allopathic state-run hospital, and a private clinic, a large residential state mental hospital and a private mental health day-clinic, and several shrines oriented toward spiritual healing. Although this was only a small sampling of the range of health care options and providers available to people in Sri Lanka, this gave me an idea of various health conceptions and the differences between individual providers. It also suggested similar patterns that emerged throughout these different settings, particularly those involving doctor-patient relationships, which I will discuss in Chapter 6.

Because I was interested in the socialization of children, I also spent a good deal of time in the local village school. I interviewed teachers and administrators and observed the children during instruction periods, schoolwide gatherings, and at less formal times. In 2006, I returned with the primary purpose of observing children starting school for the first time. Since parents often said that children learned proper behavior when they went to school, I concentrated my observations on the first- and second-grade classrooms and interviewed those classroom teachers, along with a few others. I was also interested in seeing how dramatic state-mandated shifts in educational policy from teacher-centered learning to student-centered learning were being taken up by teachers and by students. I will discuss these observations in more detail in the second half of the book.

Throughout this research, issues of desire and attachment arose repeatedly in different ways and in different settings. Before I conclude this introduction, I will discuss some of the resonances of those concepts, both in the field setting and in the scholarly resources I use.

Desire and Attachment

One of the central concepts in Buddhism is *tanha*, sometimes translated as "cling-ing and craving." It is this, according to Buddhist teachings, that is the root of all suffering. The residents of Viligama knew this Noble Truth well. To them, this troubling feature of human nature was not just the subject of esoteric doctrine but the stuff of everyday life. Desire and attachment were topics of ordinary dis-cussion, central to the ways that people reflected on their own and each other's motivations. Understandings about desire and attachment were foundational to the ways that people related to each other, including their children, inculcating these understandings and emotional orientations into the next generation.

The observations I sketched out at the opening of this chapter all have something to do with desire and attachment, with wanting and relating. Tod-dlers wanted objects and activities and attention from people around them— and those people indulged them. But when children did not assert their own desires, those who cared about them worked to make sure their needs were met, granting the younger person approval and affection as well. These and other interactions I explore in this book involve desires to have and to do and to be, and they involve attachments to people and ideas and identities, as well as to things in the world.

While I will be arguing that these desires and attachments are shaped in the course of growing up, I will also argue that they are the very tools of that shaping. It is through participating in relationships with important others that children learn what to expect from others, how relationships should be conducted, and how they to want to be in these kinds of relationships and not in others. It is through the experience of enacting their own desires that children learn how dangerous desire may be, that it might destroy a coveted object or a valued relationship. Conversely, experiences of having their needs met without ever voicing them builds trust in certain kinds of relationships and attachments to particular people.

Desires and attachments are not just important in this Sri Lankan village, of course. They are at the heart of social life everywhere. In any social group, there is a nexus of individual wants and social ties. Within groups of people who interact regularly, these individual wants and social ties have a pattern and are mutually intelligible. If that group is to endure, there must be ways for new members to develop these patterned desires and ways of relating.

Accordingly, much of the academic thinking about individuals and society has something to say about desire and attachment. In coming to make sense of what I observed in Sri Lanka, some of these theories have been particularly helpful. Before going on to analyze and interpret those observations, I mention the most relevant of these, which I draw from the broader fields of psychology and anthropology. These bodies of literature and scholarly thought frame much of my analysis in this book. My treatment of them here will be brief, but I will return to them at future points in the book as I draw on them to make sense of the ethnographic encounters I describe and use those ethnographic encounters to think through aspects of this literature. In the concluding chapter of the book, I will return to these theories as I discuss the contributions of this study.

Psychological Connections

Psychology, as it has developed in the West, is replete with theories about desire and attachment. Why do people do what they do? What motivates them? These are foundational questions, and there have been many kinds of answers. The analyses in this book draw on these resources, particularly those in the psychoanalytic tradition. This is a rich area of theory and research, beginning over a century ago with Freud's earliest writings, and one that this introduction cannot hope to review in depth.[10] However, I do want to point to a few themes within this body of work that have been useful to me in trying to understand the actions and interactions I observed in Sri Lanka. One of these themes regards desires and motivations, recognizing that those are not always conscious nor are they rational, that they are rooted in and shaped by early experience, and that they can produce anxieties and conflicts against which we develop unconscious ways to defend ourselves. Yet these desires bleed through, finding ways to assert themselves, if only in covert or indirect ways. Psychoanalytic theory and the object-relational approaches it led to also offer productive ways to conceptualize the attachments that people have to each other, to ideas, and to images of themselves. This area of psychodynamic theory that considers the way our earliest interactions with others are reflected in an internal object world, which then shapes how we experience future relationships, presents a way of understanding how people are shaped by their relationships with each other and how that is transferred to and reworked through future interactions. These approaches are integral to the analyses in this book, helping to shed light on the interactions I observed in Sri Lanka. At the same time, the observations themselves challenge and extend these psychodynamic theories that have been developed within and largely applied to a limited Western context.

Another area of Western academic psychology, one with roots in psychoanalytic thinking, that my work simultaneously draws on and critiques is what is known explicitly as "attachment theory." This area of developmental psychology offers an account of how it is that infants come to attach to their caretakers, what might go wrong in this process, and how these attachments matter as children grow up. Although cross-cultural observations of early childhood call attention to the ethnocentrism built into this theory, attachment theory as it is classically articulated still provides one version—albeit a culturally restricted one—of how attachments to caretakers may be developed and shaped.[11] As I will demonstrate in Chapter 4, this theoretical model demarcates some of the key factors in early attachment processes, although the particulars of this model need to be expanded to include the cultural variation in "normal" attachment that exists across the world.

Anthropological Connections

Investigating desire and attachment is also at the heart of what anthropology is up to. Over the past century or so since it was established, sociocultural anthropology has been concerned with documenting and seeking to understand the various manifestations of human life, with particular attention to social interactions and cultural meanings. It is connections between actual people that compose and enact the social structures which anthropology has traditionally described. Desire propels people to produce those structures of social life and to act within them. More recently, anthropologists have attended to individual practice rather than rules, to the subject positions people take up, to the habitus they acquire, to the enactment of agency, and to the possibilities for change and contestation. Integral to these contemporary concerns are questions about how desire is enacted, developed, recruited, regulated—or is resistant to pressure from others—even though the details of these processes typically remain unspecified.[12]

The subdiscipline of psychological anthropology has been more explicitly concerned with these issues of desire and attachment that underlie much of what the wider field of anthropology investigates. This subfield of sociocultural anthropology examines the interplay of mind, culture, and society. In addition to observing the cultural and individual shape of desires and attachments, psychological anthropology asks how it is that particular kinds of desires and attachments come to be learned, cared about, and transmitted by particular people.

These questions about how culture is internalized were pursued by early anthropologists such as Margaret Mead, Ruth Benedict, and Edward Sapir as part of what was called "culture and personality" studies.[13] These anthropologists worked during the first half of the twentieth century to answer questions about how people are shaped in culturally patterned ways by childhood experience and how individuals may vary within those patterns. Although the culture and personality approach was viewed as central to anthropology in the 1940s and 1950s, it has been critiqued by anthropologists—sometimes fairly and sometimes not—on several fronts. This work has been criticized for seeing cultures as overly bounded and distinct, for overlooking both individual variation and intrasocietal diversity, for not taking account of the possibilities for change, for being too wedded to Western psychological notions and to psychoanalytic theories in particular, and for reducing the broad sweep of human history to single infant care practices. Under the weight of these critiques, which, as LeVine points out, were largely focused on "only the most visible and vulnerable parts of it" (2010: 11), culture and personality studies fell into disrepute.[14]

Even so, ethnographic work with children continued, albeit less focused on questions of personality and its relation to culture. One of the primary efforts in this area was led by John and Beatrice Whiting (1975), who coordinated a multisited, multiteam research project to observe and compare children's behavior across societies. In recent years, there has been a resurgence of interest in children and childhood within anthropology. This is evident in the robust and growing membership in the Anthropology of Children and Youth Interest Group created in 2007 within the American Anthropology Association, as well as the many new publications focused on children's lives in particular settings (e.g., Burr 2006, Fong 2004, Huberman 2013) and around the world (e.g., Lancy 2008, Montgomery 2009, Schwartzman 2001). However, the questions earlier culture and personality studies pursued about how culture is transmitted and how it shapes people remain largely unanswered.

This book takes up those questions by earlier anthropologists about how people come to know, care, and act in culturally patterned ways. As I will elaborate in the conclusion to this book, however, it does so with newer theoretical tools and models to add to the careful observation and attention to ordinary, everyday interactions that characterized the best of that older work.[15] The work of those interested in language socialization, as represented in the collection of papers edited by Schieffelin and Ochs (1986), provides one important source for those tools and models for how they might be used. By paying close attention to what transpires in communicative episodes involving children, these researchers are able to investigate not only how children learn to use language but also how they learn about social arrangements, emotions, and themselves. The work of Jean Briggs (1998) provides another important model for this work. She also pays close attention to communications between Inuit children and those around them, but with an eye that is more attuned to the psychodynamic dimensions of those interactions. In these interactions she calls "dramas," she describes how children are presented questions about who they are and where they fit that they must make sense of. What all of this work shares with mine is not only the close attention to everyday practices but also the recognition that it is the action and agency of individual people that brings social forms to life as they interact with each other. Further, it is not only adults who have this agency, but children themselves, children who are not just the recipients of enculturation messages but actors, communicators, and sense-makers in their own right.

Foundational to my approach are the innovations of cognitive anthropologists, work led by Roy D'Andrade (1995) and Claudia Strauss and Naomi Quinn (1997). According to this way of thinking about culture—a way of thinking that I share and use in this book—culture is a set of schemas derived from experience.

A schema is a mental representation—an idea, an understanding, or a way of doing things. These schemas may represent something relatively specific—like "ball," or they may be larger schemas that incorporate more basic schemas—like "a game of baseball." Although it may not turn out to be quite literally true, these schemas are visualized as interconnected neurons whose connections are strengthened through use. We derive our schemas and strengthen the associations between them through our experiences, whether those are physical experiences in the world or more internal kinds of experiences, thoughts, or reactions.

No one person's full set of schemas is identical to another's because no one person's full set of experiences is identical to another's, let alone the sense they make of them or the innate dispositions and capacities they begin with. However, to the extent that those experiences are similar to those of others and to the extent that the sense that is derived from those experiences is similar, we can say that those are culturally shared. Thus, culture is made up of patterned practices in the world and the shared schemas that people derive from them, schemas that in turn are used to generate further practices and interpretations. The only difference between a belief and a cultural belief is the extent to which it is shared; the only difference between a practice and a cultural practice is the extent to which it is shared. Conceptualized in this way, "cultures" are not distinct and coherent wholes, nor are cultural beliefs and practices unchanging or endorsed equally by all members of a society. "Culture" is not only what is "traditional" but also includes all the lessons and sense making people do in response to their necessarily social experiences.

But people are not just shaped by their ideas and actions. Feelings get attached to these schemas and are evoked by them. Some schemas are more motivating than others. And some feelings prompt other feelings, reactions, patterns of reaction, and defenses against them. In order to think about how it is that people come to feel and care about ideas, practices, each other, and themselves, the resources from psychodynamic theory as it has developed over the past century can be integrated with more cognitively oriented anthropology, as I will demonstrate through my analysis.

What these cognitive and psychodynamic lines of thinking, as well as the work of those who examine communicative episodes discussed above, all call to our attention is the importance of social interaction and experience in the transmission of culture and the formation of people. It is through these social interactions that children's desires and their responses to them are shaped in culturally patterned ways, leading them to participate in and care about relationships in the ways that they do. This book will describe some of the ways that happens among people in one particular community in Sri Lanka.

2

Sri Lanka

Setting the Ethnographic Context

People often ask me why I chose to do this study in Sri Lanka. I find it a difficult question to answer. In some ways, I could have conducted this study anywhere, but I had to conduct it somewhere. In order to study the ways that children are shaped through their experiences with others, I needed to find some particular children who were being shaped.

In my initial project design, the one I proposed to my doctoral committee, I aimed to study the intergenerational effects of community violence on children. Before coming to graduate school, I had spent eight years working with children and adults affected by sexual violence in the United States. For some of the women with whom I worked, I saw how their exposure to violence and their ways of dealing with those experiences influenced the ways they parented their own children. In my doctoral research in anthropology, I wanted to investigate how people in a different cultural setting, exposed to different kinds of violence close to home, might respond, and how those responses might shape the ways they raised their own children. In the late 1990s, at the time I was looking for a field site to situate such a study, there were many possibilities—Rwanda, Bosnia, Haiti. But it was Sri Lanka that drew me.

Sri Lanka had been the site of an extended ethnic conflict since the anti-Tamil riots in 1983, the seeds of which had been sown long before that, as the nation emerged from centuries of colonial occupation.[1] These conflicts escalated into a civil war in which separatists in the north and east of the island fought for an independent Tamil state, a fight they continued until crushed by government forces in 2009. In addition, there had been two recent insurrections in the Sinhala-dominated south, the first in 1970–1972, and again on a more massive scale in 1988–1989.[2] These movements brought violence into the streets throughout much of that region. Many of the teenagers who witnessed episodes of community-based violence in the 1980s would be parents by the time I began my study, ten years later. This made a promising site to study the kind of questions I had in mind.

In addition, there were more practical reasons to choose Sri Lanka. I would need to learn a language—and Sinhala, as an Indo-European language with a simplified spoken version, was said to be relatively easy for an English speaker to learn. I would be traveling with my husband and young son, so the relatively high levels of health and safety in Sri Lanka made that seem possible.

But there were other reasons, reasons that have more to do with attraction and are harder to explain. I had been thinking about Sri Lanka for a long time. When I was young, living in Guam, where my father was stationed with the U.S. Navy, I briefly knew a girl whose mother was Sri Lankan. When I was just out of college, I had another Sri Lankan friend, a young man who talked endlessly of the civil war he had been sent away to avoid, and who cooked delicious Tamil food from a cookbook he had bought in the States. When I got to graduate school in San Diego, I was assigned *Medusa's Hair* (Obeyesekere 1981), a strange and wonderful book about possessed priestesses in Sri Lanka, which led me to write a master's thesis on the topic. By the time I got to choosing a place for my doctoral research, I felt in some ways as if the choice had already been made.

Eventually, my project moved away from questions about the effects of violence to deeper, more general questions about the ways that culture is communicated from parent to child, how it is lived out, and how it might change. I came to realize that my initial questions were far too specific, too embedded in my own previous understandings about "trauma" and PTSD and the ways that parenting shaped children. My observations about more general patterns of relating did not stay neatly inside the boundaries marked out by the focus on an event ten years in the past. Instead, my research became concerned with the experience, relationships, and internal life of the people I got to know, and centered on the things important to them, rather than on this event that had seemed important to me. As those research questions deepened, so did my interest in this place and the people who made their lives there.

Before presenting the results of that research, I want to give a brief orientation to the nation, its history, and its people, emphasizing aspects relevant to this study.[3] I do this for readers unfamiliar with Sri Lanka, in order to give them a frame of reference for the research this book presents. However, it is with some trepidation that I do so. This is not only because such a brief sketch is inevitably partial and simplistic but also because historical narratives have been used in Sri Lanka—as they have elsewhere—to legitimize ethnic divides, political claims, and violence.[4] I refer the reader to the many accounts of Sri Lanka's history, politics, and people cited throughout this book for a more nuanced reading of the features I have space here to sketch out only briefly.[5]

Politics and History

The Democratic Socialist Republic of Sri Lanka is an island nation off the southern tip of India. This tropical island, formerly known as Ceylon, is roughly 25,000 square miles—just a little larger than West Virginia. The official capital, Sri Jayawardenepura, is located on the outskirts of Colombo, the island's major urban center, located on its west coast. In the north of the island is the city of Jaffna, which served as the central city of the Tamil separatist movement that was fighting for an official homeland in the north and east of the island throughout the time of my fieldwork. The southern coastal lowlands are the site of coconut, rubber, and cinnamon estates, an active fishing industry, and beautiful beaches that draw international tourists. The dry plains in the north-central part of the island are the home to ancient kingdoms, temples, and irrigation systems. The central highlands are famous for tea plantations and, in the southwestern part, gem mines. Kandy is the principal city of this central part of the island where I conducted my field research. It was the seat of the last of the indigenous kingdoms and continues to be an important ritual, administrative, and tourist center.

Sri Lanka's population, reported by the 2012 census to be just over 20 million, includes diverse ethnic, religious, and language groups.[6] The largest of the island's ethnic groups—the one among which most of my research was conducted—is made up of those who identify as Sinhala. This group dominates the national government and the southern and central parts of the island. Most members of this group speak the Sinhala language and most identify as Theravada Buddhists. At the time of the 2001 census, which estimated the total population at just under nineteen million people, those identifying as Sinhala made up three-quarters of the total population.[7]

The nation also includes two distinct groups of Tamils. One group, usually referred to as "Sri Lankan Tamils," trace their ancestry in Sri Lanka back more than two thousand years and compose as much as 12 percent of the population.[8] The majority of the members of this Tamil group reside in the north and east of the island, the area that were contested during the nation's civil war. The other Tamil group is made up of the so-called "Up-country Tamils" who are the descendants of Tamils who came from south India in the 1800s, often as bonded labor, to work on tea plantations established by the British. They now make up 5 to 6 percent of the total population.[9] Both groups are predominantly Hindu and speak Tamil, a Dravidian language also spoken in a large part of southern India.

Members of the country's third main ethnic group, making up 9 percent of the population, are usually simply identified as Muslims, many of whom speak a variety of Tamil. Historically, members of this group have been distinguished by whether their ancestry was understood to be "Malay" or "Moor," although this distinction is falling out of use. Muslim communities are dispersed throughout the island, although they make up a significant part of the population on the east coast, where the populations of Muslims, Tamils, and Sinhalas are more balanced.[10]

In addition to these main ethnic groups, the population includes approximately 7,000 people of other ethnicities, making up less than one-half of 1 percent of the total inhabitants.[11] Among these are Burghers, who are said to have Dutch ancestry, and Veddas, identified as descendents of the island's earliest inhabitants.

Each of the island's ethnic groups is identified with a language and religion, as I have noted above; however, these are more fluid than they appear. Across these groups, there are significant numbers of Christians, including long-time Catholic and Anglican families, as well as more recent Protestant converts. Many of the island's inhabitants speak English as either a first or second language. In addition, many people have some fluency in one or more languages besides the traditional language of their ethnic group, particularly if they reside in regions that are less ethnically homogenous. There is also some flexibility to the religious practices as well, as they borrow from and share with their neighbors, sometimes intermarrying. Despite the violence that has marked Sinhala-Tamil relations in particular, members of all these groups share many practices, beliefs, and values.

The island's position at the crossroads of multiple trade routes and its rich natural resources have shaped its complex demographics, culture, and history. Both Tamils and Sinhalas were well established on the island by the third century BCE, although both claim to have arrived on the island first. The Tamils immigrated from southern India, bringing Hinduism and their Dravidian language with them. It is widely believed that Sinhala people migrated to the island from further north in India, bringing their Indo-Aryan language and some version of Brahmanism with them, although as with other origin stories the veracity of this account is in doubt. By the first century BCE, Buddhism had been established in their principal areas of settlement. Sinhalas, Tamils, and various south Indian invaders built powerful kingdoms with advanced agricultural projects and elaborate religious institutions, kingdoms that periodically brought the island under the authority of a single regime.

European powers also established holds on the island. In the early sixteenth century, Portuguese traders began to arrive, eventually gaining control over a small but productive portion of the island concentrated in the coastal areas. In 1638, after nearly 150 years of this domination, the king of Kandy enlisted the help of the Dutch to drive out the Portuguese. However, the Dutch, who were the rising power in the surrounding waters, kept the land they had taken from the Portuguese for themselves. The Dutch eventually controlled all but the kingdom of Kandy until, in 1796, they were pushed out by the British under a similar arrangement with Kandy's monarch. Like the Dutch before them, the British kept the island for themselves, eventually ousting the last Sinhala king from Kandy in 1815 and capturing all of Ceylon, as the nation was then known.

On February 4, 1948, Ceylon became politically independent of Great Britain, although it remained part of the British Commonwealth. At that point, English remained an official language and continued to serve as a common language for business and politics. In 1956, however, the "Sinhala only" language agenda came to the political fore, gaining support from the Sinhala majority and beginning to divide the country—divisions that had been fostered by previous British policies. In 1972, a new constitution was adopted that changed the nation's name from Ceylon to Sri Lanka and officially converted the tri-language, secular nation into an officially Buddhist and Sinhala-language government. This effectively declared the minority religious and linguistic groups to be second-class citizens and barred their participation in many forms of government work and activities due to language barriers.

Tamils, the largest and most prominent of these groups, were increasingly shut out of the government and universities and became frequent targets of mob violence and government surveillance. The Tamil separatist movement began to reinforce its own efforts with sporadic acts of violence. In 1983, one of these acts touched off massive anti-Tamil rioting, beginning in Colombo and spreading to other areas of the country. These acts inflamed the growing support among Tamils for armed rebellion and a separate Tamil state in the north, a call that was taken up by the paramilitary LTTE, the Liberation Tigers of Tamil Elam, who waged a civil war against the Sri Lankan government for over two decades.

At the time I began my research in Sri Lanka in 1999—despite the presence of soldiers and check points along the roads, despite the families I knew whose son or brother or father was in the army, and despite sporadic bombings and assassinations carried out by the increasingly desperate Tigers—the ongoing civil war felt far away from Kandy. In February of 2002, just after my initial fieldwork period, a Norway-brokered ceasefire was signed by Sri Lankan prime minister Ranil Wickremasinghe and LTTE leader Vellupillai Prabhakaran. That fragile ceasefire continued through my visit in 2004, but by the time I returned in 2006, hostilities had begun to escalate once again. This continued for the next three years until the Sri Lankan military fully crushed the LTTE forces, ending the conflict in May of 2009.

Religion

Buddhism, the religion of the majority of people in Sri Lanka, is given a place of preference in the national constitution and public life, although Hinduism, Islam, and Christianity are also practiced by significant portions of the

population, as described above. The 2001 census reported that, for the areas of
the island that were surveyed, roughly three-quarters of the population considered themselves Buddhist, 8 percent Hindu, 9 percent Muslim, 6 percent Catholic, and 1 percent Protestant.[12]

In practice, there is a degree of blending among these religious practices, as well as an incorporation of other indigenous and astrological beliefs.
Sri Lankan Buddhists and Hindus, in particular, share a number of ritual practices and foundational beliefs. Adherents to these religions recognize a similar pantheon of gods, spirits, and demons, into which many local deities have
been absorbed. These beings may be male or female, benevolent or malevo-
lent, moral or amoral, but they are all considered subject to the same laws
of death and rebirth as other beings. Devotees of particular gods—including
some Muslims and Christians—appeal for assistance with a variety of concerns,
mostly worldly. In addition to this involvement with the gods, Hinduism and
Buddhism share several core beliefs. The moral codes of both recommend mod-
eration and restraint, with Hindus stressing the discipline of one's behavior
and Buddhists advocating "the middle path." In both, the concept of karma and
rebirth are central, ideas which posit that one's actions in this lifetime determine the kind of life into which one will be reborn through the quantity of
merit one earns. While both Buddhism and Hinduism propose that one can
escape the cycle of rebirth, a goal that is elaborated within Buddhism, much
of the religious activity of the laity in Sri Lanka is oriented around generating
spiritual merit.

The vast majority of Sinhala people identify as practicing Theravada Buddhism. In this version of Buddhism, the *bhikkhus* (monks), members of the
Sangha (monastic community), are meant to seek salvation through enlighten-
ment and escape from the cycles of rebirth through detachment from the world
and from the desires and suffering connected with it. The laity, at least until
recent years, has sought to earn *pin* (spiritual merit) for a better rebirth for
themselves or their loved ones through their support of the *Sangha* and pursuit
of ethical conduct, mental discipline, and wisdom. Traditionally in Sri Lanka,
practices and beliefs derived from pre-Buddhist beliefs, Hinduism, and Tantric
Buddhism exist alongside these more orthodox beliefs, although some of these
may be fading away among the urbanized upper classes.[13]

Living Conditions and Economy

Sri Lanka boasts unusually high indicators of well-being, relative to other South
Asian nations, especially considering the political violence of recent decades
and centuries of colonial exploitation before that. As the government's Department of Census and Statistics reports,

Sri Lanka is far ahead of her South Asian neighbours in the accomplishment of human development goals. Life expectancy at birth is currently 72 yrs. and is close to the estimated lifespan in the developed countries. High literacy rates, low mortality rates and the steadily declining population growth, reflect the country's progress in the sphere of social development. All these human development indicators are a tribute to Sri Lanka's social service net work, which was established in the latter part of the 1940 decade, ensuring sound educational policies, an extensive health care programme and an effective medical system for all sectors of the nation. (DCS-SL 2011a)

Despite relatively low household incomes, the health indicators for children and families were strong during the period of my fieldwork from 1999 to 2006. In 2002, the Sri Lankan government reports that the average monthly income for households in the central district where I conducted fieldwork was 11,175 SL rupees (approximately 120 US dollars). This figure was close to the Sri Lankan national average, but only half the average for the urban center of Colombo.[14] In 2000, the average age of first-time mothers on the island was twenty-five, with a fertility rate of approximately two children each.[15] Those children were spaced an average of four years apart, a figure that bodes well for child survival. During roughly the same period, the infant mortality rate was a relatively low 15 out of 1,000 live births, compared to a rate of 6.75 infant deaths per 1,000 births in the United States and 58 per 1,000 in India.[16]

With free and universal education, subsidized transportation, and national health care, the quality of life in Sri Lanka is high in comparison with other developing countries. In addition to the reported long life expectancy and relatively low mortality rates, there is a well-developed infrastructure that provides fairly safe drinking water and latrines to at least two-thirds of its inhabitants, an adequate food supply, and a well-developed network of health care providers.

However, since the major change in economic policies of 1977 that opened the markets to international trade and reoriented the state away from its previous welfare agenda, the quality and availability of these government services have been eroding and increasingly replaced by private resources accessed by the middle and elite classes. Besides the difficulty posed by reductions in state funding, the civil war created additional challenges to the welfare system, as up to one and a half million people have been displaced, a group that has been targeted for relief and resettlement by NGOs and private donors. These NGOs and others operating in Sri Lanka have increasingly come under scrutiny from a government wishing to gain control over their resources, particularly following the strong NGO response to the 2004 tsunami and the 2009 end of the civil war, which opened up areas for development in the north and east.

Accelerated by changes in government policy, Sri Lanka's economy is shifting away from its traditional agricultural base to include production for an international market. While agricultural production continues to be a major industry, in recent years, the sale of garments manufactured in Sri Lanka has outstripped the more traditional exports of tea, rubber, spices, and coconut products. Together, these are among the largest exports, along with locally mined gems. Workers themselves are one of the major exports, and their remittances are a major source of income for the island's economy and for its families, one in twelve of which has an adult abroad. By the mid-1990s, roughly one-quarter of the population was employed as skilled workers in agricultural, fishery, or animal husbandry, one-quarter in skilled craft or factory production, one-quarter in administration, professions, sales, service or clerical work, and one-quarter as unskilled laborers. In spite of this shift away from agriculture, Sri Lanka has recently reported near self-sufficiency in rice production and other staple foods.

Sri Lanka's towns and villages, as well as its urban centers, are typically active sites of commercial exchange. People raise fruits and vegetables, spices, and sometimes chickens, goats, and cows near their homes, as well as rice on nearby paddy fields. Most of this nonplantation agriculture that is not consumed in the home is sold at local markets. These markets and stores also carry other home- and factory-produced goods, imported commodities, and traditional craft products such as brass, pottery, and baskets that are often made by hereditary caste groups. Transportation, repair, construction, tailoring, printing, and other services are always in demand, as is teaching and private tutoring. In some locales, especially in the coastal beach areas, tourism is also the focus of a range of commercial activity.

Hierarchy and Social Relations

This book is primarily about relationships—how they are learned, how they are experienced, what they teach, and why people want to participate in them. Here I introduce some of the broad dimensions which pattern social relationships and hierarchy throughout Sri Lanka—among them class and caste, gender, and kinship—with a particular focus on how those emerge in Viligama.

Caste and Class

Caste was not something people liked to talk about in Viligama, insisting in response to my questions that caste was not important any more and that "everyone in Viligama is the same." I could only guess the caste identities of my neighbors. Although it is sometimes possible to identify someone's caste by family name or home village, it is often not clear. Adults in Viligama not only avoided talking with me about caste, they avoiding talking about it with their children. Mothers told me that their children did not know about caste, that their children certainly did not know what caste they belonged to, and that the mothers would not tell them. To my question about what she would tell her son if he asked about caste, one woman's said, "I would explain to him that there is no difference between castes. . . . I would explain to him that it is not serious, not to pay attention to it, not to think so much about it. Then he would not think about those problems. I would explain it like that. But otherwise I would not do anything." On the other hand, this mother allowed that some high-caste people still taught their children to discriminate on the basis of caste. Although people in Viligama were reluctant to talk about caste, it continued to be part of the context in which they live their lives.

Caste is a traditional part of both Sinhala and Tamil society in Sri Lanka.[17] It is determined by one's lineage's place within a predetermined status hierarchy, a position into which one is born as a result of one's karma, as a reward or retribution for one's deeds in previous lifetimes. Historically, caste identity has been marked by personal and place names, ritual roles and occupations, regulations of dress and housing, forms of address, language, seating arrangements, and other practices of deference and superiority. Today, where these hierarchical relations continue, there is a degree of uneasiness or even resentment toward them, particularly among the educated younger generations.

Although caste is a part of Sinhala social life, it is not supported by state law or Buddhist doctrine.[18] There are also features of the system that have been considered to lessen the historic importance of caste in Sinhala society in comparison to other communities in South Asia. First, the Sinhala caste structure does not include the top and bottom rungs of the standard Hindu caste system. Among the Sinhala, there is no high Brahmin (priest) caste nor are there true outcastes. Second, the vast majority of Sinhala people are members of the highest caste, the *Govigama* (cultivator) caste, although there are gradients of prestige and obligation within this group. In the coastal areas, the *Karava* (fishermen) caste sometimes claims equal status with Govigama, although this is not necessarily reciprocally recognized. Ranked below are an array of smaller castes, often associated with a particular place, occupation, or ritual role, the relative status of which is not clear cut and so is a matter for contestation and maintenance. Although caste may not be formally supported among Sinhala people, whether Buddhist or Christian, and may be less salient than in other casted societies, it continues to shape social life in Sri Lanka. Caste concerns often surface in marriage arrangements, and they continue to influence politics, place of residence, friendships, social connections, and beliefs about people.

Although the importance and legitimacy of caste is being eroded throughout Sri Lanka by political and economic developments as well as by popular sentiment, differentiation by class is of growing importance, as well as increasing disparity. Class status is marked not only by differences in wealth but also by differences in education, employment, speech, dress, transportation, and housing. In general, the most elite classes can be identified by their possession of imported commodities and access to international networks, whereas the lower classes are associated with traditional behavior and local relationships. Education, a command of English, and access to urban centers are significant determinants of both employment and class status.

Class and caste status do not always correspond, nor has their relationship to each other remained steady over time. Some high-caste families are poor and relatively uneducated, while some low-caste people may be well-educated, well-heeled professionals. Efforts to improve one's status, especially when unaccounted for by more traditional differences in rank, often spark gossip, suspicion, and envy, as I will discuss in Chapter 5.

The Status of Women

Although men's and women's circles in Viligama were usually separate, women had a significant degree of respect, autonomy, education, and say-so. Women and girls often walked through the village or went on busses alone, at least during daylight. Girls were expected to do well in school and, while their virtue and reputation had to be guarded in ways that their brothers' did not, girls were expected to have good judgment and self-discipline. Although there was a general preference for sons, this is not as strong as in other South Asian communities. People said it was best to have a daughter first, since she would set a better example and be more responsible in caring for younger siblings than a son would. Married women had more autonomy, mobility, and authority than unmarried women, although certainly not as much as their husbands. Although they deferred to men in many ways, their opinions and their work—both in and out of the home—were generally valued.

Such observations on the relatively high status of women in Sri Lanka, especially in comparison to other South Asian nations, are widely noted by social scientists and lay people alike.[19] Practices of child marriage or widow burning that ignite concern elsewhere in South Asia have never been reported in Sri Lanka. Even though most groups on the island prefer that new brides to move into their husbands' homes, women typically retain strong ties with their own natal families. Additionally, it is expected among most groups that the bride's family will provide a dowry, at least if it is an arranged marriage. For the Sinhala people I knew, as I describe in the next section, this dowry was generally understood as belonging to the bride, although it may be used by the family.

Political leadership positions in Sri Lanka are largely held by men, although there are important exceptions. Sri Lanka elected the world's first female prime minister in 1960, Sirimavo Bandaranaike, whose own daughter was later elected president. Although this is likely to be more indicative of the importance of family lineage than of the political power of women in general, Sri Lankan women have held voting rights since the vote was instituted in 1931 and have long held property rights.

There is a strong tradition of both men and women working, with men focusing more on income opportunities and women focusing on the household. Currently, women's participation in the paid labor force is significant, although not evenly distributed, concentrated in professions such as nursing, teaching, tea picking, and garment manufacturing.[20] In manual labor and agricultural work, men are typically better paid and assigned tasks that are considered more physically demanding, while women are assigned the more repetitive, detail-oriented work at which they are thought to be more adept than men. Opportunity for foreign employment for women, while relatively available and well-paying, is restricted to domestic work, whereas opportunities for men are more varied, ranging from manual labor to engineering.[21] Within the home, regardless of their engagement in paid labor, women and girls do nearly all food preparation and most other domestic work.

Although private schools and some of the more prestigious government schools are often sex-segregated, education has long been important for both boys and girls in Sri Lanka. Overall, school enrollments for boys and girls are relatively even.[22] The literacy rates for men and women are similarly high; the 2001 census found that 89.7 percent of females over the age of ten years were literate, compared to 92.6 percent of males.

Despite both traditional practices and the full rights of citizenship that women in Sri Lanka enjoy today, women in all ethnic groups consistently defer to men across the domains of life, including the workplace and the home. Among all but the most urbanized, they are expected to defer to men of relatively equal status and to avoid all implication of sexual impropriety by keeping themselves appropriately covered, refusing all alcohol and tobacco, and refraining from interaction with unrelated men. Women bear the greater weight of social expectations and sanctions for noncompliance. I found a strong expectation and practice of virginity for unmarried women and girls, although individual young women had a range of sexual experiences, usually short of vaginal intercourse. In addition, sexual harassment and assault, while seldom reported to the authorities, was a common experiences women discussed. Casual or affectionate physical contact between men and women was rare in public, even between husbands and wives. However, there was a great deal of physical contact that emphasized closeness between members of the same gender and with children.

Kinship, Family, and Marriage

Getting married is something people in Sri Lanka are generally expected to do, and this was certainly true in Viligama. Whom this marriage is to—what the spouse is like, what the family is like, what kinds of resources they have, connections they offer, and children they will produce—is crucial to one's future and one's family's future, for good or for ill. In marrying and in the ideally accompanying steps of setting up a new household and having children, young people move into new positions in new sets of hierarchically organized relationships—within their newly established household, within their newly acquired in-laws' networks, and possibly within new neighborhoods, villages, or cities.

Even so, their own natal home will continue to be an important point of reference and of relationships for them, whether they move away at marriage, to seek employment, or because of displacement. In Sri Lanka, the notion of ancestral place and the kin group associated with it is very important. The hereditary home is the site of life-cycle rituals and celebrations as well as day-to-day interaction with extended kin. It is most common for this kin group to belong to the father's family, as there is a preference for women to move to the homes of their husband, raising their children nearer to his relatives. However, it also happens that husbands join wives' families instead, particularly among the matrilineal people of the island's east.

The basic Sinhala family unit is bilateral, nuclear, and preferentially neolocal, unlike many other South Asian groups which have a preference for patrilineal joint family households composed of grown brothers and their families living together.[23] This means that children in Sinhala families are considered equally related to their mother and their father, with whom they form the central family unit. Ideally, a Sinhala husband and wife will live in their own household with their unmarried children. As demonstrated in the village surveys I collected and draw from later in this chapter, the ethnographic and statistical record consistently shows a strong preference for and pattern of households composed of a husband and wife and their unmarried children.[24]

This practice is flexible, however. Widowed parents may move in with grown children and their spouses. Other family members, for one reason or another, might come to stay for a short time or for good. Grown children might not get married or might not move out right away after they do. A youngest son, in particular, will often stay at home, raising his own children in his parents' house, which he will inherit at their deaths. At times, the "new household" that a couple sets up might actually be a small section of an extended family home. Individual households are identified by cooking practices, so that, even within a larger house, a wife may cook for her husband and children independently from others who may live within the structure, perhaps sharing the same kitchen. At other times, the women who live in the house may cook jointly or one may do most of the cooking, although men rarely cook unless no women are at home.

In all ethnic groups on the island, marriages are traditionally arranged by the families of the couple. However, marriages initiated by the couples themselves have a long history and seem to be becoming increasingly common. Although not arranged by parents, these "love matches" did not necessarily meet with parental disapproval. In fact, love matches carried the advantage of diminished costs to parents who are not expected to pay dowry or host elaborate celebrations for these types of marriages—an advantage for families of limited means, like those in Viligama, in addition to their potentially valued association with modernness and romantic love. Further, for young people who have found ways to circulate within more prestigious sections of society, such as at university or in the city, love matches may provide an upward mobility otherwise unavailable to families with limited connections.

Although families may aspire to find a match for their child—and especially for their daughters—that will improve their social standing and opportunities, they are not likely to agree to a marriage with someone they consider beneath them. Regardless of who initiates the marriage, the bride and groom are typically of the same socioeconomic status and are expected to be of the same ethnicity, and, for Buddhists and Hindus, caste status. It is also considered best if the couple are of similar age, with the husband being slightly older than the wife. Additionally, there is a preference among Tamil and Sinhala groups for marriages between cross-cousins—the children of a brother and sister—although this does not always show up in practice.[25] In any case, marriage between parallel cousins, those children of two brothers or two sisters whom one calls siblings, is not an option.[26]

The age at which people marry is relatively high in Sri Lanka. Government reports for the Kandy area over the past two decades indicate that twenty-five is the average age for women to marry, and twenty-nine for men, which is consistent with national patterns.[27] Divorce, while increasingly common, occurs in less than 1 percent of marriages. Remarriage following divorce or the death of a spouse is possible for both Sinhala men and women, although it is unusual; it is especially rare for previously married women to marry never-married men.

The majority of Sinhala families practice bilateral inheritance, giving a portion of the family possessions to all children in the family. This inheritance pattern has been linked to the relatively high status of Sinhala women. In practice, fixed property such as land generally goes to sons, and the family home itself typically goes to the youngest son. Mobile property such as cash, furniture, and jewelry is more likely to go to daughters, often in the form of dowry. Unlike dowry practices in India that may put brides at risk, dowry among the Sinhala families I knew was considered the property of the bride herself and served as a kind of safety net for her children and herself, often eventually passing on to the bride's own daughter as dowry. However, dowry is usually only included in marriages that are arranged, at least to some extent, by families.

By the time a marriage comes to be, whether it is initiated as a love match by the bride and groom themselves or whether it is begun for them as a proposal marriage, the bride and groom usually know each other well. For the Buddhist majority in Sri Lanka, marriage is not a religious ceremony per se, although the marriage ceremony feels sacred and full of meaning, with each ritual act done to ensure the auspiciousness of the marriage and the family ties being created. One of the usual acts during this ceremony is to wrap a plain white sheet around the bride's waist, the sheet on which the new couple would have intercourse for the first time. Following this ceremony, and after many pictures were taken and a meal was provided by the bride's family, the couples I knew in Viligama as well as in more affluent areas usually spent a few days on their own in a hotel or guesthouse. During this time, the bride and groom, who had come to know each other over the long process of negotiating the marriage, were expected to have sex for the first time. When this little time away was over, the couple returned to the groom's parent's home. During this "homecoming," the groom's family would host another elaborate meal. At some point during the party, the bride, now traditionally wearing a red sari rather than a white one, should present the white sheet with her virginal blood on it to the groom's mother and other older female relatives. This homecoming celebration concludes the wedding festivities, establishing a new family unit and new networks of kin.

Although much of the recent anthropological work on Sri Lanka has focused on broad sociopolitical processes, there are accounts of more intimate, ordinary life that are helpful in understanding more about Sinhala families.[28] These ethnographies present a consistent picture of expectations regarding gendered family roles. Although a woman may assist her husband in his work and may have her own income, she is primarily responsible for child care, food preparations, buying food and clothing, and other household tasks. In fact, when I asked children during play interviews to put the family dolls into the house, they invariably put the mother dolls in the kitchen. Women may have a great deal of power within a family; however, ultimate authority belongs to the oldest male member of a household, whether that is the father, husband, brother, or son. Though there is some debate about whether there was great egalitarianism between the sexes prior to the introduction of colonial law, the husband, when present, is the undisputed head of household.[29] In this role, he is generally characterized as a sort of beneficent and gentle patriarch, and he typically consults his wife on important decisions and leaves her to manage her own affairs. His primary responsibilities are in his work outside the home, and he does little in the way of household tasks or child care. He traditionally sleeps and eats apart from the rest of the household. He expresses no overt signs of affection publicly, either to his wife or grown children. The only exception is in his relationship with very young children on whom he lavishes physical affection, taking on a stricter disciplinary role, particularly with sons whom he is responsible for controlling. Corporal punishment is quite common, especially from older males to boys. Although mothers perform most of the child rearing, they are more responsible for their daughters' discipline and tend to be more indulgent with their sons. In Viligama, I found a similar division of household tasks and relationships, both in my direct observations and in people's reports. As will be referenced in the chapters that follow, however, I did not find men to be as isolated from their children or even their wives as portrayed in most of these older ethnographies, although a kind of distance clearly existed.

As it is usually discussed in Sri Lanka, marriage is a ranked relationship with the husband in the senior position. Although husbands are seen as having more authority, there are ways in which they are dependent on their wives, particularly in regard to food preparation. In still other ways, the spousal relationship is conceived of as one between peers. Cross-cousins are not only the preferred marriage partners but the only colloquial Sinhala kin terms which do not indicate elder-younger relationship. In addition, although husbands and wives should not display signs of marital intimacy, a deep attachment between them is the ideal. These themes of hierarchy and mutuality are clear in the response from a woman in Viligama to a question about husbands hitting their wives, something which was often expected, if not acceptable, under certain circumstances:

> Getting married means that every day, both are in a relationship together for their life time. If even for a little mistake, the husband beats the wife, that is a very cruel act. . . . I think it is a weakness in his mentality. That is his weak mentality. Now truly, when both are in bed, does he have the strength to beat a person who is so peaceful? . . . He is bringing food, drink, sarees, everything for the woman. But the women are doing all the work—washing clothes, giving food and drink. Doing all the work in the home and the children's work. . . . Doing everything. They have to do all those things. Then to pacify sexual needs. Sometimes when they go to bed, he does not allow her to be, needing to be satisfied. So hitting someone like that is a sin (*paapaya*).

In this, as in most marriages in Viligama, authority, caring, and obligation are woven together in complex and dynamic ways. These same threads help make up the fabric of more explicitly and consistently hierarchical relationships both in and out of the home, as this book will demonstrate.

The Everyday Life of Sinhala Families

It is striking how little description of childrearing and family life is included in the ethnographic work on Sri Lanka, let alone how infrequent are the efforts to analyze the effects of those practices.[30] What little documentation there has been is generally consistent with the findings from my own fieldwork, although the interpretations vary, and I will present them along the way. This paucity is, of course, one of the main reasons for my having undertaken this research and written this book. Throughout the chapters that follow, I will present descriptions of childrearing practices as they connect to my analysis of how desire and relationships are shaped in this Sinhala village. Here I will introduce some of my more general observations regarding family life and childcare in order to provide context for the analyses to come and to fill out the ethnographic record on childrearing in Sri Lanka.

Day and Night

A typical day in Viligama started early, often before dawn. Mothers would make tea, sometimes bringing it to husbands, older people staying at the house, or sleepy children who needed to get up for school. They would make breakfast and lunch for those who were going to work or to school. Later in the morning, when the morning housework was done and the others out of the house, women who stayed home sometimes took a nap or had a bath before doing the afternoon chores and cooking. When children came home from school, they might have lunch if they had not eaten at school. They might fall asleep for a bit, but there is no formal practice of either afternoon naps for children or siestas for adults. In the afternoon, there was often tea and snacks. Dinner was served late in the evening, after dark and just before the adults turned in. Many nights, young children did not make it that far, falling asleep somewhere after tea. When children fell asleep, they might be carried to a bed, where they were often covered with a mosquito net, although older children and adults did not usually use these in Viligama. Later, when the rest of the family was ready to turn in, little children would be taken outside or to the bathroom to relieve themselves. Then without the elaborate routines involving bathing, dressing, toothbrushing, and reading that are typical for both children and adults in the United States, the family would head off to bed, often in the same room, often in the same bed—a practice of co-sleeping that was the result of preference rather than space limitations.

In the early part of my fieldwork, I would ask new parents if they were getting any sleep, expecting that they were not and expecting to commiserate with them. This was an experience and conversation that is so common in the United States that I had taken for granted that it was a universal experience of new parents. However, Sri Lankan parents were consistently confused by my question. As I was there longer, I came to understand their confusion.

Babies in Viligama were not expected to follow a strict sleep schedule. They were not expected to go to sleep at a particular time at night, to sleep alone, or to sleep all night through, as many parents in the United States try to get their babies to do. In fact, no one of any age in Viligama was really expected to do those things. Since babies slept next to their mothers, nursing whenever they liked, mothers did not have to get out of bed periodically throughout the night to feed them, nor did their crying wake the rest of the family. In any case, periodic nighttime activity was not unusual or disconcerting for people I knew in Sri Lanka, who did not seem to expect or value uninterrupted sleep nor did they seem to have trouble falling back asleep.[31] Indeed, new mothers if anything seemed to sleep *more* than other adults, since they spent so much time in bed with their babies during the day as well, and fathers' sleep remained pretty much the same.

Another reason that my question about whether adults were getting enough sleep produced confusion was that this was not something that people in Sri Lanka talked about or even seemed to think about very much. I did not find the elaboration of ideas about sleep that is part of the common sense and conversation of so many in the United States. I did not encounter people complaining that they were behind on sleep or could not fall asleep, that they needed a routine, special sleeping circumstances, or quiet to sleep more. When I asked people how much they thought a person should sleep at night, they seemed not to have considered the question before. When people did respond, the answers ranged quite a bit, but no one told me they thought a person needed as much as eight hours, the standard recommendation in the United States. People I knew in Viligama did think sleeping was a kind of indulgence, associated with laziness and boredom, with sickness, and sometimes with leisure. As indicated above, proper wives and mothers were expected to rise very early. Students were expected to stay up late studying. Monks were supposed to restrict their sleep, as they were to take the middle path with other bodily needs, avoiding attachment to these as either pleasures or austerities. But mostly people did not pay sleep much attention, letting it fill in where there was time—more for those who were very young or very old, less for those who were busy, more during the nightly power cuts that were so common when I was there, and none at all during certain all-night celebrations.

A New Baby

The ideal in Viligama as in other Sinhala areas of Sri Lanka is for new couples to establish their own homes and raise their children there, as discussed above. However, when a new baby is born, the mother typically returns to her own mother's home where she will stay with the baby for the first three months, something allowed even to working mothers under the state-mandated three month's paid maternity leave. During this time, the mother's female relatives care for her and the baby, doing their laundry, cooking for the mother, and sparing her from her usual household chores.

When I visited new mothers during this period, they were usually in their housedresses, lying in bed with the baby, who dozed and nursed as it wished. As new mothers began to feel stronger, they would get up more frequently, often leaving the baby on its back on a cloth on the bed, awake or asleep. Fathers would come to visit the mother and baby, sometimes bringing along the couple's older children. These older children usually continued to live at their own homes, looked after, perhaps, and cooked for by the father's mother or sisters. Relatives and neighbors would stop by to visit, leaning over the baby, smiling exaggeratedly and cooing "uu-kuu, uu-kuu"—which I was told was a sort of baby-talk word for milk. Seldom did I hear babies crying, and mothers, too, seemed happy and well cared for during this period.

Babies I knew in Viligama were nursed frequently and for several years, with little fuss but a good deal of warmth. It was assumed to be something that both mothers and babies enjoyed, and this seemed to me to be true. While still at the mothers' natal homes, babies I knew in Viligama were kept close to their mothers, nursing as often as they liked and on no particular schedule. Once the mothers returned to their own homes, they were much busier, cooking, sweeping, and washing clothes for the family. While mothers attended to these tasks, babies were laid on their backs on cloths or held by other family members. Still, babies were not usually very far from their mothers, who continued to nurse them frequently, though not necessarily for very long at any one time. Mothers did not seem concerned about how much milk the baby was getting or which breast the child nursed from, nor did they encourage a child to drain the breast fully at one time, as mothers in the United States are sometimes advised. If a mother had to go out for a short time or return to a job for longer periods of time, babies were typically left in the care of their grandparents or a nearby aunt. If there was no family living close by and a mother's responsibilities were particularly heavy, one of the baby's grandmothers might come to stay for a time. During those times when a mother was away, babies who did not yet eat solid foods were given formula or *kottamalli* (coriander tea). But at nighttime, all of the babies and toddlers I knew in Viligama nursed as much as they liked from their mothers whom they slept next to, usually in a bed shared with the baby's father and siblings.

These breastfeeding practices I observed in Viligama are consistent with reports from around the island. At the time I began my fieldwork, most children in Sri Lanka were breastfed well beyond their second birthday, and nearly all were nursed at some point.[32] This breastfeeding was usually the exclusive form of nourishment in the first few months, while water, formula, and solid foods were added gradually. The authors of one study reported that these rates regarding the continuation of breastfeeding and the introduction of solid foods were the same for the mothers who worked at jobs out of the home as it was for the rest who did not, although those who worked at jobs tended to nurse more on a schedule, whereas the at-home mothers did not (van den Berg and Ball 2008). These authors concluded that this ongoing breastfeeding, regardless of work, was facilitated by the practice of co-sleeping and nighttime nursing.[33] This relatively long duration of breastfeeding was consistent with the mothers' own experience as children.[34] These mothers also said that it was from their own mothers that these women received guidance in feeding their own children, though they reported being even more influenced by advice from their doctors—all of whom seem to have shared the understanding that mothers ought to nurse their children for the first few years of life.

Parents as Providers

Knowing what children need and providing it is central to and even definitive of the role of parents in Viligama. Whenever I asked people to tell me the best ways to raise children, they invariably focused on what parents should provide children. Mothers and grandmothers would begin by telling me about how children should be fed. Fathers talked about providing children with a good education. This idea of parents-as-providers frames many of the different tasks that Sinhala mothers and fathers do for their children. Parents must provide food, clothing, and shelter for their children while they are young, as well as the education, property, and social contacts they will require to ensure their material needs are met into adulthood. This emphasis on providing as central to the role of parents and other senior people figures prominently in the analyses in the chapters to come.

Because parents must provide for their children, they must take care not to have more children than they can afford. This was something that people in Viligama insisted on. As a mother of three grown daughters explained in response to my asking about how many children a family should have,

> That depends on the economic situation. If there isn't any financial prob-
> lem, it is better to have four or five babies, you know—to see them all
> grown, with good jobs, living luxurious lives. That is a happiness, and I
> would like that. But we must be able to afford their education and every-
> thing. We must feed them properly. If you cannot take that responsibility,
> it would be better to have one baby and raise it. If you cannot afford it, it
> is better to have one than to have four or five children and put them in
> trouble and suffering. That is how I think.

This is the way many people in Sri Lanka think, and it shapes what they do. The rate of live births in Sri Lanka has been only 2.26 per woman in recent years.[35] The message that it is irresponsible to have more children than a family can afford to take care of has been promulgated by national public education campaigns and facilitated by widely available and affordable birth control (De Silva 1994). But it is a message that fits very well with how people in Viligama think about what it means to be a parent. At the same time, parents did not make these decisions without occasional regrets. One man with a successful village shop, whose two grown children now had children of their own, told me that during the early years of his marriage he thought he did not have enough money to have a lot of children, but now he thinks he does not have enough children.

Although it is the responsibility of both parents to make sure their children are provided for, the fathers' role focuses on providing economic resources while mothers are typically responsible for day-to-day direct provision and supervision. Given this division of labor, most of the instantiations of this provider/recipient dyad in young children's lives involved their mothers and sometimes grandmothers or aunts. However, both mothers and fathers were responsible for making sure their children have what they need. This means that it is not inconsistent with being a good mother to a small child to go work abroad as a nanny for foreign children in order to send money back so that her own family could finish building their house, be able to buy a three-wheel taxi to offer for hire, or save up for school fees for a prestigious private school. It also means that, while men were not typically involved with the hands-on care and feeding of children, they seemed to find it well within the requirements of the role as fathers or even grandfathers, uncles, or brothers to provide this kind of care when needed. Frequently, other members of the family helped out with child care, educational and employment arrangements, or housing—but it is the parents who were the ones through which this was arranged.

On the face of it, it may seem that providing for children is the fundamental responsibility of parents everywhere. However, I want to point out at least three ways that this Sinhala idea has a particular cultural shape. First, as evolutionary and cultural anthropologists have repeatedly pointed out, the personnel of caretaking may and usually does involve many people beyond the child's own biological parents (see, for example, Hrdy 2009, Seymour 2004). This was certainly true in Viligama. Grandparents, aunts, siblings, cousins, neighbors, and teachers sometimes took care of children. In some families I knew in town, servants also looked after children. But even when other people provided the bulk of the child care, children were considered the responsibility and right of the biological mother and father, at least unless some other arrangement was made.

Second, evidence from a wide range of societies demonstrates that various caretaking tasks and responsibilities for providing may be parsed and distributed among caretakers in different ways. For instance, among the Murik of New Guinea, a child's own primary mother figure provides comfort while other mother-like figures correct the child's behavior (Barlow 2010). On the other hand in Bhubaneswar, India, paternal grandmothers, aunts, and other family members cared for children, while children's own mothers were discouraged from looking at them or holding them for extended periods of time (Seymour 2013). So while the Sinhala belief that it is the *parents*—both mother and father together—who bear the primary responsibility for seeing that their children's needs are met may be unsurprising to many in the United States who hold similar ideas about the primacy of parents, these beliefs and practices are by no means universal.

A third way that this construction of the role of parents is culturally shaped is perhaps more obvious in its contrast with practices among contemporary middle-class families in the United States. This cultural shaping has to do with the emphasis given the task of providing over other aspects of what Sri Lankan parents do for their children. In different societies, parents hold different cultural models about what a parent's role is and what children need, foregrounding different aspects of basic child care and training. In some communities, parenting may be seen as most importantly about protection; in others, it may be focused on character development; in another, it might be to make children feel loved and special. For the people I knew in Viligama, however, it is *providing* that is the aspect of what parents do for children—and they of course do many things—that is paramount.

In the chapters that follow, I will continue to explore ways that people in Viligama think about parenting and how they go about providing for their children. I will examine these ideas and practices as they play out in everyday, ordinary interactions, asking what it is that children learn through these encounters, how culture gets transmitted, and how the children themselves are shaped.

3

Socializing Desire

Demanding Toddlers and
Self-Restrained Children

From early on in my fieldwork, I was impressed by the quiet, restrained, and self-denying manner of the Sri Lankan children I came to know.[1] Bashfully pulling behind their mothers who came to my house for a visit, these school-age children would mouth a silent but smiling "*baa*" indicating that they "couldn't" accept my offer of milk-tea or biscuits. When I came to their houses, they would stand, smiling shyly, their arms hanging limply at their sides, not moving to take the small wrapped gifts I presented, until finally their mothers accepted the gifts and put them aside to be opened after I left.

This behavior was so different from what I expected from children of the same age in the United States, children who would plead to unwrap birthday presents before the guests even got through the door, tearing off the paper as soon as they were allowed, and exclaiming with pleasure at the gifts inside. How, I wondered, as had other Western visitors to Sri Lanka, did Sri Lankan children become so well-mannered? How had they been taught such self-restraint? And why were they not more interested in these gifts?

Although groups of school children might shout at foreign tourists for "school pens," clinging to each other with laughter at their bravado, in more usual circumstances these same children were deferent to adults and unlikely to try to get things that were not theirs or even to display possessiveness of things that were. In the few places where Sri Lankan children are talked about in anthropological accounts, they are typically described as shy, displaying a valued disposition of *lajja-baya* (shame-fear), that is strongly associated by both Sinhala villagers and by ethnographers with self-discipline, control, and restraint (e.g., De Silva 2002; Lynch 2007; Obeyesekere 1984; Spencer 1999). In her ethnography of life in a rural community in the south of the island, Baker speaks admiringly of the "unselfishness and honesty" of the village children.

She relates an incident in which a ten-year-old boy with whom she was walking refused to keep a coin they had found on the road, slipping it out of his pocket when he thought she was not looking and putting it back on the path, saying in response to her surprise: "Some small child might have lost it and might come back looking for it" (1998: 105).

As I came to know families in Sri Lanka more intimately, I came to spend more time with their younger children. And I came to see glimpses of a very different kind of behavior in these young children, behavior that seemed nearly the opposite of the mannerly self-restraint I had observed in their older, more fully socialized brothers and sisters. The littler children would assert their wishes boldly, demanding to have whatever they desired. Mothers were clearly embarrassed by this behavior and would try to distract and quiet their demanding children, smiling uneasily and whispering unrealistic promises or threats. If this failed, the mothers would give up and give in to the demands of the children or leave with the child altogether.

These observations added a new dimension to the puzzle of how it is that Sri Lankan children became so restrained and undemanding. If they were being taught this restraint by their parents, it was not a lesson I recognized. Rather than being strict with their children, as I might have expected, teaching them to control their own demands by setting firm and consistent limits from an early age, the mothers and others I observed in Viligama usually gave in to what babies and young children demanded.

As I will explore in greater depth and to different ends in the next chapter, this responsiveness to children's needs began in infancy. Adults were typically attuned to subtle signs of infants' needs and responded to them quickly. Mothers nursed babies as much as they liked, sleeping beside them at night, practices that continued for years. Baker also observed that "toddlers and babies are coddled and indulged" in the impoverished village in which she worked, describing how they are dressed in expensive clothes, given attention and doted on by all who come within their vicinity. She, too, notes that they are fed on demand and says, "It is rare to hear an infant cry in the village" (1998: 100).

This acquiescence did not stop as these babies became toddlers and young children. Instead, children just seemed to make fewer and fewer demands. When children did insist on having their way, despite attempts to distract or remove them, parents appeared powerless to resist their demands.

Far from helping me understand how it was that Sri Lankan school-age children were so well-behaved, this apparently indulgent parental behavior intensified the puzzle. My expectation—one so widely held in the United States as to be taken as self-evident—was that giving in to children when they stubbornly insist on getting their way certainly does not teach them patience, self-restraint, and generosity. To the contrary, this kind of parental submission to children's demands was what I, like many in the United States, would have called and predicted to be "spoiling." I assumed that giving in to children like this would reward and encourage demanding, selfish behavior, leading those children to become demanding, selfish, unappreciative older children and, eventually, self-centered adults.

However, in the Sri Lankan case, mothers, fathers, siblings, shopkeepers—everyone I saw gave in to the demands of little ones, no matter how outrageous; and yet, by middle childhood, Sri Lankan children stopped demanding. Somehow, little two-year-old tyrants, marching around their world, throwing tantrums, being served and indulged by all around them, transform—beginning around age five and certainly by age ten—into shy, compliant, restrained, and self-denying older children.

This chapter is an exploration of this puzzle. I begin by introducing a little girl I call Rashika. It was she who first called my attention to the way people in Viligama give in to the demands of small children and led me to ask the question of how this "spoiling" could fit into a pattern of child rearing that produced older children who were so self-restrained. In what follows, I trace out my quest to answer that question, including an examination of how children's desires are managed in other cultural contexts. I then use my close examination of this indulgence in Rashika's family and my subsequent enlistment of other mothers in Viligama to figure out what might be going on in this cultural context.

In the end, I argue that this indulgence is part of a culturally normative pattern of child rearing that encourages a growing child to make a transition in behavior and emotional orientation from being a demanding baby to disavowing his or her own desires by middle childhood. I propose that crucial to this transition are the subtle negative messages that accompany the indulgence. Children come to recognize that when they assert their desires, their demands will be met, but that in the process the affection from and inclusion with those they care about may be disrupted. This early socialization to the destructive potential of desire makes fertile ground for subsequent cultural doctrines that explicitly link desire, suffering, and destruction. I also suggest that mothers and others who have already internalized these understandings of desire as dangerous then react to their children's assertions of desire with intense discomfort combined with indulgence, even if they think there are better ways to parent, replicating their own socialization in the experiences of their children.

But let me begin by introducing Rashika.

Rashika

I first met Rashika when she was two years old. She had been born soon after my first stay in Sri Lanka to my neighbor Sii Devi, a woman whom I had come to know and like especially well. When I returned to the village after having been away for two years, one of the houses I stayed at was Sii Devi's. And what I found there was that this delightful little girl, Rashika, now ran the household.

Everything that Rashika wanted, Rashika got. If she wanted to be held, she was held; if she wanted to sit on the table, she sat on the table; if she wanted her older brother's new game, he must give it to her. If she wanted to put all the potato curry on her plate just for the joy of ladling it, then no one would stop her. If she wanted to sit up on the kitchen counter and cut okra with a sharp knife like her mother was doing, then there she was. No matter whom she inconvenienced or what the consequences might be, Rashika's desires were indulged.

On that return visit, I had brought Rashika's older brother, Sampath, the game of Yahtzee as a present from the United States. Toward the end of the visit, I finally sat down to teach him to play it. His mother had been encouraging me to do so since I arrived, motivated by her belief that by "getting used to" Western things, Sampath would be drawn to them and thus be more successful in the long run. Ensuring Sampath's success in school and eventually in a career was one of the central concerns of Sii Devi's life.

But at ten, Sampath was too shy to be alone with me so he wanted his mother to stay with us. This, of course, meant that his little sister Rashika was there as well. I gathered that what Sampath wanted was to play the game with his mother and me and to have his sister go away. What his sister wanted was to have all the dice and all the shakers to herself all the time. This meant that no one else could roll the dice without her screaming.

My inclination was to ignore Rashika's screams, take our turns as quickly and undemonstratively as possible, involving her in the dice rolling and other parts she could help with, and then give her more frequent turns in between each of us. Given my own cultural understandings about children and childrearing, my approach seemed to me a reasonable way of handling the situation so that everyone's desires were met at least a little bit.

Rashika's mother understood and responded to this situation differently. At first, she tried to find different spaces where she could distract Rashika while Sampath and I continued playing. However, each time she left the area, Sampath would get up and drift after her, too shy to stay alone with me. So eventually, there we all were, trying to play the game together. And Rashika screamed anytime anyone else tried to use the dice. After many attempts and with mounting but unarticulated frustration from all, we were forced to abandon the game, because, as Sii Devi said, "She will not let us play."

To this and countless other incidents in which children expressed a desire for something they should not have, the adults and older children at first responded either by ignoring the desire or by distracting the child toward another thing or activity or space. Often parents tried deceit, promising later treats or warning about unrelated disasters that might befall them. But if the child persisted in his or her demands, and especially if the child cried, the elder person would give in.

So, if a child wanted her brother's new toy, she was ignored, given something else, or, eventually, allowed to play with it. If she really wanted the matches, even after they had been hidden where she could not reach them, she was given them. At one point toward the end of this visit, Rashika and Sii Devi were in the kitchen and Rashika had started crying. I walked into the kitchen and asked what the trouble was. Sii Devi told me that Rashika wanted one of the antibiotic tablets that she had just seen her father take. Although Sii Devi had not given her one, I could see that she was finding it hard to resist, wincing as she said in response to my (admittedly ethnocentric) exclamation that she could not give it to her, "I know, but she *wants* one."

At another time, earlier in my stay with Sii Devi, I was sitting in her kitchen while she was cooking. Rashika came up to me and tried to take my new digital camera that I was holding in my lap. Without thinking, I off-handedly said "*epaa*," the refusing "no" in Sinhala. To my surprise, Rashika burst into angry, horrified tears. Her mother scooped her up, trying unsuccessfully, to comfort her. I was mortified and, somewhat defensively, told Sii Devi that all I had done was to say "epaa," at which Rashika screamed louder and angrier, alternating between burying her face in her mother's shoulder and glaring at me. Later, after paying attention to how others in the household responded to Rashika's requests, I asked Sii Devi, "No one says 'epaa' to her, do they?" "No, Bambi," Sii Devi said gently.

Why, I wondered. And more importantly, how was this kind of parenting ever going to get Rashika toward being an appropriately restrained, self-denying child like the older Sinhala children I knew?

Parenting Theories and Responses to Children's Demands

That two-year-old Rashika wanted things, was trying to get them, and was quickly frustrated when she did not was not surprising—not surprising to me and not surprising to her mother. We both assumed that children around this age will want things and will try to get them, that they are easily exasperated if they do not, and that they do not yet understand the social rules and consequences of such demands. However, the ways that we thought we should or shouldn't respond to these childish requests, how we thought toddlers would turn into well-behaved older children, and even how we defined what "well-behaved" meant were fundamentally different in ways I only slowly came to see.

There is some debate about whether or not the so-called "terrible twos" is universal. Anthropologists Sara Harkness and Charles Super write in their volume on parents' cultural beliefs in different societies, "Two-year-old tantrums are one of the great universals of human behavior, appearing expectably in simple as well as complex cultures" (1996: 2). However, developmental psychologist Barbara Rogoff concludes from her review of reports from around the world, "In many communities, such a transition to negativism and obstinacy around age 2 is not observed or expected" (2003: 167). Although the jury may still be out on the extent to which this kind of behavior is universal for this age group, reports from a wide range of societies including those in both Rogoff's and Harkness and Super's volumes, show two-year-old children expressing their desires.

What clearly does vary across cultures, though, is how parents interpret and respond to such wishes—and to what effects.

Parental Ethnotheories

What parents believe about children—about what children need, about what they are capable of at different stages, about whether they are vulnerable and to what, about their moral dispositions and spiritual character, about what it is that changes as they grow up and how that change happens—shapes how parents behave toward children, how they structure children's experiences, and how they feel toward them. This can vary between and even within individual people. However, many of these ideas are shared with others with whom we interact. This is not only because our ideas are developed in conversation and exchange with others but also more fundamentally because our own experiences are often similar to those of others within our social group. Similar experiences in the world lead us to develop similar ideas about how that world works. The ideas that relate to one another and are broadly shared among members of a society form what cognitive anthropologists would call a "cultural model" (see D'Andrade 1995, Strauss and Quinn 1997). Cultural models about children and childrearing are what Harkness and Super call "parental ethnotheories" (1996).

What is particularly important about the cultural models parents have about children is not so much the ideas themselves—although those ideas are often interesting. If we are to understand how it is that ideas are transmitted and people are shaped, what is important about parents' cultural models is how they are instantiated in practices—how cultural beliefs shape what people *do*. These practices may be regularized through institutionally structured activities like schooling or religious rituals. However, they also emerge on the fly, as those who take care of children rally the understandings at their disposal to make sense of situations and decide what to do. In this way, ideas about children shape the experiences children encounter, and so shape children. The extent to which these ideas are shared or diverge contributes to the patterning of children's experiences and so to the patterning of children.

US Ethnotheories about the Danger of Spoiling

When I interacted with Rashika, I was drawing on my own cultural models of children and childrearing—models that it became clear Sii Devi did not share. My responses to Rashika's grab for my camera or insistence on having the Yahtzee dice felt natural to me, flowing as they did from my own "common sense" about children.

Although my actions were surprising to Rashika and to her mother, they were very much in line with what others in the United States might have done. In fact, my improvised strategy of letting Rashika take extra turns with the dice was similar to the ways the middle-class European American mothers in Christine Mosier and Barbara Rogoff's study handled conflicts over toys between toddlers and their older siblings. In contrast to the Guatemalan mothers in their study, who expected their older children to give the younger ones the coveted toy, the American mothers tended to emphasize the equal rights of the children, wanting them to follow the same rules and negotiate turn taking, although they were more lenient with the little ones (2003: 1055). The US mothers in that study and I were operating out of a shared ethnotheory, part of which held that all children should be treated equally, with only minimal allowances made for the littlest ones. We shared the idea that by insisting on "cooperative" behavior we could teach children "proper behavior" and "counter willfulness" (2003: 1048).

I was acting out of my cultural assumptions that children must be taught to share, to take turns, and to follow rules by having firm but gentle limits set. I believed that it was my obligation, as a responsible adult, to say "no" to demands that were out of bounds—and that once I said "no," it was my responsibility to stick to that. If I were to give in to Rashika's screams, I would be reinforcing that behavior, teaching her that "no" did not really mean "no," teaching her that she could and should manipulate people around her with displays of temper, and that she could always expect to get her own way. To give in to Rashika, I believed, would be to "spoil" her.

US PARENTING ADVICE: SET CONSISTENT LIMITS EARLY. One way that these ideas about children are captured and circulated in the United States is in the form of expert advice in child-rearing guidebooks. As Judy DeLoache and Alma Gottlieb point out, although such parenting guides may introduce new perspectives and even contribute to lasting changes in the ways children are seen and raised, they primarily "reinforce common cultural practices" (2000: 21). Despite the array of perspectives and approaches taken by guidebooks available to US parents, there is remarkable consistency in their belief that setting limits is essential in raising good and happy children.

The discussions of discipline and setting limits that these books commonly offer reflect similar beliefs about the dangers of spoiling to those I was acting out of when I interacted with Rashika. This is certainly the case in Dr. Spock's perennially popular child care manual in which he warns that "the more parents submit to babies' orders, the more demanding the children become" (2004: 105). He urges parents to take steps to correct this pattern with children between six and twelve months old so that babies "begin to build frustration tolerance," which is, he says, "a much harder lesson to learn later on" (106). Barton Schmitt, writing in another oft-reprinted child care guide, recommends parents begin discipline with children as young as four months so that "parents can begin to clarify their own rights. If your child kicks and wiggles during a diaper change, making the process difficult," he says, "you can say firmly, 'No, help mommy change your diaper'" (2005: 311). He recommends beginning "external controls" such as these because, he says, "Children don't start to develop internal controls (self-control) until 3 or 4 years of age. They continue to need external controls (in gradually decreasing amounts) through adolescence" (309). Similarly, *The Children's Hospital Guide to Your Child's Health and Development*, a popular guide put out by the Children's Hospital in Boston, says:

> It is important for parents to set clear, consistent limits for their children, which form the basis of discipline. Although an infant under 1 year old is not ready for regular discipline techniques, the use of simple commands and an authoritative tone of voice can be effective when your child is doing something that may harm him, another child, or the upholstery on your new sofa. When he misbehaves, pull him aside immediately and say, "No biting," or "Stop!" . . . Your baby can't follow elaborate explanations, . . . but he does understand the word "no," even though he doesn't always obey you when you say it. (Woolf et al. 2001: 165)

An important part of this US ethnotheory that is being spelled out to new or uncertain parents is that children need this limit setting in order to learn self-control—and further, that children themselves *want* adults to set limits for them, as it makes them feel safe and loved. The *Children's Hospital Guide* continues in this vein:

> If you set consistent, loving limits for your child, he can learn, gradually, to set limits for himself. That is, he can learn self-control. To do this, he needs to know where the boundaries are, and within those boundaries, he needs freedom to make his own choices. It may surprise you to know that children want to have clear limits set by adults. These limits make them feel secure because they fear unpredictable situations where the

rules are not clear. So set your limits, and let him go. If he exceeds those limits, it's time to step in. (Woolf et al. 2001: 166)

There are, of course, many differences and points of disagreement among parents and among parenting experts about the best ways to discipline children; however, underlying these are many shared cultural assumptions. One example of this can be seen in Penelope Leach's "baby-led" approach, in which she aims to offer new approaches to parenting. In this popular guide, she advocates that parents refrain from punishment and anger with children under one year old, which she says is both ineffective and damaging for babies. She says that you cannot "spoil" a baby with too much love and positivity, and that it is in fact those very things that foster good development. However, she still sees consistent limit setting as important early on, allowing that "yes, children need clear, comprehensible boundaries" and that "'no' has to be understandable and it has to mean 'no' always" (2010: 274). Similarly, attachment-oriented US parenting guides, which emphasize the importance of the early bond between parent and child and encourage parents to respond sensitively to infants' expressions of needs, see this type of early parenting as laying the groundwork for subsequent limit setting. Sears and Sears, authors of some of the most popular of such guides, argue that "true discipline is the product of a trusting relationship between parent and child" (2003: 563). During the first year of life, parent and child are becoming attuned to each other. "On this foundation both the connected parent and the connected infant can more comfortably graduate to the next stage of discipline—setting limits" (364). By the time the child is around two, Sears and Sears emphasize the importance of boundary and limit setting and the importance of consistency.

US PARENTING ADVICE: DO NOT GIVE IN TO TODDLER TANTRUMS. These beliefs about the importance of limit setting in preventing children from becoming "spoiled" lead to specific recommendations about how to handle conflicts that are presumed to arise inevitably when toddlers' demands butt up against those limits. In the United States, "toddlers" are expected to be increasingly self-assertive and stubborn. When these two-year-olds do not get their way, "temper tantrums" may ensue, in which children may scream, cry, and throw themselves on the ground, inconsolable until and unless they get what they want. This poses problems for parents fearful of reinforcing that kind of terribly unwanted behavior by giving in to it.

The experts suggest to parents an array of tactics and tricks for responding to these difficult toddler demands and temper tantrums, but they are in agreement about the basics: remain calm, try to ignore the behavior, and do not give in. The *Children's Hospital Guide* is clear about this: "There are two things to avoid when your child throws a tantrum. First, don't lose your temper. . . .

Second, don't give in to your child's demand." They recommend that, in order to help a child get through a tantrum, parents should silently remove the child from a public place, if that is where it begins, and then "ignore him until the tantrum is over" (Woolf et al. 2001: 188). They emphasize that tantrums are "normal for toddlers," beginning around eighteen months old, because they have less self-control and communication skills than older children. They say that these tantrums are the result of a child "trying to work through his inner turmoil" (187). By doing so, "toddlers learn from them that they can come through such rage and survive it. With time, they will accept help in avoiding tantrums and eventually learn how to do this themselves" (187–188). Sears and Sears, coming from an attachment-parenting perspective, offer similar if somewhat more flexible advice, reminding parents that it is important to "convey who's in charge" (2003: 365). In responding to tantrums, they recommend examining the causes of the tantrum, staying calm, redirecting the behavior, removing the child from a public scene, and offering children choices when possible. They advise parents to consider what rules must be enforced and what ones can be compromised, but they advise against regularly giving in to children's tantrums: "If you sense that your child is consistently using tantrums behavior to get his own way, don't change from a reasonable 'no' to a wimpy 'yes.' . . . This reinforces negative behavior" (570).

The danger of giving in to tantrums is clear: the child will be spoiled, setting him or her up for future social difficulties.[2] In his advice book, Schmitt lays out what is "common sense" to most people in the United States, whether or not they are parents themselves:

> The main cause of spoiled children is a lenient, permissive parent who doesn't set limits and gives in to tantrums and whining. . . . Without intervention, spoiled children run into trouble by school age. Other children do not like them because they are too bossy and selfish. Adults do not like them because they are rude and make excessive demands on them. Eventually they become hard for even the parent to love because of their behaviors. As a reaction to not getting along well with other children and adults, spoiled children eventually become unhappy. Spoiled children may show reduced motivation and reduced perseverance in schoolwork. There is also an association with risk-taking behaviors, such a drug abuse. Overall, spoiling a child prepared him poorly for life in the real world. (Schmitt 2005: 327–328)

However, through reasonable but firm limit setting and a refusal to give in to children's tantrums, children will learn self-control and respect for others. As Schmitt summarizes, "Good discipline gradually changes a self-centered child into a mature teen who is responsible, thoughtful, and respectful of others, assertive without being hostile, and in control of his or her impulses. Reasonable limit-setting keeps us from raising a spoiled child" (2005: 309).

The Puzzle about Rashika

According to these cultural beliefs that I brought with me to Sri Lanka, allowing Rashika to do or have whatever she insisted upon was going to spoil her, was going to make her into a selfish, inconsiderate person whom no one would enjoy being around. This would have been a problem in the United States, but would be an even greater anomaly in Sri Lanka, where older children were typically so much more reserved, compliant, and self-denying than those I knew in the United States.

One possibility was that perhaps Rashika was, in fact, anomalous. In every society, some people fit less well than others with what their society expects of them. Perhaps Sii Devi was raising Rashika in a way significantly out of synch with other children in Sri Lanka, including Rashika's older sibling, who was quite well-behaved.

Yet, I had seen other small children in Sri Lanka treated much the same way as Rashika, allowed to do and have whatever they insisted on. And when I went to other mothers in Viligama, asking about the way Rashika was being treated, they found it perfectly normal and sensible.

So what was going on?

"We Have to Give"

During my return trip to Sri Lanka in 2004 when I first met Rashika, I had scheduled follow-up visits and interviews with the women I had come to know well during my initial fieldwork in Viligama. During these visits, I asked about the kind of indulgent behavior I had been witnessing at Sii Devi's house. I related an actual incident that happened during my stay with Rashika, although I said it was with a family I knew near the city, and asked the other mothers to explain it to me.

This incident began with Sii Devi's request that I prepare an "American dinner" for her family. For dessert, I planned to serve banana splits, overlooking the local health belief drawn from Ayurvedic traditions that held that "cooling" foods—such as ice cream and some bananas—should not be eaten in the evening lest they produce phlegm and illness, a particular concern with young children. Rashika seemed to be particularly predisposed to colds, phlegm, and wheezing, which greatly worried Sii Devi. When Sii Devi reminded me of this, I cancelled my plans for dessert. However, at the end of the meal, Sii Devi insisted that I eat some of the ice cream I had bought, which she thought would be all right for me since I came from a "cool" country. When Rashika saw that I had ice cream, she demanded some for herself. Sii Devi tried to distract and offer substitutes, but Rashika began to scream. I tried to put mine back in the freezer but Sii Devi would not let me. Then Rashika's father and older brother, seeing me eating ice cream, helped themselves to dishes of it, as well. By this time, Rashika was in a full-on temper tantrum. So, in the end, Sii Devi gave her a dish of ice cream. In response to my look of surprise and confusion, Sii Devi gave a shrug and said, "She was crying."

Each mother I told about the incident chuckled and nodded, seeming to anticipate the end of the story before I got there. I asked them if this was typical behavior, for a child and for a mother. Everyone agreed that it was. Several said that it was wrong of the mother to give the child the ice cream, but agreed that it was understandable that she did. "What could she do?" one said, "the child was crying." I asked what the problem was with allowing a child to cry. This mother's reply was apparently obvious to everyone other than me: "Well they are crying. They cannot understand. We suffer when we hear that. We have to give."

Then I asked each of the mothers to explain how it was that young children learned to stop crying for their every wish to be fulfilled. They agreed with my observation that older children did not cry like that. When I asked them what was different for the older children, each told me that older children did not cry for things because they had "understanding" (*tereneva*). When I asked what had changed for the children, I was told that they simply get understanding. Some said that this happened around the age of seven or eight, others said it happened gradually between five and ten. But all agreed that there would be something wrong with a child who was still crying and pleading for things past the age of ten.[3]

As I probed further into what was, to the mothers I interviewed, a very obvious and common-sense process, there seemed to be two main aspects to what it is that children would come to understand. First, they come to understand that there will be concrete, negative material consequences from them asserting their desires. For instance, they will get a cold if they insist on eating ice cream in the evening or will cut themselves if they grab for the knife their mother is using. The mothers felt that children will inevitably come to see this for themselves; however, I regularly noticed parents facilitating this recognition by pointing out to children and other novices what would happen if they insisted on their way and then calling attention to negative consequences when they occurred. I myself had often been the target of these messages, as mothers in Viligama routinely warned me against doing foolish things like bathing in the evening or letting my son eat a little red fruit called *jambu* when it was damp out. Such things were known to cause colds. So when sometime later I would cough or my son would sneeze, someone would be sure to remind me of my earlier heedlessness and point out that this was the result.

The second theme in the mothers' explanations of what it was that children come to understand was that it is "hard for their parents to give," a phrase repeated throughout the explanations I received. I asked the women how this happened. Did they tell the children that they could not afford to buy things or that it made them feel embarrassed when their children asked for things in public? The women tended to laugh at this idea, dismissing such possibilities as ridiculous. When I pressed for them to identify the techniques they used to teach children that it was hard for their parents to give, they said that children "just get understanding" and before they developed that capacity, it was useless to try to teach them.

Since young children do not have such understanding, they cry for things. Therefore, if one cannot distract them, physically or with lies, then one must give in to their demands. To do otherwise, would mean the child would keep crying, and that was intolerable.

The Puzzle Remained

So what was going on that led these indulged children to become well-mannered, self-controlled older children? My own US-based ethnotheories about how children develop could not explain it. Yet, among Sinhala parents, the transition I noted with such surprise was something they fully expected. It was taken as natural and obvious by these mothers that young children would cry for things and be given what they wanted until they reached an age when they could understand the difficulties their requests posed for others, at which point they would stop making them. In fact, this kind of developmental path was not so different from those reported elsewhere in the region and in some other communities around the world.

From Indulged Baby to Well-Behaved Child:
Observations and Explanations from around the World

People all over the world—whether in Sri Lanka, the United States, or elsewhere—treat infants and very young children differently from older children, offering the littlest ones greater nurturance and responsiveness. In Beatrice Whiting and Carolyn Pope Edwards's 1988 analysis of systematic observations of mothers and children's interactions in twelve very different communities around the world, they found that mothers consistently initiated more nurturance and responded more compliantly to their young children than their older ones. An earlier "Six Cultures" study found that children themselves in all of the communities observed offered infants more help and support than any other kinds of behaviors, and were more nurturing to infants than toward any other age group (Whiting and Whiting 1975: 153–158). Whiting and Edwards point out that this "transcultural generality involves the power of young children to draw or elicit more nurturance" (1988: 118), a capacity that helps ensure the survival of infants themselves and, as Hrdy has persuasively argued (2009), the survival of the human species as a whole. As children grow and are expected to behave more maturely, these nurturant and compliant responses to them decline, though in amounts and at rates that vary significantly both within and across societies.

The variation in the rates and ways that people in different societies respond to children is connected with their ethnotheories relating to children. As described above, US ethnotheories hold that children will learn gradually to follow social rules if those rules are consistently enforced. In many other societies, however, young children are considered incapable of following social rules and so are not expected to do so until they reach a certain age. As Barbara Rogoff explains:

> In some communities, infants and toddlers are accorded a unique social status in which acts and responsibilities are regarded as being of a different sort than those of older children and adults. As such, they are not simply "immature" and needing to quickly learn how to behave by the rules of social behavior. They are in a period of moratorium in which they are not expected to follow the same rules and are not hurried to do so.
>
> In such communities, babies and toddlers are expected not to be capable of understanding how to cooperate with the group. . . . So there is no sense in hurrying them to follow the rules. They are patiently given their way until they leave infancy and are regarded as capable of intentional acts and of understanding how to cooperate. In the meantime, they are accorded a privileged status in the family. (Rogoff 2003: 163–164)

Rogoff points out that "such treatment of infants and toddlers has sometimes been termed 'indulgent' by researchers from communities in which children are seen as willful from the start" (164)—communities such as those in the US middle class from which I came.

This transformation that struck me as inexplicable—that what Mosier and Rogoff (2003) have called a "privileged baby" will transform into a well-behaved older child as a consequence of the child's own emerging capacity for understanding—is, in its broad outlines, similar to the ways that children grow up in societies found across the globe. As David Lancy and Annette Grove point out in their examination of the role of adults in children's learning across cultures, "Examples of young children treated as being essentially uneducatable are legion in the ethnographic record" (2010: 153), including reports from societies as distant from each other as Fulani pastoralists of West Africa, Javanese town-dwellers in Indonesia, and Maya farmers and weavers in Central America. Ethnographic reports from elsewhere in South Asia also frequently include descriptions of parental beliefs and behavior which assume that it is pointless to try to teach children until they reach an age where they can understand things. As part of what Susan Seymour calls the "laissez-faire atmosphere" toward raising young children among the families with whom she conducted research in Orissa, India, "One is simply allowed to grow-up at one's own pace. Self-conscious 'child rearing' is not a relevant concept" (1999: 82), at least until age six or seven, when more explicit training begins for both boys and girls (85–87).

Part of what is driving these transitions may be changes in children's neurophysiological organization and cognitive capacities, though these are clearly facilitated by, as well as facilitative of, changes in behavior. A qualitative shift in cognitive performance and social participation of children between the ages of five and seven has long been remarked on in the West and observed in the ethnographic record from societies across the world. Before this transition—which is marked variously by increased responsibilities for helping with child care, involvement in subsistence activities, and the commencement of formal schooling—children appear to be less capable of reason (Sameroff and Haith 1996).

But neither parenting behavior nor child development is simply a response to children's innate needs and capacities. The variety of maternal behavior evident in close examinations of mothering as it is practiced in various cultural settings makes it clear that mothers are not just responding to the unfolding development of their children (Barlow and Chapin 2010a). Further, their children's development is itself necessarily shaped by participation in social activities (Rogoff 1996). But how does this happen? How does what mothers do and how children participate allow children to transition between being demanding little ones to being reasonable older children?

Other anthropologists and cultural psychologists have also been interested in this puzzle. Although cultural accounts of this basic transition between privileged baby and deferential older child may be similar in their basic outlines across many communities, researchers' explanations for this shift vary. For instance, Mosier and Rogoff point to the birth of a younger sibling as catalyst for this transition among Guatemalan Mayan children (2003). When a new sibling is born, the now-elder sibling affords the new baby the same "freedom of choice" and respect that they themselves had received. Jean Briggs, analyzing a similar developmental shift undergone by an Inuit child, emphasizes the role of teasing in fostering the transition (1998). She describes how this subtle teasing prompted the little girl to realize, while in the midst of enjoying her babyhood, that there were also costs to being a baby, such as being thought foolish. Heather Rae-Espinoza, drawing on research among urban, middle-class families in Ecuador, argues that the very treats and pleasures afforded as a part of daily social activities there encourage children to want to behave in socially approved ways so that they will continue to be included (2010).

In the literature on South Asia, psychoanalytically oriented theorists working from reports from adults in India have explained this developmental transition as catalyzed by an abrupt cessation of maternal indulgence, perhaps complemented by a sudden increase in expectations (Carstairs 1958, Kakar 1981). Such a sharp discontinuity is interpreted as creating a developmental crisis for a child that results in submission. However, these accounts are not borne out by the ethnographic record of childrearing in India, as Seymour persuasively argues (2004). In contrast, it is often the incompleteness of maternal indulgence—seen, for example, in the frequent but brief breastfeeding provided to children who demand it—that is seen as the key to its socializing effects by close observers of childrearing practices there (Minturn and Hitchcock 1963, Seymour 1999, Trawick 1992).

In any case, I did not observe such a discontinuity in the ways that children's demands were responded to in Sri Lanka—neither an abrupt discontinuity at some point during childhood nor periodic discontinuities in the midst of meeting a child's requests. Neither my own observations nor Sinhala mothers' accounts of this transition noted a change in parents' behavior toward children; instead, these explanations focused on the change within the children themselves. However, the ways that Sri Lankan mothers and others responded to children's requests did convey multiple, contradictory messages which, as I will argue below, allowed children to make this transition from demanding two-year-olds to self-controlled older children.

What Children in Viligama Come to Understand

How mothers in Viligama said they responded to their children's demands was just what I had observed. Little children who could not be distracted or discouraged from their demands were simply allowed to do or to have whatever they were crying for. But as I continued to observe these types of interactions more carefully, I became aware not just of the material transactions and overt demand-acquiescence enactments, but also of the less concrete but equally palpable emotional interchanges occurring.

What I began to attend to was how the emotional atmosphere felt when a child was demanding: it felt tense. I began to notice that while the child's overt demands were often met, the emotional tone of the granting was negative and withdrawing. People looked away from the child, made cringing or disgust faces. With the demanded outcome, the child also received disapproval, warning, discomfort, and dislike. Sometimes this came overtly, as from Rashika's sulking brother, and sometimes more subtly, as in her mother's wince.

I propose that this negative emotional tone that accompanies indulgence is what eventually makes Sinhala children stop asking for what they want. As these children grow, they become more aware of the negative states of others and learn to prevent them by disavowing their own desires. Children come to understand that when they express a desire they will get that thing—and that they will suffer the consequences of that met demand. They realize that they just do not know what is good for them—that wanting a knife might lead to a cut. But further, they come to anticipate that any expression of desire may result in a negative shift in their emotional environment, an environment necessarily composed of the emotions of others. The lesson that relationships with others are important to their well-being—something they presumably already knew implicitly—is made vivid, along with the emotionally charged and experienced lesson that these relationships can be lost through demanding self-assertion. The child learns that expressed desire is dangerous and that, to maintain a safe world and valued relationships, desire must be disavowed.

It seems to me quite likely that very young children are not able to link the voicing of their own demands with the unhappiness it creates. The unhappiness probably does not register as being caused by their demands at first. However, this link is continually reenacted in countless iterations, giving children endless opportunities and ample motivation to recognize this. This constancy is something that Quinn has identified as a technique used universally in child-rearing to make important cultural lessons "unmistakable, motivating, and memorable" (2005b: 477). In these demand-acquiescence "dramas," as Briggs (1998) might call them, there is also heightened emotional arousal and the risk of being approved of or rejected, two more of the techniques Quinn says are used around the word to teach key lessons. Further, these dramas about desire, as I will discuss below, prime children to be "emotionally predisposed to learn" important cultural lessons about the dangers of desire, a final common child-drearing feature Naomi Quinn identifies (2005b: 477).[4]

Through these repeated, emotionally salient experiences, I believe that Sinhala children eventually come to "understand" several things. First of all, they come to understand that when they voice their desires, those desires are ultimately undeniable and potent: they cause things to happen in the world, within others, and between people. Second, they see that, although their desires may be met in material ways, they will not be satisfying, as the pleasure and power of receiving is undercut by the pain and terror of rejection and the withdrawal of love. These lessons foster the development of a third understanding in which they begin to see that their own self-assertion and uncontrolled desires cause pain for others, others whom they depend on and love.[5]

In other words, children "come to understand," just as mothers had been telling me. Children come to understand that they cannot know what is best for them and so should defer to their elders. They come to understand that it is, indeed, "difficult for their parents" when they ask for things—difficult in practical ways, but difficult emotionally as well.

As children begin to develop these understandings, they come to fear and mistrust their own desires, desires that feel dangerous and seem to have the power to directly affect things in the material and social world. The anxiety generated by these understandings, I suggest, leads children to ignore, repress, or disavow their own desires, generating the self-denial and concern to share so notable in older children.

The Disavowal of Desire

How is it that, having learned about the destructiveness of desire, a Sri Lankan ten-year-old does not want to keep the rupee found on the road side? How is it that the nine-year-old girl I am interviewing refuses my offer of cookies, professing not to be hungry? I believe these disavowals of desire can occur at many levels. There may be conscious and practical choices that lead to such denials. Whoever lost the rupee will be looking for it. You may appear needy by accepting the cookies and shame your family. These children have learned that there are many potential negative consequences to admitting that they want something, and so it is better to ignore and deny those feelings.

In the child's experience, any admission of a feeling of desire might be taken as a demand that must be met. These children have never received a direct and firm "no," nor have they had chances to practice justifying, negotiating, and compromising to get some of what they want, while giving up other parts. These children have had little chance, therefore, to experience their own control over their desires, of articulating and prioritizing multiple wishes, or of consciously accepting a refusal that is not a rejection. These children have repeatedly experienced their own desires as acting beyond their own intentions, often to destructive ends. And so better not to have the desire at all.

For some people and in some circumstances, the refusal to admit a desire may not be a conscious decision to ignore one's own wishes in order to preserve a social relationship. The decision may instead be a decision not to articulate the desire even to oneself, and not to admit to oneself that this decision has even been made. This is what Herbert Fingarette (1969) calls "disavowal," a turning away from a part of one's self and refusing to claim it as one's own. Interestingly in the Sinhala case, it may be that the mother's actual looking away, which I have often observed in the moment of meeting the untoward demands of a child, serves as a gestural enactment of the psychodynamic move the mother has made and a model for the psychodynamic move the child will undertake.[6]

This avoidance of "spelling out" some piece of one's experience to one's self in an effort to deceive one's self is motivated, Fingarette says, by an effort to maintain one's sense of one's identity; that which is being actively not noticed is that which does not fit with the identity avowed. "A person may avow or acknowledge *as his* an action, a feeling, an emotion, a perception, a belief, an attitude, a concern, an aim, a reason. In avowing them as his a person is 'identifying himself as' one who feels, suffers, perceives, believes, etc., thus and so" (1969: 70–71, emphasis in the original). Conversely, when there is something that one is motivated not to identify as part of the self, that person may adopt a tacit policy of "*persistently* avoid[ing] spelling-out some feature of his engagement in the world" (47, emphasis in the original), a policy whose adoption the person must also refuse to acknowledge in order for the self-deception to work. These disavowed pieces of themselves are then cordoned off from the normally articulatable, explicit consciousness, leaving them to emerge in sometimes surprising ways.[7]

Disavowal helps explain how children in Viligama may come to experience their own desires as not their own, to turn away from them, refraining from acknowledging them even to themselves. As a child becomes more practiced at recognizing the earliest tingles of desire and the anxiety that this desire prompts, the disavowal comes swifter and easier. Each time a child disavows a desire, this unconscious action is rewarded in that it prevents the destruction that the desires might otherwise have caused and dampens the anxiety that was triggered in anticipation of that destruction. Further, the disavowal is rewarded by the pleasure of inner security and social approval.

This way of thinking about how children are shaped by their experiences requires that we take into account the unconscious aspects of a person's mind and the dynamic ways those operate. It requires that we go beyond conceptualizing socialization as a direct and rational process. It requires that we attend to the complex feelings evoked by experiences and the ways that we develop to protect ourselves from difficult or contradictory feelings, experiences, and recognitions. These psychodynamic processes play a powerful role in shaping how children develop and relate to others, and they do so in culturally patterned ways and throughout the life course. Although these processes are not directly observable as they happen within a person, they are vital to attend to if we are to account not only for individual development but, as I will argue in the final chapter, for how it is that culture is patterned, internalized, transmitted, and altered.

Related Cultural Models: Dangers of Desire and Receiving

Children's developing understandings about the dangers of desire, and the psychodynamic moves and behavioral expressions these understandings motivate, intersect with more explicit cultural tenets about wanting and getting. I propose that, as children are introduced to these cultural beliefs, they are prepared to find them particularly sensible, resonant, and true, given what they have come to understand about the dangers of desire and the difficulties posed by receiving. In turn, these ideologies elaborate and reinforce the understandings of desire developed in childhood. As these grown children go on to parent children of their own, these deeply layered understandings of desire lead them to reproduce the circumstances in which they themselves were socialized.

Adults in Sri Lanka have robust and elaborate understandings about the dangers entailed in desire and receiving. Such understandings are entailed in folk models of envy and greed, Buddhist doctrines of suffering and merit, and traditional caste relations. The feelings, understandings, and behavior around desires and receiving that children are developing are simultaneously affirmed by and incorporated into these more overtly articulated cultural belief systems and practices.

Dangers of Desire: Envy, Greed, and Attachment

In Viligama and throughout the region (cf. Gosh 1983, Pocock 1991, Sabini and Silver 1982), envy is understood to be powerful and destructive, to result from unmet desires that come through people but that are not really within their control. *Irishiyava*, the Sinhala term that I am glossing as "envy," is the emotional complex resulting from situations in which a person desires something that another possesses, a topic I will explore at length in Chapter 5. What is relevant to my argument here is how these cultural models of envy resonate with and co-animate understandings of desire derived from childhood interaction. Further, the defense against the dire accusation of being envious is to disavow one's desires.

When a person feels envious, when that person covets something belonging to another and feels that it should be his or her own, that desire is understood in Viligama to have power to harm the desired object or its owner. People spoke of *aes vaha* (literally "eye poison") which comes through the gaze of an envious person and has the power to destroy the desired object. They spoke of *kata vaha* (literally "mouth poison") which may undo someone's good fortune if envious others praise it. When I was walking down a road in Viligama with a young woman named Wasana and another young woman remarked on how beautiful Wasana's hair was, Wasana felt it as a threat. Later, when Wasana found more than the usual number of loose hairs when she shampooed, she remembered the other woman's praise and knew this was the cause. Expressions, verbal or gestural, that indicated someone might desire something belonging to another may be threatening—and so to admire something openly would be to threaten destruction. Each person I spoke to denied ever feeling envious, although they described others who had threatened or actually harmed them with their envy.

People protected themselves by hiding what they had, by putting marks on their babies, by putting masks of demons on new houses, or by giving away a coveted wall hanging or other pretty thing.

The understanding of desire as destructive shows up in other cultural models and practices, even ones that people did not usually talk about as having to do with envy. This is evident, for instance, in ideas and practices around eating.[8] One of these involves the idea of feeling *kaedara*, which is typically translated as feeling "greedy" or, as one person translated it into English for me, "very much desire." If someone feels kaedara for food someone else is eating, it might cause the eater to become ill. For instance, I was told that if someone looks at your food while you are eating and his mouth waters and he swallows that spit—a crucial dimension to this phenomenon—then you will get a stomach ache. The best way to avoid such problems, I was told, was not to let anyone see you when you eat. So, the polite thing to do when someone is eating in front of you is to look away. In that way the person can eat without having to hide or to worry— worry which may itself, as one person proposed to me, be the true mechanism of the illness.

Although this is more likely to happen with strangers, it can also happen with relatives. And although anyone could do it, there are some people—greedy people—who have a tendency to cause it. For instance, one elderly woman claimed that her son's daughter always made her sick because the girl was greedy. This could happen with nursing mothers, as well. When a mother is nursing a baby, if someone watches, the baby's stomach may become upset.

It could also happen that someone sees the milk leaking from a new mother's breasts, as a mark soaking through her shirt, and feels greedy for that extra milk. This can stop a mother's milk entirely. As an example, a new mother told me of her father's sister who, when her first baby was born, had her milk stop in both breasts as a result of someone seeing her leaking milk. This aunt then developed hard places (*gedi*) in both of her breasts, which the doctors had to drain. Not only did this happen with her first child but with all six subsequent children as well. As the young mother told me of this happening to her aunt, her own mother who was listening chimed in "aes vaha," eye poison.

New mothers were also advised not to eat in front of their babies, lest they make the baby sick. If babies see adult food, their mouths may water and that saliva would upset the baby's stomach. Again, it is the saliva that is held to be the medium of illness, though here it is the observer that suffers rather than the eater.

The dangers of others' desires is not confined to the living, human world. A *yaka* (demon) may be attracted by certain meats, fried foods, and sweets. Those who must walk alone with such treats, especially at times when demons are known to be about—dawn, dusk, noon, and midnight—are wise to carry limes or pieces of iron to ward them off.

The spirit of a dead person may also contain these dangerous longings for food until they go on to their next incarnation or enter *nibbana*.[9] This spirit is called a *perethaya* (Sanskrit: *preta*), which can also be translated as "a greedy person." At funerals, special foods—especially oil or sweet things—are set aside in a special place for the perethaya to eat, during the period while mourners work to give *pin* (merit) to the deceased so that they can go to a good rebirth. Some spirits may be stuck in this space between, this *perethaya atmaya*.[10] In such cases, a diagnosing religious adept may advise the relatives of the deceased to give a *dana* (almsgiving) on his or her behalf, earning spiritual merit so it can leave that space and go on to be reborn.

Indeed, in Buddhism as it is understood and practiced by the people whom I knew in Viligama, it is desire and attachment to the world that makes a person be reborn at all, keeping one tied to the cycle of rebirth rather than escaping to the nothingness of nibbana. One can only leave this cycle by eliminating all "clinging and craving," all *tanha*. And it is desire, as the second of Buddhism's Four Noble Truths asserts, which is the root of all suffering—the usual gloss for the Pali word *dukkha*.[11] In his classic study of a Buddhism as practiced in rural Sri Lanka, Richard Gombrich explains this truth as follows: "*Dukkha* exists because of desire: it is desire's corollary. If we have no wants we shall suffer no disappointments. . . . It is desire, notably the desire for life, which gives the impetus for rebirth. . . . The destruction of unhappiness is consequently the destruction of desire. Those who cease to desire life will not be reborn, and experience no more dukkha" (1971: 69).

In Jonathan Spencer's 1990 ethnography of another Sinhala village, he sees everyday behaviors and explanations involving ideas of desire and detachment as being rooted in these "basic assumptions in the Buddhist view of the moral universe" (1999 [1990]: 165). For example, in behavior indexed as *lajja*—either in reaction to humiliation (as in the English "shame") or in defense against it (as in the English "shyness"), Spencer asserts that what it is people are doing is "holding back from the gaze of others, keeping intense encounters at arm's length" (171). He also sees this attitude of distance and detachment as a defense against accusations of showing *adambara* (pride, self-aggrandizement) or, conversely, of showing envy, both problems of desire. In addition, he sees this strategy of pulling away in everyday practices of lying and concealment and in the common suspicions that polite behavior is a cover-up for hostility. In all of these cases, people are enacting or understanding others to be enacting a withdrawal from dangerous engagement with the social world. These social strategies of detachment and cultural models of desires that must be hidden are similar, I would suggest, to the kind of psychological moves of disavowal children are learning to adopt in order to defend against their own desires.

That desire is grasping, uncontrollable, and destructive—that it can reach out and grab at things, that it comes through people but is not contained within them—are ideas that are found throughout Sinhala culture. That the best way to defend against the difficulties it poses is to avoid it in others and eliminate it in oneself is also suggested in such cultural models. These complex cultural models draw on understandings of desire that are consistent with the ways Sinhala children experience their own desires and those of their siblings in their early home life. Their experiences of their own desires as both irresistible to others and unpredictably destructive of the very things they want most helps make these more explicit cultural models particularly resonant, meaningful, and right when children encounter them. This culturally normative orientation to desire is part of what children are assembling internally as they are developing in the context of a Sinhala family and in interaction with vitally important others.

Vulnerability in Receiving: Food, Intimacy, and Hierarchy

When children get what they demand and are unhappy for it, they are learning not just about the dangerous, fickle nature of desires but also about the ways that receiving makes one vulnerable. When they receive something—even something they want—they may be harmed in the process in unforeseen ways. To receive something from someone is to lay yourself open to that person, to allow their actions to shape one's own physical, emotional, and relational world. This felt-concept about the vulnerability entailed in receiving shows up in adult life as well. It is central to hierarchically ranked interpersonal relationships, which I will explore in the next chapter, as well as to structures of caste and class that organize much of social life in South Asia.

When my family and I were preparing to move to Viligama from Kandy, our very cosmopolitan next-door neighbors in town warned us not to talk to people in the village, not to let them into our house, and especially not to take food from them. This food was likely to be poisoned, we were repeatedly warned by Sri Lankans from the town and from other villages as well. When, during our first few weeks in the village, a woman looking to do a bit of work for us brought us a plastic baggie of jak curry she had made, our housekeeper insisted we throw it out. When the woman who had given us the curry asked about it later, I thanked her, pretending that we had enjoyed it. When next she came to visit, she brought more curry, setting it confidently on our kitchen counter.

What our concerned friends were trying to communicate to us was about more than the food. They were warning us against entering into relationships with these, from their perspectives, uncouth and untrustworthy villagers. In this, they drew on some ideas I shared and some I did not. I, too, believed that sharing food helped foster relationships, establish trust, and build intimacy. That, of course, was what I had moved to Viligama to do—to build relationships with people so that I could understand more about their lives from their points of view. While my city friends and high-caste housekeeper knew I was there to study life in the village, they could not imagine that I would really want to become like them, that I would want to—as they saw it—descend to their level. What I at first missed in what my Sri Lankan friends were saying was that to take food from someone would change who I was. It would not only make me indebted to the giver, it would make me become like them.

This notion that sharing food creates and affirms sameness is found in ethnographies throughout the region. In *Notes on Love in a Tamil Family*, Margaret Trawick (1992) describes the intimacy that prompts, justifies, and is intensified by eating from the same plate within the family she lives with in Tamil Nadu. Steven Parish says that for the Newars of Nepal, "The act of sharing food even more than dwelling in the same house defines a family. . . . It asserts you are 'at one' with those who eat what you eat, who eat with you, from the same pot and hearth, from the same common store of food." Parish goes on to say, "Through food, a person can incorporate something of the other into self, and contribute something of self to the other—eating together, people blend their natures or essences, making themselves alike, forging a bond" (1994: 61).

Households in Sri Lanka, as in Nepal, were defined by the sharing of one hearth.[12] This marked who belonged together and where there were divisions. For instance, when the father in one family I knew had to move to Colombo for work and his wife and young children moved in with his parents, the wife explained to me that she had a separate cooking area from her in-laws. By emphasizing this, she was asserting that she was still running her own household, rather than being a dependant. In another instance, an old woman in the village, angry at her husband's drinking, had refused to cook for him.

The sharing of food was often associated with sexual intimacy in Viligama. Euphemisms for sexual affairs were phrased in terms of women cooking for men. As the content of gossip attested, women who gave men food could be assumed to be giving them sexual access as well. One teenaged girl I knew got into a great deal of trouble with her older brother when he heard she had handed a boy from her school a lunch packet out of a window during a *dana* (almsgiving). In the university dining hall, young men and women would eat from one lunch packet open on the table before them, gazing at each other as they ate by hand, their fingers intertwining and lingering.

But food sharing does more that create intimacy or mark divisions; it creates hierarchy. Within a household, rank was reflected in the order in which people ate, with guests eating first, then senior men, children, and finally women—although this order was flexible in practice. However, there is power not just in eating first, but in being the one to give the food. To receive food from someone is to allow a bit of them to enter into you, becoming part of you.

When that food sharing is unidirectional, it enacts a social order and establishes a ranked relationship. Parents feed children, gods return *prasad* to their supplicants, and high castes give to low castes.[13] When good superiors give what they determine is appropriate and necessary for their juniors, those gifts and the ranked relationships which they evidence are valued, something which will be developed in detail in the following chapters. However, there is also risk entailed by accepting something from an inappropriate person—risk that the attractive gift will disguise something damaging, and risk in the submission accepting a desirable gift necessarily entails.[14] To receive willingly is to make yourself junior to or at least equal with the giver, to make yourself vulnerable, to trust. To take what a senior person judges to be unsuitable entails risks posed by the thing itself and risk of undoing the relationship with the senior, a relationship within which one is cared for and secure.

I have said that Rashika is learning that what she demands often turns out to be harmful or unsatisfying—the knife cuts, the ice cream makes one sick, the game isn't any fun if no one else plays. She is learning that, when she insists on having her way, it ruins relationships she cares about—her mother cringes, her brother turns away. She is learning that her own desires are powerful, potentially destructive, and that their effects are outside of her control. These repeatedly enacted, deeply felt, and intimately meaningful lessons lay the ground in which cultural models about desire and relationships can take root.

Why Mothers Respond as They Do

Such cultural doctrines about the dangers and sufferings that accompany desire are things all the better known to the older people with whom children interact. I believe that these rich, intersecting, and robust understandings about the dangers of desire are key in shaping adults' responses to children's demands. These explicit pieces of knowledge make family members and others uneasy with expression of desire, even from their children. This leads them to make the kind of alarmed, disgusted expressions they do when children begin to scream for what they want and to pull away from them. It also leads them to do whatever they can to make the screaming stop, even if that means giving in to unreasonable demands. In addition, as I will argue below, these reactions are not only fueled by adults' explicit cultural knowledge about desire but also by their own childhood experiences in which that knowledge is rooted.

Recognizing adults' own complex orientations to desire helps make sense of what I observed in mothers' behavior and of a common refrain in their explanations of why they give in to their children's demands: They repeatedly asserted that no one can tolerate hearing a child cry. They seemed to be talking about something more specific than our species-typical arousal at the cry of an infant.

On reflection, I realized that no one I knew in Sri Lanka seemed to be able to tolerate demands or even requests from anyone—child, beggar, poor relation—for very long without either escaping or acquiescing.

The acute discomfort that the demands of others can induce is, I believe, related to the granters' own fears of desire and psychological habits of disavowing their own. When, through their crying and whining, children make flagrant assertions of desire, those around them fear the demand as a manifestation of something they deeply know to be dangerous. Desire is morally, spiritually, and socially troubling; it is also something adults learned to avoid or suppress in their own early childhoods because of the unpredictable havoc it can create. Therefore, mothers and other caretakers act swiftly, almost compulsively, to stop the demands children make by distracting them, appeasing them, or withdrawing from them.

But the crying can also, I would argue, trigger empathic recognition in others. A screaming, demanding, wanting child represents the kind of naked desire adults and older children ordinarily forbid themselves from displaying, but might sometimes feel twinges of, despite their motivated disavowal. That this identification with the child and with the feelings expressed is unsettling for onlookers is clear to observe. It may be that this scene triggers shame and fear in the identifying onlookers in reaction to the glimpse of their own desirous nature that it provides. Giving children what they are screaming for simultaneously serves to end the unsettling scene and to allow the identifying onlookers to see desire win out, something they do not pursue for themselves.

This empathic identification with and response to demanding children may be all the stronger for mothers and others who closely identify with these children, seeing them as both their primary responsibility and extensions of themselves. Further, given that in Viligama it is women who largely provide care for small children, this identification may be particularly strong with girls. As Chodorow (1974) points out, mothers may have a kind of double identification with their daughters as both an extension of themselves and a mirror of themselves as a child. This may be a contributing factor toward what seems to me to be the stronger socialization in Sinhala women than in men to disavow their own desires. But whether the child is a boy or a girl, Sinhala mothers strongly identify with and feel responsible for their children.

When they hear their children's screams, I would suggest that mothers are especially likely to experience empathetically what it is to feel strong and undisguised desire. This empathetic response triggers not only their ordinary fear and avoidance of desire but also the feeling of desire itself and the frustration of not having that desire met, frustration they normally ignore along with their desires. Having identified her own disavowed feelings in her child, the mother wants to make the triggering stimulus stop, judges the desire expressed to be bad and dangerous, but simultaneously, if covertly, wants to have those desires met, thereby enjoying vicarious gratification through the child who has not so long ago been part of her.[15]

These multiple goals are pursued by the same course of action: Give the child what she wants. In this way, mothers stop these children they are responsible for raising from behaving in such unseemly and dangerous ways. That this behavior is unseemly and dangerous is confirmed by cultural beliefs about desire and proper relationship. It also makes sense in terms of Sinhala ethnotheories of child development, which say that it is useless to try to teach young children not to ask for things because they do not yet have the capacity to understand such things. Emotional power is added to these beliefs and theories by mothers' own psychodynamic habits of disavowal rooted in their own childhood experience. Together, these load mothers' interactions with demanding children in a way that feels right to the mothers, is highly charged, and communicates a complex message to children, perpetuating the socialization of desire into the next generation. Through these interactions, children transform from demanding, indulged toddlers into well-behaved older children predisposed to find subsequent ideas of desire and ways of relating meaningful and compelling.

But these are not the only ways that parents and children interact or the only lessons about desire and relationships conveyed. In the next chapter I will describe a very different kind of interaction, one in which, rather than asserting their desires, children wait passively, accepting the actions, gifts, and decisions of their superiors. Through these everyday interactions that children like Rashika are also having, children learn that when they refrain from asserting their own desires, things will go much more happily for them and for those around them.

4

Shaping Attachments

Learning Hierarchy at Home

Children, like adults, participate in different kinds of relationships. Even between children and their parents, there are different types of interactions within these relationships.[1] In the last chapter, I focused on one type of interaction in which children receive. In that type of interactions, children boldly asserted their desires and those around them gave into those demands. However, there was another, more common and more valued way that children were given things in Viligama—and this giving and receiving was accompanied by a very different emotional tone and a very different, if complementary, lesson.

In this type of giving and receiving interaction, children waited passively while their caregivers—most commonly, but not exclusively, their mothers—gave them what those caregivers deemed to be necessary and appropriate. In these interactions, in contrast to those described in the last chapter, children's own particular wishes or opinions were not voiced, nor were they solicited. Adults initiated the giving interaction, offering children what they determined those children needed. I argue that this type of early interaction is key in shaping children's attachment to particular caregivers. I also argue that these interactions establish a template for future relationships with others, relationships that have a particular cultural shape and value. Through this type of interaction, in which seniors provide what juniors need, reiterated from infancy through adulthood, children learn about and learn to value culturally sanctioned relationships between people of different rank. Such hierarchical relationships are not only important within family life; they form the scaffolding of much of Sri Lankan society.

In this chapter, I describe how this template for interactions between juniors and seniors is experienced, learned, and infused with feeling through family interaction. I begin by relating the incident that first crystallized my

recognition of this cultural style of hierarchical relationships and its enactment in everyday childhood experience. I then explore various ways this style
emerges over the course of children's growing up. I describe the basic model
of hierarchical relationships that is manifested in and communicated through
these kinds of interactions between parents and children. I examine ways
that people might violate the expectation of this model, and how participants
within these relationships might respond to such violations. Along the way,
I discuss how this pattern of parent-child interaction compares to those discussed by developmental psychologists who study attachment and caregiving in
the United States and how Sri Lankan-style attachments might lead to different
socially valued outcomes. In the end, I suggest that this model of relating that
children experience in Viligama is something they take with them and draw on
as they participate in relationships outside of the home, something which is the
topic of subsequent chapters of this book.

But first the incident with the fish.

"I Feed It to Him, So He Eats It"

One day, when I was first getting to know Sii Devi, several years before her
daughter Rashika was born, she was complaining to me about her four-year-old
niece who was visiting her, saying, "She doesn't eat." When I asked Sii Devi what
she meant, she explained that her niece would only eat milk and sweets but not
rice or fish. I asked if Sampath, her own son who was seven at the time, liked
fish, to which she replied, "He eats it." Thinking she had misunderstood, I asked
again if he *liked* it. Sii Devi laughed a little and said, "I don't know, he *eats* it." In
response to my puzzled look, she added, "I feed it to him, so he eats it."

Like most Sinhala mothers, Sii Devi fed meals to her child by hand, massag-
ing together each bite of rice and curry from the plate of food she had prepared
and placing the food directly into his open mouth with her fingertips, while her
son waited passively, undemandingly, for each bite. I had seen this interaction
before. It was repeated at mealtimes each day, as Sii Devi fed Sampath—and as
she would feed her daughter, Rashika, once she came along. Likewise, at mealtimes in households throughout the village—and, indeed, all over the island—
caregivers placed food directly into the mouths of waiting children, giving those
children regular experiences of being directly nourished and nurtured by caring
and capable superiors.

The basic pattern of this daily practice was not limited to feeding, I realized. I had seen it in so many other interactions between children and their
caregivers. In all of these interactions, caregivers provided for children what
the caregivers determined each child to need, without consulting that child
about those needs or preferences. And children, if they were good, waited

patiently and uncomplainingly, taking what they are given. Further, I realized that this pattern of interaction between juniors and seniors appeared not only in the caregiving interactions I had been witnessing. I had seen it in relations between those of different ranks in other domains as well—between students and teachers, between patients and healers, between citizens and politicians. In subsequent chapters, I will describe ways that this model of interaction emerges in those relationships. In this current chapter, I will trace out some of the ways this model patterns child care and family interactions through adolescence, arguing that it is through these experiences that children learn—and learn to value—this model of hierarchy.

Providing for Children as They Grow: Changing Activities and Enduring Patterns

When people in Viligama talked about raising children, they focused on the parents' role as providers—providers of food and clothing, providers of education and advice, providers of social connections and opportunities. As discussed in Chapter 2, this obligation to provide was the central idiom through which parenting was understood and legitimated. This may be yet another reason why it was impossible for mothers to refuse to give their children what they cried for, the topic of the previous chapter. It may also be part of why Sii Devi gave in to her niece's demands for milk and sweets, and why Sii Devi was so annoyed by the girl's refusal to accept the rice and fish she gave her. Ideally, senior people should determine what is best for children and provide that. Children, in turn, should receive this provision passively, gratefully, and respectfully. And it is by their acceptance that these relationships continue.

This concern with the parent's role as provider and the complementary role of the child as passive recipient patterns not only how people think and talk about parenting in Viligama but also how they do it. The particular cultural form of these everyday actions then shapes the context in which children develop. As children grow, parent-child interactions are patterned by this basic model of relating, although the kinds of activities they engage in change. During infancy, the child's passivity and dependency are reinforced, and caring actions are sensitive and warm. As children become verbal, they are not encouraged to identify and articulate their needs but are instead trained to wait passively until their parents choose to provide for them. Parents foster children's developing capacity to understand, but have only limited exchanges of explicit, verbal information. As children enter adolescence, they are expected not just to act more appropriately respectful around their superiors but also to feel more appropriately *lajja*, more shy, and—especially for girls—more properly afraid, exercising good judgment and self-control as they defer to the decisions of their elders. In other words, these young people are expected to have internalized the cultural model of hierarchy fully so that it frames not only their understanding of relationships but also their feelings within these relationships, motivating them to participate in these relationships and making the relationships meaningful. As young people come to take on their role as adults, their consent to participate as the junior person in hierarchical relationships is more explicitly required, although consent is important throughout.

This developmental path is marked by a series of rituals that enact and reinforce the proper hierarchical relationship learned in day-to-day interactions. These ritual celebrations mark culturally significant developmental steps, and the ways these rituals are conducted illustrate the proper complementary roles of seniors as providers and juniors as passive recipients. In each, the child who is the focus of the ceremony is physically ministered to, but the child him- or herself is largely passive. This is clear in the first feeding ritual as well as in the marriage ceremonies discussed later in this chapter, as it is in other life-cycle rituals. These celebrations mark things that are done for or happen to a child—the first time a child receives a bite of rice and curry, is taught a letter, has his or her hair cut, or the first time a girl's body begins to menstruate. The rituals around these events are done to and for children by their parents in order to ensure children's good fortune as they pass into new stages of life, rather than marking an active achievement of the child or some demonstration of agency.

In contrast, compare these to the milestones many contemporary parents in the United States look to and celebrate in their children's development such as their first steps, the first time they sleep through the night, their first words, learning to use the toilet on their own, the first day of kindergarten, high school graduation—all things that represent increasing skills, agency, and independence. Although "Sinhala" parenting and "US" parenting are neither opposites nor mutually exclusive, I want to emphasize the difference in elaboration and focus. This difference in focus is a difference at the level of parents' ideas or ethnotheories about their children's development. But this difference at the level of ideas entails a difference in what people actually *do* with their children—and therefore a difference in the worlds that children are experiencing and the internal worlds they are developing.

Caregivers' cultural models shape how they interact with and around their children. These actions create and pattern the contexts in which children develop their own models of the world around them, how relationships work, and who they are. Since these internal, working models of the world are developed in this culturally patterned context, the models themselves are culturally patterned. This chapter describes one particularly important working model that children in Viligama develop out of their experience—a cultural model of hierarchical relationships.

Of course, children do not develop these cultural models only or even primarily out of their experiences during these rituals of passage. Rather, these ritual celebrations mark out culturally recognized changes in children's ongoing development. That ongoing development is shaped by ordinary, everyday experiences that alter as they grow. These patterned and changing experiences that children are having are structured, as Barbara Rogoff points out, by their "changing participation in the socio-cultural activities of their communities" (2003: 36). By engaging in changing but patterned social activities—the everyday as well as the ritually marked—children in Viligama learn about hierarchically ranked relationships and how to participate in them. Through these patterned interactions with important others early in life, they also come to value these kind of hierarchical relationships, to feel about them in particular ways, and to want to participate in them. As we will see in subsequent chapters, they will bring this knowledge and these feelings with them as they enter into other sociocultural activities and other relationships.

In what follows here, I will trace out some of the more ordinary sociocultural activities and the changing ways in which Sinhala children participate in them, activities through which they come to learn, care about, and enact this model of hierarchical relationships. In these daily experiences with intimate seniors, the particular cultural shape of these types of relationships are conveyed to children and also made clearer to those of us observing from the outside. What becomes particularly clear in these everyday interactions, as in the ritual markers, is that seniors provide what juniors need without providing explanations or receiving input from those juniors. However, the interactions only continue with the compliance of the junior person, building in a kind of choice for the junior person. What is also clear in the way care is provided is the nonverbal attunement and sensitivity that are required and conveyed by these interactions, infusing hierarchically ranked relationships with the warmth, closeness, and security that accompanies respect, deference, and distance in Viligama.

Caring for Babies

While all human infants have a set of needs that their caregivers must attend to, these needs are recognized and met in culturally specific ways. All over the world, parents and other caregivers must do similar types of things for and with their children—feed them, transport them, tend to their cuts and colds, teach them skills—but the *ways* these are done, the ideas behind them, and the messages they communicate are always culturally shaped. Some of these activities may receive more attention in some places than others, while others may be thought to be unimportant. In Sri Lanka, parents and others paid a great deal of attention to the provision of food and accompanying concerns about health maintenance, while they paid little mind to elimination and sleep. Among US parents, in contrast, how and how successfully babies are put to sleep and toilet trained is a matter of great concern. But regardless of whether particular care-giving activities are regarded by adults as significant or not, the ways that they are all carried out reflect and communicate cultural patterns—communicate them to other parents, communicate them to observing anthropologists, and communicate them to growing babies.

In Viligama, the ways these everyday caregiving activities are carried out are patterned by and convey basic principles of a Sinhala model of hierarchically ranked relationships. In daily infant care, as in most parent-child interactions, the child is not encouraged to recognize and intentionally express his or her needs. Instead, the parent recognizes the child's need and acts to meet that need, providing direction by physical ministration and manipulation without verbal instruction. These everyday caregiving activities are carried out casually and con-fidently, but with warmth and physical intimacy. All the while, parents and others conceptualize the child's activities and development as things the child *chooses* to do, having been provided with the opportunity by the parent.

Sleep

The ways that babies slept in Viligama exemplified and contributed to the foun-dation of warmth, intimacy, responsiveness, and solidarity upon which ranked relationships stand. Babies and young children in Viligama slept next to their mothers at night, nursing off and on as they liked. Fathers and older siblings often shared the bed. Not until children were around ten did they begin sleep-ing away from their mothers, and then they often slept with same-sex siblings. These co-sleeping practices in Viligama, which I described in more detail in Chapter 2, were the result of preference rather than space limitations. They were guided by what Richard Shweder et al. (1995) called "moral goods" in their study of sleeping arrangements in India and the United States. As that study makes clear and my own research supports, the ways that families put their children to sleep reflect the ways that children are thought about, related to, and aimed toward becoming. In addition, although Shweder and his colleagues do not make this point, sleeping patterns do not just emerge out of and make sense in terms of moral, cultural principles; these sleeping patterns also com-municate these moral, cultural principles to the children who grow up with them. These early sleep experiences teach children valued ways of being and relating in each of these societies, as in others.

What children in Viligama were learning was to trust that those around them would not abandon them and would respond to their needs. They had the nightly experience that these hierarchical, dependant relationships among family members were warm, comforting, and safe. They did not experience extended periods of being alone that required them to develop strategies for self-soothing under conditions where no one was there to help them or to interrupt them. Whether or not parents thought about sleep as an important part of life, these experiences contributed to infusing the model of hierarchical relationships that children in Viligama were deriving with associations and expectations of warmth, security, togetherness, and nonverbal intimacy, all of which characterizes the ideal model of ranked relationships expressed by adults.

In addition, the casualness around children's sleep reflects the conception of children and other juniors within this model. Parents and others did not worry about when or how much children slept. They did not see themselves as having to teach their children to sleep at particular times or in separate spaces. Children were allowed to fall asleep when and where they would. If they fell asleep before others in the family had retired for the night, then they were carried into the bed they shared. In sleep, as in most caregiving activities and other hierarchical interactions, young people were seen to act according to their own capacities and inclinations, having been provided with the proper opportunities by their elders. This is in line with how people in Viligama thought about child development, but it was also in line with how people thought about appropriate relations between seniors and juniors of any age.

Feeding

The ways that babies in Viligama were fed also demonstrated and conveyed what could be expected from relationships with a caring superior. Unlike sleeping, though, feeding children is something new parents and others in Viligama paid a great deal of attention to. Right from the beginning, the provision of food is the central concern of new parents and the symbolic enactment of the relationship. In feeding children—first with breast milk and later with solid food—mothers and others know what children need and provide it, without asking about what children want. Children receive this passively, gratefully, and are understood to do so by choice.

BREASTFEEDING. Babies in Viligama were nursed frequently and for several years. As I described in Chapter 2, breastfeeding was the usual way that babies were fed in this village and across the island. Newborns were kept close to their mothers, day and night, finding a nipple close by whenever they might feel hungry or in need of comfort. When their mothers were up and about, babies were laid on their backs on a cloth or held by other family members. However, babies were not usually very far from their mothers, who interrupted their work frequently to breastfeed, although not necessarily for very long at any one time. As children began to toddle about, they would climb up on their mothers, reaching for a breast as they felt inclined, or would tug at their skirts whining to nurse.

Mothers might sometimes be inconvenienced by these needs, but they did not refuse them.

When mothers were away, others would work to bounce, comfort, and distract children, offering them substitutes like specially prepared teas or, occasionally, commercial infant formula. In the past, I was told, a mother's sister or best friend might nurse a child, and as that child grew, it would call the woman *kiriamma*, literally "milk mother" in Sinhala. Although this co-nursing arrangement does not seem to occur any longer, the term continues to be used as an affectionate name for a favorite aunt, grandmother, or other older woman who was central in one's raising. By recognizing and providing for a child's needs and by that child's acceptance of what is offered, an enduring and intimate hierarchical relationship was created.

The ways that babies were fed—just as the ways that older children like Sampath were fed—reflected key pieces of a cultural model of hierarchy. When children seemed hungry or unhappy, mothers and others noticed and responded. These senior people did this, confident in their ability to understand what children need and to provide it. The mothers I knew in Viligama did not look at the clock to see if it was time for a child to breastfeed, nor did they require a great deal of privacy to do so. As in other relationships between juniors and seniors, mothers identified and delivered what children needed casually, quickly, and competently.

However, these breastfeeding episodes were not all business; they were also expected to be warm and intimate. Both babies and mothers were expected to enjoy these interactions. One of the reasons people often gave me for why mothers might breastfeed their children into their third or fourth year or even far beyond is that mothers felt pleasure in this activity and were sad to have to give it up—especially if they knew this child would be their last. As in other hierarchical relationships, the senior person in this interaction was expected to enjoy his or her role. Juniors, too, were expected to enjoy performing their role, without the ambivalence that might be expected to accompany taking a low position in other cultural contexts. In my conversations about breastfeeding, as about other interactions with esteemed elders, people I knew in Viligama reflected on these experience without the shame or discomfort that many in the United States might show. During a discussion about infant care in Sri Lanka with a young woman who had not yet had her own children, she turned the tables and asked me about breastfeeding in the United States. When she pressed for me to explain why people in the United States would think it was inappropriate for toddlers to nurse, I suggested that some might think it would be disturbing for children to be old enough to remember sucking on their mothers' breasts. She was baffled by this, since she herself had such fond memories of breastfeeding from her mother.

Breastfeeding in Sri Lanka is valued as more than a way of nourishing children. The giving of milk is the iconic act of motherhood. Milk in many forms represents bounty and auspiciousness—from mothers' milk, to the Hindu-rooted symbolism of cow's milk, to the coconut milk that features in both meals and rituals, as it boils over to mark an auspicious start to the new year or a new home. Milk is given by those who are loving, powerful, and protective. This is true not only for actual mothers but for other senior people who evoke similar emotions and commitments. Mothers-in-law welcome their new daughters-in-law into their home with a glass of cow's milk that they hold while the new bride drinks it. Senior men in a family or a neighborhood enact their position as caring and capable seniors by feeding coconut milk rice (*kiribath*) to junior family members and admirers at the April New Year's Festival, placing it directly into their open mouths. In turn, by receiving this milk, one enters into an intimate, protective relationship with that superior.

The way that breastfeeding is thought about and carried out in Viligama not only reflects important pieces of the hierarchy model but also conveys those pieces to children. The experience of receiving milk that is perfectly suited and deeply satisfying from a loving mother who is sensitive and responsive to subtle indications of need is one of the first experiences a child has of relating within a hierarchical relationship. The nursing child-mother pair serves as both a model of idealized subordinate-superior relationships and a model for them. In these and other early experiences of receiving from seniors that are infused with warmth, gratification, and nurturance, children learn to want and to expect these kinds of interactions with seniors. These kinds of receiving episodes also provide a contrast from the kind described in the previous chapter in which children receive unsatisfying and destructive things when they try to direct the giving episodes, rather than accepting what their seniors offer. In these early and ongoing experiences of being given breast milk and then solid food directly by those who are their closest and most indispensible seniors, without verbal interaction or discussion of the particular wants and opinions of the receiving child, children learn and learn to value this central piece of the Sinhala model of hierarchical relationships.

WEANING. Aspects of the basic model of hierarchical relationships are as evident in the cessation of breastfeeding as in its delivery. In both, the parent makes all determinations based on their own knowledge and observations, without drawing the child in to a discussion of their own desires or encouraging such expressions. The children are understood and encouraged to be the passive recipients of their mothers' ministrations, ministrations which the child is seen as choosing to accept. In weaning, perhaps more than in feeding, the right of the child to choose whether or not to continue the give-and-take relationship is particularly clear.

Weaning from breast milk is typically a gradual process in Sri Lanka, as in much of the world. It begins with the introduction of solid food and ends with the cessation of breastfeeding. In Viligama, it was the first part of this process that received the most public attention, while the ending of breastfeeding was left up to individual mothers to manage as they liked. Given the identification of the role of parents with providing in Sri Lanka, perhaps it makes sense that culturally elaborated rituals would mark when solid food is given, rather than when breast milk is taken away. Likewise, perhaps the typical US focus on weaning as the time when breastfeeding is ended makes sense in terms of the common understanding in the United States of the process of growing up as one of increasing achievement of autonomy.

In Viligama, the introduction of solid foods is one of the marked life-cycle ritual celebrations mentioned above. Babies might be given liquids other than milk or even mashed fruit during their first few months, but this was not really considered solid, adult food. It was the child's first bite of *indul*, adult-style food that has been curried with peppers and other spices, that was the focus of this ritual occasion. As with other rituals and important events in Sri Lanka, this first bite is arranged so that it will take place at a precise time determined in consultation with an astrologer to be most auspicious for the child. At the appointed time, regardless of the child's physical hunger or interest, the parent places food directly into the child's mouth. Children do not particularly seem to like this spicy, unfamiliar food at first. Parents often report that their children cried when the indul was first put in their mouths, although parents laughed this off, not regarding it as important. Repeatedly I asked, "*kamatida?*" (do they like it?), curious to know how children responded to these first tastes of the kinds of pepper many adults I knew outside of Sri Lanka would have found painful. But the response was always a triumphant "*kannava!*" (they are eating it!).

As at Sampath's mealtimes described earlier in the chapter, this ceremonial act of placing food directly into a junior person's mouth is reenacted regularly in the daily life of households—and not only with little children. One day, a young woman who had recently finished her B.A. at a university near the capital was at my house helping to translate some documents. When we stopped for lunch and had dished up our plates of rice and curry, I began to eat using my hand. However, the young woman hesitated. When I asked her if there was something wrong, she said that she needed a spoon. I was surprised that she did not eat by hand herself and asked if they had not done that in her household. I knew that she was from a well-off family, an only child, and had grown up speaking English at home, so perhaps, I thought, they used silverware. No, she said—it was that her mother had always fed her with her own hand, so she had never learned to eat properly by hand herself. Outside the home, she had learned to eat with a spoon. Even now, when she came home after being away for some time, her mother would feed her by hand, something she liked and found comforting.

Although I never saw mothers feeding grown children, I asked other adults about this. Many said that they, too, liked their mothers to feed them on occasion, especially if they were sick or had been away from home for a long time. This concrete instantiation of ranked relationships as nourishing and nurturing, safe and enduring, also appears at a symbolic remove in other parent-child interactions and, as I shall argue in Chapter 6, in other hierarchical relationships as well. Similarly, food sharing enacts the kind of intimacy and sameness that siblings experience when being fed together by their mother from the same plate, something which I will talk more about in the next chapter.

In contrast to the first introduction of solid food, the age at which breast-feeding stops is more of an individual, unmarked affair in Viligama. When mothers decided it was time for a child to stop breastfeeding entirely, they typically applied *kohomba tel* (bitter margosa oil) or another bitter substance to their nipples to discourage their child from nursing. If children objected, their mothers did not offer explanations for the bitter taste or rationales for why they should stop breastfeeding. Instead, mothers continued to apply the oil surreptitiously until their children no longer attempted to nurse. For some children, I was told, this took only one taste and they no longer tried to nurse. Other children might persist in their efforts to nurse from the bad-tasting nipples, even trying to wipe off the bitter oil, as one mother said she herself remembers having done as a little girl. But eventually, the children will stop wanting to nurse.

In this process as in other interactions between caretakers and children, the person in the superior role determines what is to be done without soliciting or attending to the expressed wishes of the subordinate. The verbal communication from senior to junior is minimal and void of directly meaningful content. Yet throughout, the parent does not overtly interfere with the child's continuance of the relationship; the child is allowed to continue her nursing behavior until she decides to stop. Although each of the mothers I knew in Viligama initiated this full weaning when they thought it was time, they simultaneously talked about it as something the child decided to stop doing.[2] These mothers made sure that children did not want the breast anymore, but it was the children themselves who chose to discontinue this particular form of their relationship. This highlights an important feature of hierarchical relationships which I will elaborate later in this chapter: relationships are brought into existence and continue only with the consent of the subordinates, to whom the option to exit the relationships is also reserved.

Elimination

People in Viligama responded to babies' bodily need to eliminate waste in ways that were also patterned by and communicated elements of a basic Sinhala model of ranked relationships. As with other needs, adults were attuned to subtle signs of infants' needs to urinate or defecate and respond to them quickly. When children learned to control their bowels and bladder and to evacuate them in an appropriate place, this was conceptualized as something children were just ready to do themselves—as it was when children decided to stop nursing or eventually left their mothers' beds. However, in contrast to the attention paid to feeding, children's elimination was not something that concerned people in Viligama very much. Like getting children to sleep, this aspect of caregiving seemed quite obvious to the mothers and others I asked about it.

Children's urine and feces were treated casually in Viligama, with only the minimum of off-handed concern that a child might soil something or someone. Babies were left bottomless or dressed in tiny panties and set on towels, all of which were replaced as necessary throughout the day. At first, babies were not removed to a special spot. If someone was holding a child who needed to urinate or defecate, that person would swiftly hold the baby out away from their bodies. They usually did this without saying anything or drawing verbal, reflective attention to it. Only when traveling was necessary did people seem to be concerned about these matters, and it was then that those who could afford to might use commercially available disposable diapers. As babies got older and there was more warning time, they were placed astride a gutter or in-ground toilet. By the time babies were around ten months old, people reported that children were in control of their bowels and bladder and used a toilet or other appropriate spot.[3]

I would argue that what allows this training to succeed—and at a much earlier age than is usually thought to be possible in the United States—is the keen attention caregivers paid to the subtle, physical signs that children are about to urinate or defecate and their immediate responsiveness to these signs. Adults in Viligama told me that babies just learned to control their bladder and bowels on their own, and that they learned where and how to go by being placed there by their caregivers. However, my observations led me to make a slightly different sense of this process. First, children's ability to control their elimination was not necessarily as complete at ten months as parents reported. There were occasional "accidents" even beyond the first year, but these did not excite the attention or concern of anyone around. Someone just wiped up the kitchen floor or changed the child's clothes. Second, as has often been noted by Western toilet training advice-givers, it seemed to be more the caregivers who were successfully trained than the children. Those who held babies were particularly motivated to notice small signs that indicated a child might be about to evacuate their bladder or bowels. When they did, they immediately held the child away from their own bodies. If they judged that there was a bit of time between the first signs and the evacuation, the caregiver would quickly get the child to a more appropriate place, placing them over one of the gutters that ran around the houses or down the edges of the streets. But it is not only the caregivers who are being trained. Caregivers' consistent, swift, physical reactions to children's subtle signs of need to eliminate, can hardly fail to raise children's own awareness of these urges and the need to do something about them. These actions are physically made to happen for children until such time as they begin to do it for themselves.

In this, as in most parent-child interactions, the child is not encouraged to recognize and verbalize his or her needs. Instead, the parent recognizes the child's need and acts to meet that need, providing direction by physical manipulation without much verbal instruction. All the while, the adults conceptualize this development as something the child is just ready to do, the parents having only provided the opportunity. Children, in turn, have the repeated experience that those who care for them do indeed know what they need, without the children themselves needing to express it.

Developing a Working Model of Hierarchy in Infancy

These and similarly patterned interactions with infants display the cultural models that are implicitly guiding the actions and delineating the options of fully enculturated caregivers—allowing them to be derived by the anthropologist through repeated observation. At the same time, these patterned interactions convey important pieces of these models to the children involved. As babies participate in these highly salient interactions with vitally important others, they are assembling their own internal working models—of the world, of others, of relationships, and of themselves. "Working model" is, in fact, the term John Bowlby (1982: 354), the father of attachment theory in developmental psychology, used to label the set of expectations children developed about what they can expect from their caregivers, especially in terms of availability and responsiveness. The basic premise of this theory accords with the more general point that I am making here, as I will discuss in the final part of this chapter. These working models that babies are developing in their earliest interactions form templates for subsequent interactions, not only with these particular caregivers but with other superiors, juniors, and peers in a range of settings. Because—and to the extent to which—children's experiences are patterned by social arrangements and sets of understandings held by their caregivers, the working models, or schemas, children are developing are also likely to be shared with others—and it is to that extent that we call these "cultural models" (see D'Andrade 1995, Strauss and Quinn 1997).

In the Sinhala cultural model of hierarchically ranked relationships that is brought to life and conveyed in early parent-child interactions, good superiors (principally mothers in these early years) provide children what they need, without consulting those children about their needs or preferences (see Table 4.1). Good juniors (children, in this case), wait patiently and uncomplainingly, accepting what they are given. Experiences like the ones described above of remaining passive while being directly cared for by a responsive and capable superior who does not expect input from the subordinate are repeated throughout the life course. These primary experiences of hierarchical relationships—relationships between ranked pairs of superiors and subordinates—are infused with solidarity, nurturance, trust, and dependence, coloring the Sinhala model of hierarchy as it is enacted and internalized within early relationships. Through these interactions children come to know, feel about, and value hierarchical relationships—knowledge, feelings, and values they will bring along as they enter into hierarchical relationships outside of the family and to their own parenting as well.

Shaping Behavior in Childhood

This style of interaction in which parents provide what they determine children need with limited verbal communication continues as children grow, though with new manifestations. As children's capacities change and develop, so, too, do the expectations and actions of those around them. As children move beyond their babyhood, parents work to shape their children's behavior through a variety of physical and verbal strategies.

These strategies arouse emotion, as I will describe below, making these important cultural lessons motivating and memorable for children, something

---

TABLE 4.1

**Developing Sinhala Model of Ranked
Relationships in Infancy: Hierarchy Pairing in Infancy**

The Parent/Senior

- identifies and provides for child's needs
- does not solicit verbal input from child
- does not justify or explain actions
- is sensitive, caring, and powerful

The Child/Junior

- is compliant and passive
- does not question or offer opinions
- does not discuss thoughts and experiences
- is acquiescent and expectant

that Quinn (2005b) has pointed out is one of the universal features of child-rearing, as discussed in the previous chapter. The particular emotions that are evoked in these interactions do more than help convey particular messages about behavior and relationships. The emotions evoked in these lessons become part of what children are learning about hierarchy and about themselves.

What becomes clearer during this period than it was in infancy is what counts as a violation of the expectations for behavior between juniors and seniors and what may be done about it. When juniors do not do what seniors want them to do, what might those seniors do? How might they shape children's behavior without violating the expectations of being a powerful, knowing, and caring senior? These options shape what parents and others in a caregiving position may and may not do in disciplining their children. What parents then do patterns the experiences children have and, in turn, the working model of hierarchy that children are deriving from those experiences.

Strategies for Developing Understanding without Words

One of the major changes that people in Viligama expect to happen as children grow is that they will develop an increasing ability to "understand" (*tereneva*). As discussed in the previous chapter, this ability is not thought to develop in children until about the age of five.[4] Starting around then, it would begin to develop "naturally" and was expected to be fully present around the age of ten. This "understanding" included the ability to reason, to see actions as having consequences, and to recognize other people's perspectives. Once children developed this capacity, they would be able to see the proper way to behave and should act accordingly. Before then, it was useless to try to teach children through direct verbal communication because they simply would not be able to understand.

With this cultural theory about what young children's minds are like, adults relied on nonverbal strategies when those young children behaved in ways adults did not like. Older people often responded to children's undesirable behavior by ignoring it, tolerating it, or even indulging it. Since children could not understand the social rules or ramifications of their behavior, they were not expected to behave as if they could. This is how Sii Devi responded to her daughter Rashika in the previous chapter, giving in to Rashika's demands, even though Sii Devi's body language and subtle emotional response communicated her disapproval. Another way that parents responded to undesirable behavior was to physically control their children's bodies, literally shaping their behavior so that it conformed more closely to social norms. Often people used exaggerated, unrealistic threats or promises—ones that even little children were presumed to be able to understand—in order to persuade children to behave as adults wanted. None of these strategies relied on or even contained explicit and accurate verbal instructions or information.

Caregivers improvised as they drew on and combined these techniques in order to extract compliance from children as needed. This is clear in the following example in which one mother, whom I will call Nirmala, employed a range of these options in response to her daughter's perceived misbehavior. One afternoon, I was doing a play-interview with Nirmala's four-year-old daughter, who was not paying much attention, picking up dolls at random and trying to pull their hair off. Nirmala, visibly embarrassed by her daughter's behavior, said nothing to her daughter. Instead, while laughing nervously, she physically restrained and repositioned her daughter throughout the interview, pulling and pushing her into some semblance of the pose Nirmala thought appropriate. Earlier, on that same day, when the girl had hurt herself and was crying loudly, this same mother clamped her hand over the child's mouth and pushed her head into her lap, saying that it was nothing. At the end of the interview, when it was time to go, the girl burst into angry sobs, although she made no effort to verbally communicate what had upset her. I was alarmed and asked what the matter was, but Nirmala kept saying it was nothing, while dragging her daughter to the door. Finally, in response to my worried apologies, Nirmala admitted that, in order to get her daughter to cooperate with the play interview, she had told her daughter that she would get to play with—or maybe that I would give her—my computer when we were finished. Worried about this unfulfilled promise upon which the girl's participation had apparently been predicated, I quickly grabbed one my son's electronic games that looked something like a computer and let her play with it. Although Nirmala indulged this, she seemed to find it totally unnecessary—even funny.

This example illustrates common features of parenting at this stage: Compliance is exacted primarily through physical means. When there is verbal communication from the parent (as in the promise of the computer), the content is not explicitly meaningful; it does not contain direct, accurate information given by the parent to the child, information which the child is presumed to be too young to understand anyway. The child is not encouraged or even allowed to use the parent's communications to make realistic choices about his or her behavior in the world. Nor are children encouraged to articulate their own perspectives, desires, ideas, or feelings. These experiences add to the working model of hierarchical relationships that children are assembling and help specify the possibilities for action within these relationships.

Private Outbursts and Public Shame

Parent and other caretakers in Viligama seldom explained their actions or drew children in to negotiations about their behavior. These actions would be at odds with parents' own model of hierarchical relationships and their ideas about children. However, they did use other techniques to shape children's behavior, techniques that often relied on emotional arousal and emotional communication. The use of these techniques, as I came to see, was sensitive to social context and the gaze of others. In using emotionally salient techniques that were in keeping with adults' cultural models of proper parenting, of children, and of hierarchical relationships, they communicated to their children not only how they should behave in a particular situation but also how hierarchy was structured. As they did so, they tied powerful emotions into the model of hierarchy that children were developing.

In the interaction described above, Nirmala worked to extract appropriate behavior from her daughter by physical shaping and making expedient, if empty, promises—techniques that made sense within the model of hierarchy she held. Parents in Viligama also used verbal chastisement (*baninava*) or hitting to correct children's behavior, techniques that were also informed by and conveyed important aspects of the hierarchy model. Scolding and hitting often featured in people's stories about their childhood. However, I never witnessed hitting or even chastisement in public, and only rarely did I see it in private. On the occasions when I did see this kind of interaction, it was with families I was staying with and knew especially well. The few times I saw a parent speak harshly to a child or strike them were sudden, angry, and somewhat disconnected outbursts—a harsh but general criticism about a child being stupid, a sudden whack on the back—that were over almost as soon as they had begun. The children reacted with shock and fear, sometimes with open mouthed but silent sobs. Afterward, the children were docile or even affectionate. One mother remarked in some embarrassment, after having hit her four-year-old girl while I was staying with them, "That was the medicine," as the previously whiny girl cuddled up to her.

The ways that scolding or hitting happened in private and the ways it did not happen in public say important things about how it is that children learn about and through relationships. But I only began to understand this after two years of living in Sri Lanka. In the fall of 2001, as I was about to leave Viligama after my initial two years of research, I was wrapping up the last of the series of extended person-centered interviews with women in Viligama. Shanthi was a daughter of one of the more respectable families in the village. At twenty-two, she had recently begun attending the highly selective university, about a two-hour bus ride away. During this last interview with her, I raised a question with her about an earlier story she had told me—but her answer only added to my puzzlement. In a previous interview, she had told me about getting stuck while climbing a tree at a neighbor's house when she was younger and her mother crying and hitting her when they got home. As I read over the transcript, I wondered how her mother had responded when she *first* found her. So, in this final interview, I asked her about this. She explained, seeming to find it quite usual, that her mother had not done anything when she had found her because there were other people there. Why, I asked, would her mother not have shown that she was upset with her in front of others, why was it that her mother had waited until they got home to show that she was angry? She said, as if it was self evident, that her mother would not scold her children in front of others because it was not good for a child—that would make the child too ashamed or too angry.

The next evening, another family was hosting a good-bye dinner for me and my family, so I put the question to various people there: was it okay for a parent to discipline a child in front of other people? And if not, why not? They were all in agreement that it was absolutely not okay for parents to scold their children in front of others—and they all offered the same reasoning for why not. As Lilu, the twenty-year-old daughter in that family explained, "The child would get angry. Or they would become ashamed"—although whether the child would become an angry or shy person or whether they would just feel angry or shy right then was not clear to me.

As I came to see how obvious and commonsensical this was to people, it began to dawn on me how terrible my own parenting must have looked to people over the previous two years. I was flooded with the realization of how the numerous chastisements I had given my son in front of others must have been perceived. I, like many mothers in Sri Lanka as in the United States and elsewhere I suspect, wanted my son to be on his very best behavior in public. But based on a quite different set of assumptions than those held by my Sri Lankan neighbors, my pursuit of this similar goal led me to very different kinds of mothering behavior than what was admired in Viligama. Since I believed that to let a child get away with something would be to encourage the bad behavior, and since I believed that a young child would not be able to link the transgression with the consequences unless those consequences where presented right away, I regularly scolded my son in public. In fact, I probably did so all the more strictly and demonstratively in public than I did at home in an effort to communicate to my Sri Lankan onlookers what a conscientious parent I was, what high standards and values I had, how unusual it was for my normally well-behaved son to behave badly, and how much I wanted my son to behave nicely to them because of my own good will toward them. I suddenly realized how misguided that effort had been, communicating not what a good mother I was and how socially sensitive I was, but exactly the opposite: what a bad mother I was, how uncaring I was for my child, what a lack of self-control I had, and what a lack of interest I had in socially appropriate conduct and the comfort of others.

Of course, there had been many earlier clues that there was some kind of mismatch happening, but I had been missing or misreading them. Occasionally people would intercede on my son's behalf when I would reprimand him, interruptions I generally took as approval that I had done enough rather than censure that I was doing too much. My own field notes are full of observations of Sinhala mothers ignoring bad behavior in public, seemingly not to be able to or interested in controlling their children's behavior. In fact, when I look back through the interviews from that time, the mother of the young woman Shanthi, who had been in trouble for climbing a tree, had told me herself in an interview eight months earlier that parents should not discipline their children in public lest it make them too ashamed. When I had asked what she did when her daughters did naughty things when they were young, Shanthi's mother had said:

> I scolded them. If they did something naughty when visitors were at the house, I waited until they left. It's not good to do that in front of the outsiders because children will feel ashamed. Once the visitors were gone, I would advise the girls not to misbehave again, saying "If you do that again, I will not like you, not love you, and I will hit you." So they listened to my advice and stopped their bad behavior.

This was not just a shared practice but an explicit tenet of parenting. And my overlooking it for so long speaks to the durability of cultural perspectives (mine, in this case), the seeming "naturalness" of assumptions about children, and the necessity of long-term field work. It also speaks to the connection between shame and public censure.

Central to the understanding that mothers should not discipline their children in public—and, indeed, to my thought that I should—are culturally specific understandings, elaborations, and experiences of shame. It is, of course, a tricky thing to talk about emotions across cultures and across languages, as anthropologists have pointed out (see Lutz and Abu-Lughod 1990). Emotions often are taken to be more natural than thoughts, more a part of the body and so the same across cultures. However, emotions are not only parsed and identified differently in different languages but they are also differently triggered, associated, perceived, expressed, interpreted, managed, recognized, and defended against. These differences exist between people and certainly between groups. Still, there is something recognizable about emotion across these differences. In order to talk about these shame-type experiences entailed in public disapproval and the ways that people think about and manage it, I take as a guide Rick Shweder's suggestion that we look for the specific cultural manifestations of what he identifies as the abstract idea of shame. He formulates this abstract idea as being "the deeply felt and highly motivating experience of the fear of being judged defective." This is the fear, he says, that results from "knowing that one is vulnerable to the disapproving gaze" of others who might see us as having "come up short in relationship to some shared and uncontested ideal that defines what it means to be a good, worthy, admirable, attractive, or competent person, given one's status or position in society" (2003: 1115).

The Sinhala word that is used for shame is *lajja*.[5] This word-concept includes things that English speakers might also gloss as embarrassment, shyness, modesty, self-respect, or even fear. In fact, as I discussed briefly in the previous chapter, it is often blended with *baya* (or "fear") into an emotional cluster term that is considered one of the means and goals of proper childrearing, especially for girls. Children who are *lajja-baya* (ashamed-afraid) are well-behaved, socially sensitive children, as they are informed and motivated to good behavior by their sensitivity to shame and fear. Being lajja-baya means having knowledge of, deference to, and respect for social norms/judgment, as well as an internal state that is sensitive to the gaze of others. This social sensitivity entailed in being lajja-baya is part of what it means to be a good person, especially for children and for women, as well as for others who are in junior positions. Not having this is to be shameless, and thus to behave in ways that are shameful. Thus saying that someone is lajja is saying that they are good and proper. To be recognized as lajja is something that, paradoxically for contemporary American English speakers, is a source of pride.

So why, I wondered, would parents in Viligama think it so important to avoid making their children experience public shame for their wrong-doing, especially given the value they placed on being sensitive to shame? As I have come to understand it, if a parent—and maybe especially a mother—were to discipline her child in public, the child who is already presumed to be sensitive to shame and fear might be crushed under the shame of the combined weight of public disapproval, his mother's negative judgments, and his mother's emotional abandonment of him. The expectation that good parents care for their children would be violated along with the expectation of shared identity that children are learning through experiences such sharing a family bed. Abandoning and betraying a child in these ways is unthinkable for parents who care about their children.[6]

But there is another way that sensitivity to shame works simultaneously to prevent parents from disciplining their children in public and to convey to the child the seriousness of their infraction. This has to do with the parent's own shame. This is something Nirmala, the mother who had promised her daughter would get my computer, talked about during an interview during one of my later trips to Sri Lanka. During that interview, I was asking about the scenario described in the last chapter in which a mother gave her daughter ice cream just because she was crying for it. Nirmala said that, if that had happened while they were in the town, she would have done the same thing as Sii Devi. She said:

> That is what I do to get relief from that type of situation. We aren't at home, no? You can do anything at home. But when a child cries in the

town . . . it worries the mother. So, the mother buys whatever the child is crying for and gives it to them. . . . That crying creates worry for the mother. She can't do the things she needs to do. . . . But when she gives in, the child becomes quiet. . . . If the child doesn't stop crying, the crying creates worry for the child too, as well as for the others. Crying, crying, non-stop. . . . Some mothers are ashamed. The people say that she hasn't made the child properly or that the children are stubborn. . . . It is a shame. These people criticize the mother. They say that the mother hasn't made the child properly from its childhood. To stop those people and the cries, we give the child what she wants, and then everything is ok.

Here it is the public setting and the potential for shame that is credited for prompting the indulgence of the child, rather than the idea that small children cannot understand and so should generally be indulged, as was the focus of the last chapter. And it is the mother's own feeling of shame, rather than the child's, that is the main issue. The mother, herself sensitive to shame and practiced in anticipating and avoiding it, indulges the child to avoid attracting the annoyance of others, although it is not clear that it is possible to avoid their criticism, as she is stuck either way.

A child's public misbehavior is in itself a potential source of shame for the family, especially if the child is getting to be old enough to be expected to be able to understand social rules and consequences. If a parent were then to lose control in public, it would be an additional source of shame. It would show the parents to be uncaring about their children's well-being, unable to provide the guidance they needed to avoid the misbehavior in the first place, and unable to do what is best for the child now by protecting them from public shame and disciplining them privately later. Disciplining a child in public would show the parent to be a bad parent and a bad person, adding to the shame for all. There is also at least the possibility that, if a parent were to scold a child in public, the child might *not*, in fact, be overwhelmed with shame. The child might defy the parent, showing him or herself to be insensitive not only to public opinion but to the judgment of his or her own parents. This would speak badly for the child but even more so for the parents who had raised such a bad child and who had earned so little respect, even from their own child.

To avoid and defend against all of this additional shame that threatens the parent, the parent behaves as if nothing is wrong. To bystanders who have not noticed the child's misdeeds, this entire shameful situation is avoided. To those who do know about the bad behavior—and in a small village, it is likely they do—this parental lack of response does not communicate a lack of concern for such an infraction (as I had fear it would when responding to my own son's misdeeds). Instead, parental restraint demonstrates that, despite the infraction of the child, this is a good parent who is sensitive to her child and to others and who eases social distress by exercising self-control—not one who lets her anger flare at a child in public. This is not, of course, something a parent has to calculate consciously. It is part of a long-practiced pattern of responding to potential public scrutiny and shame by hiding and avoiding notice, and part of a pattern of interacting within a matrix of hierarchical relationships.

There is another aspect to the parents' avoidance of their own feelings of shame, and this has to do with how these feelings are communicated between parent and children. The empathic identification with the shame their children are or might be experiencing as a result of their bad public behavior adds, I believe, to the parent's own feelings of shame. This further fuels the caregivers' avoidance of a scene of public censure as a way to protect the children as well as themselves from added humiliation. But this nonverbal communication of feeling and emotional attunement between parents and children, intensified as it has been by child care practices described earlier, goes both ways. Not only do parents feel their children's shame, children feel their parents' shame. As the parent stands there, tense and alert, pretending that everything is as usual, even a child who did not already know something was amiss does now. The intensity of shame and covering up that the parent is enacting may heighten a child's awareness of the alarming shaming potential of situations like this and model the importance of covering up such badness.

So there are several lessons being presented to children during these situations that I had initially seen as an absence of disciplining. While parents refrain from public comment on their children's wrong-doing, they do not fail to communicate their horror at the child's misbehavior. Their reactions, stiff and artificially nonchalant, braced against the shame that threatened from so many angles, must be registered by children, aroused as they may be by their own shame and fear at the public disapproval and the private punishment to come. The parents' shame feelings and behavior are surely noticed and perhaps empathetically felt by the developing child, a disorienting feeling accentuated by the lack of direction about how to change his or her own behavior or make amends. Instead, the parents' response gives children a model of public comportment that does not address the particular misdeed but rather shows oneself to be placid and self-restrained in social interaction, aware of and compliant with community norms. Further, when parents conveyed to their children—as clearly Shanthi's mother had to her, and Lilu had learned from her mother— that to be caught doing something bad in public might be shameful and bad, but that there was something far worse that could happen if their mother did not spare them the total humiliation of a public reprimand: it preserved the ominous nature of the threat. That a public reprimand is seen as intolerably shame-inducing builds up the importance and power of public scrutiny and sensitizes children to public opinion. As a result, the private punishment may work *better* than a public one to persuade a child not to shame the parents and themselves in public.

I came to see these moments in which parents protected their children from excessive shame by refraining from publically disciplining them as active places of socialization. This absence of discipline was, in fact, disciplining. In these public interactions with their mothers, interactions with high shame valences, children are learning about culturally specific ego-ideals and ways of relating self to others. This was true for my son as well as the Sinhala children we knew—although the specific cultural lessons my son was learning were quite different. They were all learning more than the specific lesson about telling their mothers where they were going or whether to take a sweet or, in my son's case, the importance of saying "hello" and "thank you"; they were learning ways of relating—of relating self to family, family to society, and self to society.

Disciplining is not a strictly dyadic communicative exchange between parent and child. The mother is simultaneously, and often intentionally, communicating to the onlookers: this is the kind of mother I am, this is the kind of family we are. This is probably true all over, but certainly true in my own case and in my observations of Sinhala mothers.

However, what "good mothering" or "good parenting" is varies broadly across cultural contexts—more broadly, in fact, than I initially appreciated in my own efforts to show myself to be a good mother. Despite similar general goals of teaching our children to follow the rules we thought important, of protecting them from harm, of appearing good in the eyes of others, and of making our children feel loved, the practices we undertook to pursue these goals and the ways we interpreted each other's behavior were worlds apart—leading not just to different and differently patterned actions on our parts but also to different and differently patterned socialization experiences for our children. As Roy D'Andrade has pointed out, it is not so much a difference in values that creates cultural patterns as differences in "what counts as what" (2008: 112). By looking not just at the cultural ideals but also at the daily practices of mothering, we can see the ways these ideals are enacted, experienced, and felt so that those differences make a difference.

Adding to a Developing Model of Hierarchy during Childhood

These experiences children are having of being corrected—or not corrected—are teaching them not only about the rules for their own behavior but also about the ways relationships work. Through these culturally patterned experienced, children supplement their internal working model of hierarchical relationships, reinforcing what they already learned to expect as infants and adding new pieces.

During this period following infancy, parents continue to identify and provide what their children need, without much verbal exchange. Even though children have an increasing ability to communicate verbally and are expected to have an increasing ability to understand, this does not lead to greater or more detailed verbal interchange about the relationship itself. Children are not provided direct, verbalized information about what parents are doing and why, nor are they encouraged to share their own perspectives, opinions, or questions.

As when they were infants, the experiences children have of being passive recipients of their parents' actions, gifts, and directives are generally satisfying, easy, and looked on with approval by those on whom the children depend. When children are sensitive and compliant with the wishes of their parents and other seniors—something they are increasingly as they grow—everyone smiles on them. In addition to these ways of behaving that were rewarding in their babyhood, children are learning that showing respect to older people, helping them, and being generous with younger children is also looked on positively.

The emotional tone of the relationship continues to be physically close, attuned, and secure, although the warmth is more subtle than when they were babies. Parents continue to care for children and are generally kind and gentle with them. Their actions with their children are confident, and children continue to experience their parents as powerful, as well as wise. However, parents are becoming more restrained and judicious as their children grow older, something that is clear in the ways that discipline is meted out as well as in the ways affection is conveyed. Children, in the meantime, continue to be approved of when acquiescent and are learning to be patient. In addition, children in this stage are developing a sensitive to shame, which is extending to socially valued feelings of shyness and fear of their elders, including their parents (see Table 4.2).

When children violate the expectations of others, the response options for parents make sense within this model. Many of the tactics popular in the United States—including isolating a child in a "time out" or insisting that they "use their words" or "make a better choice," in addition to the ways that I reacted above to my own son's misbehavior—do not make any sense in a Sinhala model and would violate important features of valued relationships between parents and children. Parents in Viligama used tactics that maintained and conveyed the ways of relating they valued. Within this relationship, ignoring, tolerating, or giving in to what a child demands, makes sense—and teaches a child about the proper ways of relating. Physically shaping a child's behavior, scolding them, scaring them with unrealistic threats, or making equally unrealistic promises are all expedient ways of letting children know what is expected of them and extracting their compliance without violating the norms of the roles. Even physical violence can be a just response when a child has failed to meet expectations, so long as it

TABLE 4.2

Developing Sinhala Model of Ranked Relationships in Childhood: Hierarchy Model in Parent-Child Relationships

The Good Parent/Senior

Obligations:	identifies and provides for child's/junior's needs
Proscriptions:	does not solicit verbal input from child/junior
	does not justify or explain actions
Emotional Orientation:	sensitive and responsive
	kind, caring, and committed
	confident and powerful
	'restrained and judicious

The Good Child/Junior

Obligations:	offers compliance, passivity, 'service, 'respect behavior
Proscriptions:	does not question or offer opinions
	does not discuss thoughts and experiences
Emotional Orientation:	acquiescent, expectant, and 'patient
	'shy/properly ashamed, 'a little afraid

*If Child Violates Role Expectations:

Parent may. . . .	ignore, tolerate, indulge
	physically control
	threaten or promise
	chastise or physically punish

'New pieces of the model being learned in childhood

does not violate the parents' primary obligation to know what is in a child's best interest and to provide for it. This means that whatever punishment is delivered, it should not permanently damage a child physically or emotionally, as public shaming would. This physical closeness in both affection and discipline combined with a verbal distance in which opinions and ideas remain private or vague emerge from this model and convey it to children.

Because children's behaviors and parental responses emerge on the fly, situated as they are in the contingencies of the moment, there is variation in what happens in any given interaction and, consequently, variation in what children are learning. However, because the older people involved in these situations are acting out of patterned and largely shared assumptions and because the situations themselves are patterned by social practice, the experiences children have are largely consistent from time to time and from child to child. This consistency in experience leads to consistency in the cognitive models they are deriving, and thus to our being able to call these cultural models. These cultural models are drawn on by children and adults alike as they enter subsequent interactions.

The Teen Years and Goals for Mature Personhood

By the time they were in their teen years, most people in Viligama demonstrated that they had internalized the full model of dependency as experienced within the family and reinforced by other social interactions. They not only understood and performed the roles, expectations, and possibilities of these relationships as entailed in the model but they had also come to feel about and within these relationships in ways appropriate to the model. In Melford Spiro's terms, this set of cultural propositions had, at least for many people, become fully internalized in that it was both "motivationally instigated and empirically grounded," meaning that its acquisition was psychologically motivated and that it had been experientially confirmed (1997: 70).

During the teen years, certain aspects of the model of hierarchy come into view more clearly. For young people in Viligama, dependency on parents typically stretched well into their twenties. But this dependency was not felt to be at odds with their increasing maturity. Indeed, young people demonstrated their maturity by showing greater recognition of social norms and greater deference to those in superior positions. This deference included, ideally, trust in the wisdom of elders in guiding major life decisions, such as schooling and marriage prospects. However, young people had to consent to these decisions, if action on those decisions was to move forward. Not only did young people have the right to opt out of particular plans their seniors had in mind for them but they could also opt out of the relationship entirely. It is during this period when it becomes clearer what options young people have if they feel that their seniors are not providing what they need.

Increasing Dependence and Deference

In Viligama, people expected that children's ability to understand would be fully present by the time they entered puberty. This was not, however, expected to lead to greater independence from parental supervision, more of a say in the decisions that affected them, or greater information exchange between parents and children. This is in marked contrast to what people in the United States typically expect for teenagers. However, beginning with Margaret Mead's 1928 work in Samoa, anthropologists have been pointing out that adolescence is not universally or necessarily filled with rebellion and *Sturm und Drang* as is usually expected in the United States—nor is it even consistently marked out as a developmental period. For Sinhala children, they were expected to be more rather than less deferential to their elders as they grew, more sensitive to hierarchy, more confident that their elders know what is best for them, and less assertive about their own needs and opinions. And, indeed, this expected behavior is what I observed among young people in Viligama. However, as I will argue toward the end of the chapter, the proper performance of this dependent, junior role within hierarchically ranked relationships should not be taken as indicating an absence of a secure and autonomous self.

Adolescence was a time in a Sinhala child's life, at least for girls, that required the most intensive supervision and guidance. Several of the mothers in Viligama worked abroad while their children were young, but returned when their daughters neared puberty because the mothers felt that their daughters were entering a period in which a mother's guidance and protection were essential. Instead of leading to more independence, the adolescent's growing capacity for understanding leads to a fuller sense of shame, respect, and social propriety and a greater trust in and compliance with the dictates of the parents, an internalization of the subordinate role and the full hierarchy model. My more limited observation of boys' interactions with their parents make me think that the basic frame of this model is also internalized by them; however, since most of my direct interviewing and social contact was with women, girls, and little boys, the material about adolescent boys' development that would round out this picture is not available to me.

As girls entered puberty, they were not only expected to act in ways that demonstrated their virtue and a properly disciplined self but they also reported feeling the emotions that are understood to prompt those actions. They said that, following their "big girl" ceremonies, which marked their first menstruation, they felt increasingly uncomfortable and shy around their fathers.[7] Before this time, they sat on their fathers' laps, but now they would leave the room if their fathers came in. They said that they acted in these ways that put greater distance between themselves and their fathers because they respected and loved their fathers so much that they felt *lajja* (shy/embarrassed/ashamed) in their presence. They also reported that they could not ask their mothers about what was happening to their bodies because they knew it was not appropriate and they felt shy to do so. Mothers, too, said that they did not think daughters would or should talk to their mothers about such matters, seeing this as something girls should learn about from their peers, from magazines, and from school. That they felt shy around their parents was something that parents approved and that girls themselves reported proudly, as it demonstrated their understanding and their virtue. These young women had not only learned to perform their roles with greater aptitude and completeness than when they were younger but they had come to feel toward their parents in ways that were appropriate and that motivated them to enact those performances.

With increased understanding also came fuller feelings of trust in the decisions of parents and a fuller commitment to follow their directions. At a time when there are major life-directing choices to be made, young people in Viligama waited patiently for their parents to make these decisions for them. By the teen years, it is clear that one part of the ranked relationship model that was internalized by young people was the expectation that parents could and should direct their offspring's lives and the trust in the parents' willingness to do so. Although for major life decisions, such as those regarding marriage, education, and employment, the young person's consent is required, the pressure of parental desires and expectations is strongly felt. The priority given to parents' wishes over the young persons' own inclinations is evident in the following excerpt from my first interview with Shanthi, the twenty-two-year-old discussed above who had called my attention to the inappropriateness of public discipline. This interview took place just after Shanthi had started attending university. Unlike most of my interviews in Viligama, my interviews with Shanthi were conducted in English, at her request, so that she could practice her spoken English skills.

BAMBI: Why did you choose to go to university?
SHANTHI: I didn't choose.
B: You didn't choose? Who chose?
S: My mother. She very [much] likes [for me] to go—but I don't like.
B: So you're only going because your mother wants you to?
S: I like to learn but I . . . (pause).
B: If you got to decide by yourself—your mother said "Oh, I don't care"—what would you choose? What would you do?
S: I would dancing choose.

In decisions about their lives, a young person's particular opinions, desires, and feelings were not solicited. But it would be incorrect to say that adolescents did not have any particular opinions, desires, and feelings about these decisions. Privately, they could articulate preferences of their own that might conflict with their elders', but they generally planned to follow the expectations of their parents, as they understood them. For example, when I asked young women whether they would like to have their parents arrange a marriage for them or choose their own husband—both of which were practiced with equal frequency in the village—they consistently said they preferred their parents to find husbands for them.[8] Certainly there are many reasons for giving this answer, not the least of which was that it demonstrated their own virtue and modesty, showing that they were the type of girl who was both respectful of her parents and not interested in pursuing sexual relationships. But the reasons they gave for why they thought it was best for parents to choose were more practical. They explained that their parents were in the best position to make such an important and far-reaching decision—far more so than the girls themselves with their limited knowledge of the world. Their parents would know what match was best for them, who would make a good husband, who was from a good family. One girl told me, exasperated with my denseness in not seeing the clear advantage parents had in making these decisions, "I would just choose someone handsome!"—clearly a poor criterion on which to hang one's future.

While the girls did have their own dreams about what kind of a man they hoped to marry, they did not seem to feel they these ideas were particularly compelling or relevant when it came to choosing a husband, especially since they had faith that their parents would be working to make them as happy as possible. Having learned to disavow and distance themselves from all sorts of desires in their early years, these dreams and preferences did not usually seem to motivate action, or to be troubling when not acted on. However, important exceptions to this emerged when it came to relationships with particular boys, as we will see below, relationships that had slight chance of blossoming in the course of their well-supervised daily interactions. What most adolescents may have wanted for their own lives was felt by them to be relatively unimportant in comparison to the commitment to stay in the relationship with their parents, a relationship which necessarily entailed deference to the parents' will.

Arranging a Marriage—Parents Provide, Young People Consent

Getting married is one of the most important steps in a young person's life, a step that marks the leaving of childhood. These days, this step typically does not happen in Viligama until people are in their twenties or even later, although it is expected that everyone will eventually marry. Until then, young people usually remain at their parents' homes. After marriage, they are expected to want to set up their own households and, especially for girls, to be oriented primarily toward their new spouses and, eventually, their children, rather than their parents.[9]

Seeing that a good match is made for a young person is one of the most important responsibilities parents have toward their children, one of the most important of the things they must see is provided. Throughout a person's growing up, parents take care to prepare children to make the best possible marriage. In Viligama, this arose as part of a more general set of concerns for their education, inheritance, and job chances. For girls, parents worked to make sure that they were prepared with the attributes that would make them desirable brides, overseeing their sexual virtue, their cooking and other homemaking skills, and their academic and religious education. For both boys and girls, parents were mindful of how the reputation of the family as a whole and of each individual member would reflect on a child in ways that could harm that child's marriage prospects.

When young people reached marriageable age, the ways that parents and other senior family members were involved in the process of securing a match reflected key pieces of the hierarchy model. In these proceedings, parents identified and provided for their children without consulting those children about their particular preferences or opinions, although the young person's consent was required throughout. Although young people may meet and develop feelings for a potential spouse on their own, they typically defer to the direction of their parents or other family elders in moving forward into a marriage with that person. Or, if the parents are not—or are suspected not to be—in favor of the match, the young people may elope, exiting the supervision of those elders who refuse to provide what the young people feel they need.

As discussed in Chapter 2, people in Viligama distinguished between "proposal" marriages and "love-matches" (usually using the English terms). However, in either case, parents were usually involved in some way in making these happen—or in preventing them. In the most formal arrangements, parents and other senior family members were central actors, identifying, vetting, and selecting marriage proposals. In others, older family members might facilitate a match of the couple's own choosing. But whatever ways a marriage was or was not arranged, the parents were understood to play a key role in guiding this process, even if this was only in their disapproval, their failure to act, or, conversely, their encouragement.

Although a young person might meet someone with whom he or she decides to pursue a love match, the default expectation in Viligama was that parents and other senior family members would identify potential spouses. In these formal arrangements, young women have no role in initiating or directing the search for a husband. When I first asked about this process of arranging a marriage, my assumption that the girls themselves might have talked to their parents about undertaking such a search produced confusion and then shocked laughter. No girl would be so shameless as to ask to be married off—but no parent should be so dense or uncaring as to not recognize that, after completing their schooling, girls would of course be waiting for a marriage.

But even in the most formal arrangement processes, consent is required of both of the would-be spouses.[10] This is classically conveyed during the visit of a potential bridegroom and his family to a potential bride's family. During this visit, the would-be-bride eavesdrops on the proceedings from the back of the house. If she likes what she hears and sees, she emerges with a glass of water for the young man. If she does not emerge, the families can part, claiming this was nothing more than a friendly visit. Although she may not select the candidates, nor is she consulted about her specific preferences in a match, a young woman has the right to refuse a suitor for any reason, as does the potential groom. While I was in the village, a young woman in her mid-twenties, with two sisters behind her in line for suitors, rejected a man because he was shorter than she was. A bachelor in his mid-thirties rejected a series of suggested women because they were not pretty enough. Parents react to these refusals with amused resignation, almost proud that their children are not too eager to be married, a similar reaction to that displayed by parents when a younger child refuses food at a relative's house, claiming not to be hungry. Since desire—and especially sexual desire—is morally, spiritually, and practically dangerous, as was discussed in the previous chapter, those who show such disinterest show themselves to be good people. But the more fundamental point here is that it is the right of a junior person to consent to receive what their seniors provide. Further, it is the right of the junior person to choose which relationships to participate in— whether that be the relationship with a future spouse and his family or with her own parents, as we will see below.

If the young people do consent to pursue a marriage, there are still many steps to take—and many places at which the engagement might be broken off. Astrologers must be consulted, dowry determined, money pulled together, and parties planned. In the meantime, the young couple can get to know each other better, visiting with each other's families and spending time alone together. One young woman who was going through this process when I was first living in Viligama described how, although she had not known her husband before his family proposed that they marry, she came to love him during their engagement, over their long walks in the botanical gardens and private lunches at restaurants in town. Once all the arrangements are made, some of which may be skipped for matches begun by the couple themselves, the wedding itself has several parts. One part of a wedding is when the marriage is registered with the state—something that even a young couple without family support may do on their own. For those whose families do support the match and can afford to celebrate it, a wedding ceremony is held sometime after that. In this ceremony, as in the rite-of-passage ceremonies in childhood that parents provided, the young people who are the reason for the occasion are not so much the main actors as the recipients of meaningful action at auspicious times. In the wedding, as in the arrangements leading up to it, the young people are not themselves the active agents in moving things along. However, it cannot proceed without their consent and cooperation.

This requirement for consent from subordinates is a crucial element of the Sinhala ranked-relationship model and a key way that the autonomy of children and other junior people is recognized and evidenced. In all kinds of ranked relationships in Sri Lanka—whether between parents and children, employee and employer, renter and owner, novice and guru—the junior person must consent to the relationship if it is to continue, and it is the junior person rather than the senior who has the option of ending it.

A Young Person's Options

As they are growing up, people are learning what participants in such ranked relationships are supposed to do. They are also learning what they are not supposed to do. By their teen years, children in Viligama had developed their own working cultural model of ranked relationships, and they understood what counted as a violation of that model—and what they might do about such violations.

Young people who felt that their superiors were not attending to their needs, and thus violating their obligations as superiors, may employ two main cultural strategies in response. The first of these strategies is to convey their distress in a variety of nonverbal ways, from moping and illness behavior to, at an extreme, spirit-possession or suicide. Because parents themselves have powerful emotional commitments to their children, these behaviors on the part of their children can be very persuasive. Such actions may also have the flavor of retaliation, when the junior person's actions involve refusal to work, costly remedies, or shame to the family. Eventually, if the parents do not provide their children with what the children feel they need, children may take up the second strategy available to them: They have the right to sever the relationship, typically attaching themselves to a new superior.

Two of the thirteen women with whom I conducted intensive person-centered interviews used this second strategy, leaving their parents in order to pursue love matches that they thought or knew that their parents would not support. Both Kumari and Jayanthi eloped with their boyfriends because they had good reasons to believe they would not get their parents' permission to marry. Jayanthi, a woman who now had grown children of her own, had eloped with her cross-cousin when she was young. Even though a cross-cousin is usually thought to be an ideal marriage partner in Viligama, this boy had been raised in Jayanthi's own home since his parents had died when he was still quite young. Because of this, they feared her parents would forbid them to marry. Without telling anyone, they ran away to the village of a distant relative, where they were married and lived for several years until they were eventually reunited with her parents.

Kumari also eloped with her boyfriend. Unlike Jayanthi, who merely assumed her parents would disapprove of her marriage, Kumari knew that her parents disapproved. After her father discovered the secret romance she was having, a terrible fight ensued between Kumari and her father, which culminated in his beating her. After that, she ran away to her boyfriend's elder brother's home, where she lived until she and her boyfriend were married. She had no contact with her parents until after the birth of her first child, at which point her father let it be known that he would like to see her, and she began visiting her natal home. Like Jayanthi, Kumari ascertained that her parents would not provide what she felt she needed and so she left the relationship. In keeping with the shape and importance of ranked relationships in this context, both of these young women entered the care of another senior relative, in this case from their husbands' sides."

For both Jayanthi and Kumari, it is important to note, the relationships with their parents were reestablished, albeit with continuing strain, when the parents let it be known that they would accept their children back, and then the children initiated the reunion. The emotional commitments of parents move them to want to provide for their children, to seek to minimize their suffering and distress, and to work to maintain the relationships. The emotional orientations that children develop within this cultural model lead them to trust and respect their parents, but also to unexpressed feelings of anger, frustration, and shame in its more negative experience. These emotions are tied into this internalized cultural model of dependency.

It is not only grown children, however, who have the option to leave the relationship with their parents if their parents are not meeting their needs. Even young children may leave their parents to find new caregivers if they choose. Another two of the women I interviewed had left their parents' homes in early childhood to live with other relatives. Nirmala, the oldest daughter in her family, went to live with her grandmother when she was two and her younger sister was born. In her own report and that of her sister, this move is considered to have been Nirmala's own choice, although not wholly arranged by her. Her age at the time made me wonder whether she was fully aware of making such a significant choice at the time or whether she came to think of the move in this way later. Either way, her explanation about the move made sense to the participants now, fitting into their shared model of parent-child relationships. This model contained the possibility that a subordinate person might leave a relationship that is unsatisfactory, as it may have been for Nirmala when a new baby displaced her from her mother's side.

Manjula had a similar story to tell. She said that when she was about three years old, she went to visit an aunt and stayed with her after her parents and siblings returned home. Although Manjula does not remember the reasons herself, she understands from what others in her family have said that she was very unhappy at her own parents' home, frequently and inexplicably tearful and difficult. At her aunt's house, she was happier, so she stayed there.

While it seemed to me, from other things that both Nirmala and Manjula said, that they harbored some hurt and anger against their own parents, everyone seemed satisfied with the explanation that a child might be unhappy in their own home and so choose another caregiver. That relationships of hierarchy continue only with the consent of the subordinate is a key feature of the model.

A Full Model of Hierarchy

By the time children in Viligama emerge from their teen years, they have richly and redundantly experienced this Sinhala model of hierarchy, a cultural model that they have learned to perform and have come to feel deeply within (see Table 4.3). They have come to understand how good parents and good children ought to behave and to feel toward each other, what behaviors are unacceptable, and what might be done if expectations are violated. They have come to expect that those seniors who care for them will know what they need and provide it. They do not expect detailed, open communication or negotiation with those seniors, although they know that it is their choice whether or not they will follow those seniors. They know that their compliance with seniors demonstrates their understanding, self-control, and maturity. If they do not comply with what their seniors expect of them, they know they may be ignored, scolded, or even hit. However, they know that if they feel they have been wronged, they too have options. They may take up one of the strategies that make sense within this model for responding to a breach of the relationship, by displaying their distress to persuade or shame their seniors or by retaliating, often in indirect ways. These indirect ways of retaliating include attacks against other junior followers of the senior who is seen as having done wrong, a dynamic that will be explored in more detail in the following chapters. Failing all else, the junior person may leave the relationship, typically entering the care of a new senior figure.

Having learned this model over the course of their growing up, young people use it to interpret and interact in hierarchically ranked relationships in the family. But they use it not only there. As they enter hierarchical relationships outside the family, this working model serves as a template to interpret and act within those relationships, too, as I will discuss in greater detail in Chapter 6. As they do, they will continue to develop this general model and generate more specific versions of it, as they relate to particular situations. In addition, this model of vertical relationships shapes interaction with peers, as I will discuss in Chapter 5.

What is crucially important about this particular model of relationships that is learned first in Viligama's homes is the way that caring is intertwined

TABLE 4.3

Developed and Internalized Sinhala Model of Ranked Relationships: Sinhala Hierarchy Model Learned at Home

The Superior

Obligations:	identifies and provides for subordinate's needs
Proscriptions:	does not solicit verbal input from subordinate
	does not justify or explain actions
Emotional Orientation:	sensitive and responsive
	kind, caring, and committed
	confident and powerful
	restrained and judicious

The Subordinate

Obligations:	offers compliance, passivity, service, respectfulness
Proscriptions:	does not question or offer opinions
	does not discuss thoughts and experiences
Emotional Orientation:	acquiescent, expectant, and patient
	shy/properly ashamed, a little afraid
	deferential and respectful
	admiring and trusting

If a Subordinate Violates Role Expectations:

Superior may . . .	ignore, tolerate, indulge
	physically control
	threaten or promise
	chastise or physically punish

If a Superior Violates Role Expectations:

Subordinate may . . .	display distress
	retaliate
	sever relationship

with hierarchy.[12] Growing out of these early and ongoing experiences of being cared for by seniors who know what is best for you, without your ever having to say it, and who are committed to and capable of providing it, leads people to expect similar kinds of caring from other seniors. This is one specific, cultural version of a more general process.

Relationships in Cultural Context:
Attachment Theory and the Sri Lankan Case

The model of hierarchy I have described shapes how parents and others interact with children in Viligama, in turn shaping children's own models of hierarchical relationships, how they feel within them, and how they behave toward others. I am arguing that it is through relationships such as these that people are shaped in fundamental—and fundamentally cultural—ways. This is true not only in Viligama but around the world as well.

Throughout their growing up, people participate in relationships. Through them, they learn about the world and about themselves. They learn what to expect from others and how they should behave. They develop working models of other people and come to understand themselves in relation to these other people. These understandings have strong emotional valences, developed as they are out of the utter dependency of infancy. Thus the models that children derive through these early interactions are not purely cognitive but are infused with emotion, as were the circumstances in which they were learned. Because these interactions with caregivers are patterned by the circumstances in which they occur and the understandings of the caregivers themselves, the lessons that children take away from these interactions are also patterned in ways that are consonant with others around them, leading to cultural patterns of self-construction and social understanding.

This argument I am making shares the basic premise that our early interactions with important others shape who we become and how we learn to relate to world with attachment theory as it has been proposed within developmental psychology, as I indicated earlier in this chapter.[13] However, my observations about hierarchy and childrearing in Viligama diverge from the usual case made by attachment theorists in significant ways. The ways that they diverge call into question the universality of attachment theory, a question that anthropologists have repeatedly raised.[14] It also prompts important questions about the value of the Sri Lankan caregiving practices I have described and the security and autonomy of people raised within them.

Attachment theory, as initially developed by Bowlby and Ainsworth in the 1950s and 1960s (see Ainsworth and Bowlby 1991), holds that human infants display biologically based behaviors designed to maintain proximity to attachment figures, principally their mothers. Mothers' responses to these behaviors, the working models that children develop out of these interactions, and the ways the attachment system interacts with other psychological systems pattern children's future emotional orientations, relationships, and senses of themselves. In these ways, the general outlines of this theory are in keeping with my approach here.

However, attachment theory and research have focused more narrowly on the sense of security or insecurity that children develop out of these early interactions and the extent to which that sense of security fosters exploration, self-expression, and autonomy. This theory proposes that children whose mothers are available and responsive in infancy develop secure views of the world that allow them to explore and express themselves in positive ways. From this secure base and the exploration and expression it allows, children develop a sense of themselves as autonomous actors. Children who do not receive available and responsive care from consistent attachment figures are likely to be—according to this theory—anxious, aggressive, or unable to connect with others. Without the confidence to explore their environment and express their own feelings and perspectives, they will stay dependent and insecure, held back from developing the kind of autonomy which is the mark of mature personhood—at least in the cultural context in which this theory was developed.

Attachment theory was primarily developed within, and so reflects, a particular twentieth-century, middle-class, American style of parenting and personhood goals. Even though some initial attachment research was based in diverse culture groups, and the paradigm is occasionally applied to non-US groups by its proponents, the bulk of this research has involved examinations of parent-child interactions in the United States.[15] Further restricting the possibilities for capturing the universals of child development, this research has primarily focused on observations of parents and children in a laboratory experiment that is known as the "strange situation," in which young children are exposed to toys and strangers while their mothers briefly leave and return to them.[16] Despite the specificity of this research, the resulting theory about the relationship of patterns of care to subsequent patterns of relationship and personhood has been posited by attachment theorists to be universal. The interactions between mothers and children this theory describes, measures, and assesses are purported to reflect universal patterns of human development that have evolved as adaptations during our species' past. Further, not only have these culturally specific patterns been taken as representing universal ones but certain ones have been determined to represent universally optimal outcomes, while others are seen as pathological.[17]

Ethnographic observations of caregiving practices and relationships in other communities are often at odds with this theory.[18] The cross-cultural research suggests, as LeVine and Norman point out in their analysis of German infant care practices, that "there is a wider range of pathways to normal emotional development than has been imagined in attachment theory" (2001: 100–101). A reconsideration of attachment theory in light of this kind of long-term, naturalistic cross-cultural research raises important questions about what might indeed be universal and how that might be used in culturally specific ways. The observations I have presented in this chapter of patterns of child care, relationships, and valued ways of being in Viligama contribute to such a reconsideration.

In some ways, the kinds of infant care practices I observed were very much in line with the kinds of care that attachment theory says lead to "secure" attachment, in that mothers were generally available and responsive to children's needs, actions which made sense within the mother's model of hierarchy. The early months of togetherness afforded to mothers and babies in Viligama allowed for lots of holding and touching and gazing, the kinds of behaviors that are thought by attachment theorists to foster the establishment of "attunement" and to promote the development of a strong and secure attachment bond from infant to mother. These early months in which proximity to the mother is maintained lay the groundwork for the infant to develop a working model of the caregiver as available and responsive, which will presumably allow that child to then explore the world confidently and with increasing independence (Weinfield et al. 2008: 79). Indeed, this intense togetherness is supported by social arrangements and expectations in Viligama to a far greater extent than is typical in the United States, in that mothers in Viligama typically spend the first three months after childbirth being taken care of, together with their new baby, at their own mothers' homes. Moreover, social arrangements support togetherness not only during the first three months but for a long time afterward, as children continue to sleep next to their parents and other family member and continue to nurse for several years.

Attachment theorists point out that "accessibility is not enough to establish security for the child. . . . The child needs to experience a parent who is not only accessible but also *responsive*" (Kobak and Madsen 2008: 30, emphasis in original). What is key in convincing infants of their caregivers' accessibility and responsiveness, according to Ainsworth, is the "sensitivity" of those caregivers to infants' signals (Kobak and Madsen 2008: 30). For children in Viligama, standard childrearing methods not only entail a great deal of proximity but also require a great deal of sensitivity to infants' signals—something that is evident, for instance, in the ways that children's needs to urinate and defecate are handled. The ways that everyday caregiving is done in Viligama gives children abundant experiences of their caregivers as attuned and responsive, which is essential, according to this theory, if they are to become "securely attached."

The manner of Sri Lankan caregivers' contact and sensitivity differs markedly, however, from what is considered desirable according to attachment theory in that it is largely nonverbal. As I have described, parent-child interactions in Viligama were largely and by preference nonverbal—and increasingly so as children matured. This was, I have argued, in keeping with a more general model of hierarchy that parents held and communicated to children. However, this is at odds with the "open, full dyadic communication" understood by attachment theorists to be required for the development of secure attachments and the subsequent achievement of autonomy (Allen 2008: 424). Unlike the parenting endorsed by attachment theorists, children in Viligama were not encouraged to express themselves in words, and caregivers did not provide modeling for verbal expression when they interacted with children. Rather, the caregivers I observed relied on nonverbal cues and physical structuring to indicate to children which behaviors were appreciated and which ones were undesirable. Children were not asked to "use their words" to articulate their needs and opinions, as they might have been in the United States, nor were they praised for doing do.[19] Instead, a parent or other caregiver, operating out of their cultural model of hierarchical relationships, recognizes a child's need, arranges things as the adult thinks best, and remarks no further. It is not that young children in Viligama never expressed their wishes—they often did, and quite vehemently, as evident in the previous chapter. However, parents did not enter into verbal negotiations about these desires.

Despite the absence of verbal information from parents, children in Viligama nevertheless came to "understand" many things as they grew older. As I have described, one of the ways that a maturing understanding was expected to manifest itself was in the reduction of these demands and in increasing compliance with social norms, deference to elders, and self-denial. This way of being, these goals for mature personhood look very different from the ways a "securely attached" individual is expected to look within the attachment literature and within the United States. Secure, Western-style adolescents are expected to be working to achieve autonomy from their parents, struggling against their attachments to parents to find their own identity, make their own choices, express their own opinions, and function independently.[20] In contrast, well-raised young people in Sri Lanka are expected to recognize and willingly defer to the wisdom and wishes of their parents and other hierarchical figures, understanding that their own identity is inextricably intertwined with their family, as well as their village, class, and ethnicity. They are not expected to express their specific feelings or ideas to parents or other superiors, but to have the respect and good judgment to keep these to themselves or share them discretely with peers.

However, it would be wrong to interpret young people in Viligama as lacking autonomy; rather, I would argue, participating properly within their relationships *requires* it. Sinhala young people evidence their maturity, capacity to make good choices, and independent good judgment not by differing from their parents and other hierarchical figures, but by complying with them. As I see it, it requires a kind of autonomy to recognize the wishes of others, to judge them as worth following, and defer to them. This exercise of self-control and discernment, and the feelings of shame when one is seen to have failed to demonstrate these qualities, display an adolescent's capacity for independent evaluation, choice, action, and self-government. This deference and self-control also afford repeated experiences of distance between one's own inclinations and those of one's family and other seniors, making the distinction between and separateness of self and other impossible to miss for most young people.

In a similar vein, Kathy Ewing argues that for young Pakistani women to behave properly and happily, especially within the families into which they marry, they must have a well-established sense of autonomy. Ewing claims that the fact such a woman "typically spends her whole life firmly embedded in interpersonal dependency relationships" (1991: 132), rather than being evidence of the absence of autonomy, requires psychological autonomy if she is to participate successfully in these relationships. Ewing takes this stance in contrast to psychologists who see South Asian interdependence as evidence of a pathological lack of autonomy, and to those like Dumont (1965), Marriot (1976), and Roland (1988), who argue that a nonautonomous self is simply an alternative way of being a person appropriate to the Indian context. Instead, Ewing builds on the distinction made by Cohler and Geyer (1982) between interpersonal autonomy and intrapsychic autonomy to argue that "there is considerable evidence to suggest that in many South Asian families, individual family members do in fact act in an autonomous fashion intrapsychically, though they operate within a highly 'engaged' interpersonal network of family relationships and expectations" (Ewing 1991: 139). Although Ewing is interested in the distress that arises when interpersonal autonomy has not been achieved, rather than in the autonomy required for the kind of self-control I am saying is the hallmark of Sri Lankan maturity, the general point is the same. Although the manifestations of autonomy we observed are quite different from how autonomy is thought about and evidenced in the contemporary United States and the psychological literature, these are, nonetheless, experiences, exercises, and evidence of autonomy.

So what is to be gained by applying attachment theory to examinations of personhood and person formation in non-Western contexts? I propose that there are at least two benefits. The first and more obvious is the potential to improve attachment theory so that it is not only a theory of development in one particular cultural context but the more universal theory it aims and purports to be. By examining attachment relationships in a Sri Lankan village, some of the ways that attachment theorists' own experiences and expectations about relationships and personhood goals have specified what is meant to be a universally applicable theory become more visible. By including this material from Viligama, we can see that sensitivity and responsiveness might be oriented and supported in ways very different from those in the contemporary, middle-class United States. In particular, the nonverbal style of attunement between parents and children in Viligama contrasts with current attachment theory's emphasis on the necessity of verbal expression and interaction. And we see that the goals for maturity in Viligama are quite different from those assumed by attachment theorists.

Simultaneously, we see that other features that are the focus of attachment theory emerge as key in this Sri Lankan path of development, though played out in different ways. Attunement, responsiveness, and sensitivity are important in establishing and shaping the bonds between children and their caregivers. They are also important in shaping what children are learning to expect from others, the working models they are forming. How children are learning to communicate through these interactions with attachment figures also figures prominently in the Sri Lankan case as well as in attachment theories, although the ways and matters of communication vary significantly. And finally, these early interactions with important others clearly matter for the kinds of selves children develop and how their separateness from others is experienced and demonstrated.

What is made clear by comparing early attachment-type interactions and subsequent styles of relating in Sri Lanka with those entailed in attachment theory is that certain features can emerge as quite different but remain just as important. This is what such cross-cultural, ethnographically rich examinations of attachment offer to the task of building a more robust and universal theory of attachment. As Heidi Keller, one of the few developmental psychologists who examines attachment in diverse cultural contexts, points out, if this kind of research were taken seriously within attachment theory, "it would imply a serious shift from the view of attachment as a universal human need that has the same shape and emerges the same way across cultures to attachment as a universal human need, which looks differently and has different developmental trajectories across cultural environments" (2011: 2).

There is a second benefit, though, from the consideration of attachment theory in a cross-cultural context—something central to the concerns of psychological anthropologists. The story of attachment in different societies is a story not just about individual development but also about how culture is transmitted from generation to generation. By thinking about the role of everyday caretaking relationships in shaping individual development, and by thinking about the role of individual development in the acquisition of cultural models of relationships, we are presented a theory about cultural transmission. This theory suggests that certain features are especially important to consider: that human infants mature late, creating intense reliance on caregivers and integrating social experience deeply into mental development; that the patterns of caregiver response to signals of need matter greatly; that in these relationships children develop communicative patterns; that children learn about the larger world and their relationship to it through these interactions; and that a person's attachment system is necessarily in interaction with other systems. In addition, it suggests that psychological autonomy may be a key piece of maturity, although this may take, I would argue, various forms. These potentially universal features of human attachment processes are important to an account of how culture is transmitted as well as how diversity comes to be—diversity between individuals and diversity across groups. It is through the attachment capacities of children and reciprocal caregiving behaviors that children come to learn and care about particular cultural forms of attachment-caregiving relationships and to become particular kinds of selves within them.

Beginning in their earliest interactions, children in Viligama experience others as sensitive and responsive to their needs. When children are compliant, passive, and agreeable, their parents and others around them anticipate their needs and provide for them in ways that are generally satisfying and safe. When children assert themselves and their own desires, the outcome is less predictable and often quite upsetting. They develop a sensitivity to the emotional states and inclinations of others, as others are attentive to theirs, a communication whose medium is glances, ways of holding oneself, and words in which the general tone is more informative than any particular content. It may be that the ways early attachment bonds are formed in Viligama through being together rather than exchanging verbal information about ones' self, and the kinds of working models of self and others that children are deriving, lead to a different kind of autonomy than that seen in the West, but one which is also required for mature and socially desirable personhood.

Through these patterned interactions with caregivers and others, children derive working models of what they can expect from others, of how relationships work, and of how they should behave. Because children in Viligama are raised in similar ways, the models they develop are similar, and charged with similar sets of emotions and expectations. As these children grow up and enter into new relationships, they bring along these models and expectations which they use to interpret others' actions and determine their own.

In what is to come, I will examine how the models and the emotional lessons learned through early and ongoing relationships with caregivers emerge and matter in subsequent relationships. In Chapter 6, I will examine how the attachment styles and understandings about hierarchy developed at home figure in subsequent relationships, and I will take up the question of social change. But first, in Chapter 5, I will examine how the understandings of hierarchical relationships described in this chapter also shape relationships between peers, and how these combine with the lessons about the dangers of desire described in Chapter 3. I will describe how ideas about envy draw on these lessons about hierarchy and desire, and I will describe how these figure in a series of interpersonal conflicts involving young women in Viligama.

5

Making Sense of Envy

Desires and Relationships in Conflict

The interlocking lessons about desire and hierarchy that children learn in their early relationships are built on and used as young people participate in all sorts of relationships. The model of hierarchy learned in childhood shapes relationships with peers as well as with juniors and seniors. The deeply learned lesson that desire is dangerous and the habit of disavowing it shape how people pursue their own interests and respond to the pursuits of others. Sometimes these broadly shared cultural understandings lead to mutually satisfying, smooth-running interactions. But these shared cultural understandings are also implicated in conflicts within relationships. As people work through these conflicts, they draw on their cultural understandings and psychodynamic resources to interpret each other's actions and feelings, actions and feelings that are themselves patterned by earlier cultural lessons. By understanding the lessons about desire and hierarchy learned early in life, we can better understand the ways people behave in and experience these conflicts.

Envy is at the heart of many such conflicts. The Sinhala conception of envy (*irishiyava*) is deeply rooted both in understandings about desire and in understandings about hierarchy.[1] If we consider envy's core definition to be the emotional complex resulting from situations in which a person desires something that another possesses, then surely this feeling is not unique to Sri Lanka.[2] But in Viligama, ideas about envy were more elaborate and more specific than this—and more threatening.

In this chapter, I examine two conflicts involving teenaged girls and accusations of envy. Through the analysis of these cases, I argue that, because inequalities between juniors and seniors are justified and valued within the Sinhala model of hierarchy, envy only makes sense between structural peers—between those who should be the same. Further, I argue that, because of the ways desire is thought about and experienced as uncontrollable, dangerous, and destructive, envy is particularly threatening. In these conflicts, the participants actively use the cultural models at their disposal—models of envy, of hierarchy, and of desire, along with a host of other models such as those regarding food sharing, track meets, and sorcery. These models overlap, reference, entail, and sometimes contradict each other, as is clear in their use.

In the scenarios I describe, the participants are not simply enacting their culture; they are drawing on it to make sense their world, navigate relationships, and process their feelings. While the cultural models available to the participants enable certain understandings, they block other ones. As I argue, this dual nature of cultural models to frame the world so that some views are clear and others obscured, can also be used to avoid or revise that which might be painful. The final scenario in this chapter offers an example of how a cultural model might preclude the recognitions of some envy-like feelings while suggesting ways to reinterpret those feelings. This can facilitate psychodynamic defenses against painful feelings, thoughts, and perceptions. In this way, what is intolerable in one's self may not only be disavowed, as dangerous desires were in Chapter 3, but also repositioned and dealt with indirectly. In this way, one's own disavowed feelings of envy may be projected, so that they are interpreted instead as coming from someone else. This allows one to avoid the anxiety of owning the intolerable feelings, while simultaneously articulating, resisting, indulging, or condemning them in another. Likewise, if envy is felt to be coming from someone whom it is intolerable to believe could envy one, that envy might instead by interpreted as coming from a more culturally sensible and manageable figure, protecting oneself as well as the valued relationship.

These ideas are hard to grab hold of in this abstract form. It takes close ethnography and actual cases to see these dynamics in action and to see why they matter. Before going on to the conflicts that will illustrate and be explicated by these ideas, I want to begin with another piece of ethnography—the incident that got me started thinking about envy in Viligama.

Nimali's Dress

Early one morning, Nimali came by my house with a message from her mother. Nimali was nineteen and just finishing up her education at the village school. That morning, I was surprised to see her in a pretty new dress rather than her usual white school uniform. Having just woken up and being unprepared for visitors, I mustered the Sinhala words to speak with her, but my cadence and sentiments were straight from San Diego. I gushed that I liked her dress so much, that I had *irishiyava* (envy), and asked her where she got it.[3] Nimali looked uncomfortable and a little at a loss of what to say, more alarmed than flattered. She said something vague about the underground market in town. When I pressed for details, actually thinking I might try to find one like it, she hesitantly offered to give it to me. I laughed and said that her dress would fit one of my legs, which was almost literally true since she was nearly a foot shorter and probably ten dress sizes smaller. At my saying that, she visibly relaxed and brightened.

Both Nimali and I were thrown off balance by this interaction. Neither responded as the other expected. When I asked other Sri Lankans about this incident, they were shocked that I had said I felt irishiyava, that I was envious. They talked of *aes vaha* ("eye poison"), the harm that can come to what is being looked at with a covetous gaze, and of *kata vaha* ("mouth poison"), which refers to the harmful effects of praise, ideas related to the dangerous effects of desire that I discussed in Chapter 3. I was told that "everyone" knew that if you desired something of someone else's, that wish would lead to something bad happening to the desired object, whether this happened intentionally or unintentionally, whether the wish was expressed or unexpressed. This might happen through some sort of vaguely mapped out cosmic order which destroys coveted items, through statements which alert *yakas* (demons) to the presence of something desirable, or through more direct and intentional sorcery by the envious person. The only sure way to avoid this is to not allow a potentially coveted item to be seen or to give it away. Further, given that everyone knows all of this about desire and envy, any statements of admiration are taken as threatening demands.

Athough people in Viligama did not declare their envy or even admiration in the way that I did to Nilami, envy was something they talked about a lot— other people's envy, that is. Envy especially figured in explanations of inter-personal conflicts and difficulties. However, the ways that people talked about envy, how they saw it working, and to whom they ascribed it did not initially make sense to me. People in Viligama seemed truly frightened at the prospect of someone envying them and morally indignant at the suggestion that they ever felt envy themselves. Further, the people whose envy they feared and specu-lated on the most were people quite close to them—friends, neighbors, relatives.

Understanding Envy: Lessons from Childhood

The Dangers of Desire

As I suggested at the outset of this chapter, in order to grasp these understand-ings and feelings about envy, it is essential to take into account the early les-sons learned at home, lessons discussed in the previous chapters. That desire can be destructive, that it is not fully under volitional control, that it seems to fly out of a person and make things happen in the world are lessons learned early in life through the kind of interactions I described in Chapter 3. Children in Viligama learn that if you want something badly enough, you will probably get that thing—but the object or the experience might be ruined in the process. More important, cherished social relationships and the feelings of the people close to you might be harmed as well. The brother who loses his toy or dessert or good time because of a younger sibling's desire is disappointed and angry. The mother who is helpless but to give into her child's cries pulls away from that child, anxious and upset. The ways that people in Viligama talked about envy working to destroy an admired object or condition or opportunity make sense, given those lessons about how people's desire works. In that earlier chapter, I argued that such lessons reverberated with doctrines about the dangers of desire, in turn reinforcing adult responses to children's demands in ways that reproduced those lessons into the next generation.

These were lessons Nimali had learned, lessons that complemented and provided the emotional underpinning for the lessons she had also learned about what was polite to say and what envy meant in social relations. So, when I admired her dress, she was surprised—but she was also alarmed. Was I threatening her? Asking for her dress? Did I really just admit that I was envious? Nimali's usual playfulness that allowed her to roll easily through other awkward encounters dissolved into fear in the face of this bold admission of desire. And so, she did what parents do with demanding children, the last resort in the defense against envy: she offered to give me the dress.

Hierarchy and Equality

But the lessons about the dangers of desire are not the only childhood lessons that are important to understanding envy in Viligama. The lessons about hierarchy and relationships described in Chapter 4 also figure importantly in how envy is felt and feared. In that chapter, I emphasized what children were learning about how to interact with people above them and people below them. This model that children learn at home provides a template for relationships between seniors and juniors in all sorts of domains of life, as I will discuss in the next chapter. But this model of how juniors and seniors should interact also shapes how those of equal status interact—and it is between those who are supposed to be equal but are not that accusations of envy get made.

In Viligama, peers are defined by being in the same place in the hierarchy. They are co-siblings under their parents and co-students under their teacher. This extends to include adult peer relationships and affiliations. They are employees under their boss and constituents under their political representative. They are "small people" of limited means in the shadows of "big people" with access, wealth, and social standing. If someone tries to raise his or her own standing, that threatens to change the positions of everyone else in the system.

Most important, in raising one's own status, one will necessarily lower the relative status of one's peers and implicitly demand from them the kind of respect and deference that juniors owe seniors. For people I knew in Viligama, this was particularly galling when it was someone close, someone who had been not just a peer but a close peer, someone with whom they had shared a position under the same leader and who now expected their submission.

It is those people who try to better their position in the hierarchy that fear the envy of their peers. Further, by calling the hostility of the peers they might be overtaking "envy," the moral responsibility for the social rift is repositioned. No longer is the root of the problem one's own desire for more than those in one's position typically have—whether that is a second story on a house or a cushy office job or special honors at school. Instead, the source of the conflict is someone else's desires—the envious peer. It is these peers' bitter feelings of frustrated desires in the face of their erstwhile equal's success that is credited as the cause of the rift between them, not the ambition of the overreacher. And it is these frustrated desires of the envious peers that threaten to take away that success, bringing the climber back into position once again.

But true peer relationships are rare in Sinhala society. In most relationships, there is an explicit junior and senior. This is not only true between those of different generations or social strata. Even in relatively equal relationships, verticality is highlighted. In everyday terms, sisters are marked as older (*akka*) or younger (*nangi*), as are brothers (*ayya/malli*). Even twins are identified as older and younger, based on who emerged first. These sibling terms, automatically extended to parallel cousins, are used as terms of address to invite neighbors, fellow students, and strangers into this ranked intimacy, along with other kin terms such as *putaa* (son) or *duwa* (daughter), *maama* (uncle), "auntie" (in English) or *nanda* (aunt), *achchi* (grandmother), and so on. The only colloquial kin terms without an indication of relative rank is *massina* and *nana*, the terms for male and female cross-cousin, the customary preferred marriage partners and, accordingly, the terms for brother- and sister-in-law.[4]

But to say that relationships between equals are unusual is not to say that they are not valued. In fact, it seemed to me that relationships between equals were especially idealized and cherished, especially in the form of friendship. People told me that friends should always be there for each other and should always want to be there, in contrast to the distance entailed in ranked relationships. With a friend, everything should be shared—property, thoughts, secret wishes. This is something explained by Lilu, a girl involved in one of conflicts I describe below:

> During times of sorrow and times of happiness, a good friend should share it equally. During a period of sorrow and a period of happiness, she should not change . . . Now if I have some money with me and she gets

close to me, but then if I don't have money and she detaches, then that is not a quality of a good friend. . . . We don't need to see each other all the time, but when we are together I should really understand her. She should understand me too. If she is my best friend, then she should know about my thoughts and wishes. And if there is something I don't like, then she shouldn't do it. I should do the same.

When people talked about friendship, this idealized vision of friendship as intimate and without bounds was something that consistently emerged. However, such expectations were difficult to meet and frequently violated. Although many people seemed to long for a friend they could share everything with, there were practical limits on what people could share in terms of both material goods and empathetic attunement. Such limits often led to a sense of disappointment and betrayal. When one friend had more than the other—whether of material goods or social advantage—that betrayal could feed feelings, fears, and accusations of envy.

It was precisely between those who were expected to be the same but were not that envy featured prominently in explanations of conflict. In fact, as I have suggested, in Viligama and elsewhere in Sri Lanka envy is only really thought to occur between structural equals who have an inequity of favors.[5] In all of the cases of envy that I heard people talk about, envy occurred only between people of the same rank and relatively close relationship, people who could be expected to have the same things, the same privileges, the same opportunities. More elite people did not worry—or at least did not speak to me about worries—that one of their servants, students, children, or lower-caste neighbors would envy their greater wealth, connections, opportunities, or authority. They sometimes did worry that these people would steal from them or even poison them, but not that their envy alone would be harmful. Likewise, people in the mostly working-class village in which I lived spoke openly about how nice it would be to have the luxuries of the rich or foreign, how good it would be to travel, to send one's children to the best schools, to have luxury goods, things I could not imagine them saying about their more fortunate peers. But these were not the kind of powerful, active desires that had to be disavowed. And this was not considered envy.

In contrast, when people mentioned something a peer had that they did not, it was usually in disparaging terms, questioning either the value of the item in question or the rightfulness of its belonging to the fortunate peer at all. This may help explain why people I knew in Viligama often spoke critically about the appearance of others in their presence. I was frequently an unwilling participant or subject in such critiques about weight gain or loss, blemishes, or hair color. While I found these comments uncomfortable and even hurtful, my Sri Lankan friends took them in stride, seemingly unbothered by them. On my most recent trip to Viligama, while I was visiting with Sii Devi and another woman I also knew well, the second woman's daughter came home from school. This girl, now a teenager, had developed a bit of acne, on which Sii Devi commented. This led to a discussion between the two women, who examined the blemishes while the girl stood by, quiet and smiling hesitantly. On the way back to her house, I raised this with Sii Devi, using the incident as an example of the kind of criticism I felt to be so cruel, covertly voicing my own hurt as the occasional target of such commentary. Sii Devi said that it was not cruel but was rather the kind of discussion that let the girl know that they were all close and that they paid attention to her. If admiration can be taken as envy or threats, then it makes sense that this kind of critical commentary may serve to affirm and foster intimacy, as Sii Devi suggested, rather than to increase distance, as I felt it myself.

This understanding of envy as only really possible between equals helps make further sense of my misunderstanding with Nimali regarding her dress— both in terms of her confusion and what followed afterwards. As an older person, an educated foreigner, a white lady, my status in Sri Lanka was clearly higher than Nimali's. And yet here I was saying that I envied her, not only breaking the social convention against admitting my envy but calling the feeling "envy" at all, something that must have been particularly confusing, since I could only really envy her if we were peers. But it is just this aspect of the incident—my positioning myself as *like* Nimali by saying I envied her—that I believe made this story such a favorite. On late afternoon visits with Nimali and a few of her close female friends and relatives, the story would frequently get retold. It was the end of the story that made people laugh so hard—the part where I said that her dress would fit my *kakul* (leg/thigh). This added a risqué note to the story, in that women's thighs are highly sexualized in Sri Lanka, which emphasized the intimacy and informality of those gathered and my own ordinariness. Moreover, the implication that I *could* envy Nimali said that I felt like one of them and that I liked the same things they did. The end of the story also reaffirmed my difference, however, a difference that made mutual admiration possible and nonthreatening.

Understanding that desire is dangerous and that envy can really only occur between structural equals is essential to making sense of the ways relationships are talked about, negotiated, and felt in Viligama. In what follows, I present two different conflicts in which accusations of envy figured centrally. In unpacking these interactions, we can see how the participants are both subject to and generators of cultural forms, as they draw on cultural lessons internalized in childhood to act in ways that are improvisational, creative, and agentive. In these conflicts, we can see how the lessons described in the previous chapters are used by people as they work to make sense of their feelings, to further their own agendas, and to pursue relationships. However, as I will argue, these cultural models about envy also preclude certain recognitions and articulations, while facilitating certain misrecognitions and psychodynamic defenses.

In the first of the two conflict scenarios, one particular articulation of understandings about envy, desire, hierarchy, friendship, and equality is brought to life as one young woman is shunned by her envious friends. This conflict is ignited when the young woman is favored with special responsibilities at school and attempts to win recognition over her friends. In the end, the equality of these girls within the hierarchical structure is reasserted and the conflict resolved.

Conflict I: Lilu's Rejection by Envious Friends

Nimali, Geethika, and Lilu were in their final year at the government-run school in Viligama when I met them. This school served children in the surrounding area from the first grade through the Ordinary-level, the equivalent of the eleventh grade in the United States. It also offered an additional two years of Advanced-level schooling in the arts for those who did well in their O-level examinations. While I lived in the village, these girls were among a small group who were finishing up this Advanced-level education and preparing to take their A-level exams. Besides marking the completion of their secondary education, the scores on these exams would determine their eligibility for admission to one of the national universities, an improbable outcome for this cohort of students, but one that a few aspired to nonetheless.

During my ongoing person-centered interviews with each of these girls, all three talked to me about a conflict they were having related to their participation at school. This conflict had erupted following the school's selection of Lilu for a special role at the field day events, after which her friends excluded and ridiculed her. The overt conflict between them ended when a monk who teaches at their school intervened. However, hard feelings, distances, mistrusts, and changes of alliances persisted. Lilu discussed this conflict in detail over the course of our interviews, attributing her friends' anger to their feelings of envy over her success.

Lilu's Understanding of the Conflict

I became aware of this conflict during my first private interview with Lilu when I asked if the six girls and one boy who were in their final year of A-level schooling were all good friends. Lilu said that they had been, but that in the last month they "had become angry" with each other. During our interviews, she discussed the situation in great detail.

According to Lilu, the conflict began during the preparations for a sports meet at the school. For this meet, all the students at the school were divided into four houses. The seven A-level students were to lead the houses in pairs—except Lilu, who would head her house alone. Lilu said that the teachers told her they had selected her for this responsibility because she was the only one among the advanced students who was up to handling this on her own.

The teachers on the organizing committee called the seven A-level students to the office and charged them with selecting the track and field events. Each of the house leaders nominated events for the meet. With the encouragement of the younger students in her house, Lilu chose shot put and discus, because the younger students said she was much better than the others at those events. All of this placed Lilu in a position in which she must oppose and seek to top her friends. But it was in deciding in which events the A-level students would compete directly against each other that the conflict broke into the open.

According to Lilu, they were all practicing throwing the javelin. Lilu said that after she had her turn at throwing the javelin, the other A-level students saw how good she was at this and were afraid of competing with her. They went off, talking among themselves. When they returned, they said they all wanted to run the 100-meter race instead of the javelin. They asked whether Lilu would like to do that also, and she said okay, telling the "sports leader," the boy making the list, to put her down for the 100-meter event along with her A-level friends. However, the sports leader refused to put her in the lineup for that event, saying that she had not practiced it, a qualifying requirement to be entered. Instead, this sports leader, who was one of the younger members of Lilu's house, and some of his fellow house members went to ask the other A-level students why they were telling Lilu to run the 100-meter instead of throwing the javelin. Lilu heard the confrontation and ran over, pulling the sports leader aside and telling him, "Do not to make a quarrel, because I want my friends."

But that did not prevent a quarrel. As Lilu told it:

> Nimali and Geethika got angry. They started shouting at me that it is all my doing and that I am the one stirring up trouble. Then Nimali started shouting at that malli [the sports leader] saying, "It is not your responsibility to get involved in this." Then I told Nimali, "He was appointed sports leader, so how can it's not his responsibility?" Then she got angry and went away.

After this, Lilu went to the teacher in charge of her house and, according to Lilu, he said, "You just wait quietly. On the day of the sports meet, there will be an event for you." Apparently this got back to the other girls through their own teachers, so they exclusively practiced for the javelin event. On the day of the meet, Lilu won the discus and shot put but came in third in the javelin throw, with Nimali taking first place.

It is clear that this conflict is about hierarchy and equality, and it is also about the dangers of desire. It began when Lilu was singled out for more responsibility than her peers. Starting in this privileged position, Lilu knew that the way to preserve her relationship with her friends was not to compete with them, not to seek to gain recognition at their expense. Within the system of relationships Lilu had experienced and internalized while growing up in this Sinhala village, friends should be equal to each other. They should share everything. One should certainly not try to win advantage over one's friends, shaming them and lowering their relative status. That would disrupt the sameness. It would make those friends angry. And it would make them envy the more successful peer. While Lilu wanted to maintain these friendships, she also wanted to do well in this explicitly competitive forum, wanted to be a good leader to the younger students for whom she was responsible, and wanted to avoid disappointing the teachers who had chosen her for this task. Based on the way she framed and sorted through this story during our interviews, I also think she wanted to be recognized as special, though she would not have admitted it, perhaps even to herself. As we talked, she rallied the cultural models she had at hand, employing them in crafting her own understand of the conflict and using them to pursue her goals in ways that would still show her to be a good friend and a good person.

Lilu clearly felt herself to be in a bind, and she identified the cause of the problem as her friends' envy. As Lilu explained it, "They were envious. I can do something that they cannot. That is why they wanted to change the event. This is because of their envy, because they did not want me to win. That is why they changed the event, and that is why they said, 'Let us run.'" Lilu did not talk about the conflict as driven by her own desires but by the frustrated desires of her peers. Further, these peers, in her rendition of the story, are repositioned as hardly peers at all, given her own superior skills and her new position in a relationship matrix including both younger students who depend on her and senior teachers who have recognized her as a cut above the others.

Eating from One Plate: Efforts to Express
Social Distance and Establish Solidarity

The trouble between the A-level students continued after the sports meet, with the other girls ridiculing and excluding Lilu. In these interactions, anger, hurt, and envy were enacted through social distance and a refusal to engage, a common means of demonstrating anger in Viligama. One of the ways the girls expressed this was through their refusal to share food. Likewise, efforts to share food were later used as invitations to draw closer together, eventually helping the girls to reestablish their relationships.

On the day of the sports meet itself, Lilu said that the other girls gave "hints" that they were angry with her, but that she was so busy rushing around to get everything organized that she did not pay much attention to them. Later, some of the younger students asked Lilu whether they should talk to the other A-level students on her behalf about the problem. Lilu told them that she did not know those girls were angry with her. But her peers continued to demonstrate that they were angry. Lilu said that one day soon after that, when she was sitting with some of the younger students in her house at school, her A-level friends

> brought a lunch packet and opened it to show me. I was eating a pomelo. Then I sent a piece of pomelo to them through one of the younger students saying, "Give this to them." They just kept eating without taking it—Geethika, Ruwani, and Nimali, with some younger girls. Then one of the girls who was with me said, "You all are angry with Lilu Akka [elder sister]." I just sat there without looking over at them, eating my pomelo. They also were eating quietly without raising their heads. After that, the younger girl asked me whether I am angry with them. I said, "No." When she asked them again, the other girls did not answer. Then I stood up and said, "Let's go," and walked away with the younger girls and boys who were with me.

In this interaction, as Lilu describes it, the girls demonstrate their anger by creating social distance instantiated in the refusal to offer or accept food, as Lilu tries to use food to bridge the distance. At the same, the other girls use the food to reverse the implications about who had something desirable and who envied whom. During the sports meet, Lilu was the one who seemed to have something the others' wanted and was not interested in being part of their group. Now these other girls explicitly showed that they did not want what Lilu had, that they were the ones with something desirable that they would keep all to themselves, and that they did not want her to be part of their group. While the ways that these girls used food to express their feelings and advocate for how they wanted their relationships to be were inventive, they did not come up with this symbol on their own. Such use of food to represent and negotiate relatedness is a common Sinhala trope, as is its direct association with desire.

As discussed in the previous chapters, food is an important medium with which people establish and negotiate their relationships. One of the ways people in Viligama commonly demonstrated and experienced their solidarity and intimacy was through the sharing of food, especially by eating from the same plate. In the last chapter, I discussed the salience of the feeding of intimate juniors by their seniors. In marked rituals and daily practice, respected caretakers fed their charges directly by hand. On occasions when there were multiple charges present, they were all fed from the same plate. For instance, mothers who had several children to feed all at once would prepare a single plate of rice and curry, taking turns feeding bites to each. At New Year's, when Inoka's father fed each of us at the auspicious time, one of the many little rituals that mark that day, he made the bites for each of us from the same plate of milk rice, and continued to do this as the neighbors came by to be fed by him. When priests at temples returned the *prasad*—the sweetened rice or other food left over from offerings made to the gods—to the waiting crowds of supplicants, they did so from a single enormous tray. In these circumstances, not only is the relationship to the provider marked by the feeding but the relationship between those sharing the food is also marked. Eating from the same plate marks intimacy and equality.[6]

Friends sharing a lunch packet is a common practice and is remarked on as a "jolly" thing to do together, more of an activity than a meal. In fact, my sharing a lunch packet with this group of girls early on in my fieldwork marked a qualitative transformation in our relationship. The family of one of these girls had arranged to bring lunch to the monks at a temple some distance away to commemorate the death of a family member five years earlier, thereby earning merit for him.[7] I was invited to attend this *dana* (as these meals given to monks are called), along with Lilu, Nimali, and twenty some other friends and relations. Afterward, while we were waiting for the bus, one of the girls produced a newspaper and cellophane packet of rice and curry she had procured from the monks' leftovers.[8] She called her friends and me off to the side behind a wall and offered to share it with them but looked unsure about what to do about me. They only had one, she hesitantly said, but maybe we could tear the paper somehow? And they did not have a spoon, said another, which they assumed I would require as they knew Westerners were not used to eating with their hands. When I waved away these concerns and expressed eagerness to share it with them, they all seemed surprised and delighted. The five of us stood huddled over the rice packet that one girl held in her hand, giggling and gathering bites in our fingertips. Adding to the intimacy was the recognition that we were doing something a little bit brash and naughty together, as none of those in the larger group had anything to eat and they might be able to see us. Plus, as discussed in Chapter 3, people in Sri Lanka are often shy about eating in public, and here we were being so bold. This event cemented my relationship with the girls. Like the story about my envying Nimali's dress, the sharing of the lunch packet was something the girls talked fondly about as the time when they first got to know me. It was immediately following this shared meal that the girls discussed with me whether they should stop calling me "madam" and call me *akka* (elder sister) instead, marking a shift in how they related to me from the more rigidly hierarchical student/teacher paradigm to the more intimate younger sister/older sister one.

In the conflict between Lilu and her friends, food was used at several turns to express and negotiate the feelings and relationships of the participants. Lilu silently offered a piece of the pomelo she was eating to her friends as a bid to draw them into relationship with her. The girls' refusal of the pomelo was understood as a rejection and a registration of their anger toward her. Their eating more substantial food together without including Lilu concretized her exclusion from their circle.

But food also became the medium through which a tenuous resolution of the conflict was formed. This was orchestrated by the Buddhist studies teacher at their school, who was also the head monk at the temple where Lilu, Nimali, and Geethika all taught Sunday school. For some time after the sports meet, he had been encouraging them to put an end to their feuding. Then one day at school, he called them together and gave them a single lunch packet of noodles and curry, insisting that the girls eat together from one plate, an activity they all understood would symbolize the restoration of their solidarity, their intimacy, and their friendship. Each of the girls talked to me about this incident. This is how Lilu described it:

> The monk came and told us to eat from one plate. . . . He had a food packet from the temple and called us into the cafeteria. Then he asked us to feed each other and become friends again. Geethika jokingly said to the monk that if he was going to give us lunch packets, then we could become angry with each other again.

Although the girls demurred from feeding each other directly by hand, as the monk had wanted, they did eat together from one plate.[9] Through this act, the monk was able to craft the grounds for a reconciliation, establishing his authority over them under which they are all the same and making them perform their intimate equality in the sharing of food.

In my interviews with Nimali and Geethika, I tried to get them to talk about this conflict. Nimali, who was wrapped up in other worries and always mindful that I liked Lilu, never spoke directly about the incident. Geethika did, however, tell a story that, though briefer, is consistent with Lilu's account. She said that, although the A-level students had all gotten along before the track meet, at that time they had gotten angry with Lilu. When I asked her to explain this, she said,

> During the sports meet, we were asked to do the javelin, the shot put, and the discus. But we couldn't really do the javelin. So two of my friends agreed to go for the 100-meter instead. We asked Lilu about this and she agreed. Then later she came with some of the younger boys in her house and scolded us, saying that we shouldn't change from javelin to running. Now, I know those younger boys. They are good with

me. Anyway, my friends told me not to talk with Lilu for a while. But recently, the teachers asked me to talk to her. Then we started talking and now we are ok.

When I asked Geetika to tell me more about how this resolution happened she said,

There is a monk. He came and said, "You are teachers at Sunday school in the temple. So you should provide a good example. And he brought a packet of string hoppers [rice noodles] and wanted all of us to eat together.... On that day, the monk asked us to shake hands and he asked us to feed each other. We didn't feed each other, but we shook hands and became friends again. Even though we did not really talk, it wasn't serious. There wasn't any hate or bad feelings.

I then asked what she thought would have happened if the monk had not intervened. Geetika responded, "Maybe things would still be the same." My research assistant, Inoka, asked if she would still be angry, and Geetika laughed in agreement.

The most notable difference in this account is the absence of any assertions of envy. In fact, in a later interview, Geethika claimed never to have felt *irishiyava*, as did most Sri Lankans I spoke with. The rest of her report, however, is in line with Lilu's, including the aspect of competition: Geethika and her friends were angry at Lilu because she resisted their efforts to put an event on the agenda at which they would be successful. As a result, Geethika and her friends refused to speak with Lilu until the monk intervened, telling them to shake hands and feed each other, although in Geethika's account it is unclear whether they ate together or not. Without this senior person's intervention, Geethika imagines that the conflict would still be ongoing.

This symbolic act of social solidarity by sharing food under the direction of a mutually respected senior led to increased social contact between the girls and changes in their feelings toward one another. Lilu explained that after the intervention of the monk, the other girls came to visit her house, although only her father was home at the time. Lilu said, "I was not at home, but later I started speaking to them. I thought, it's bad not to speak to people who visit my house." When, a little while later, I asked Lilu if she still felt angry at those girls, Lilu said no, not even a little. She said, "I am not angry, because I realized that if we get angry with each other over this kind of minor thing, then if something serious happens to me, they will not be there for me." Through this interaction, Lilu has come to realize—or has been reminded—that gaining more than one's peers leads to envy, to anger, and to exclusion and loss of the relationship. Having these relationships is more important than pursuing one's own desires.

Cultural Models, Feelings, and Action

In these interactions, the cultural models of hierarchy, friendship, desire, envy, and anger fit together to create a world in which Lilu and her friends can make sense of one another's behaviors, in which they experience powerful emotions, and in which they can act and interact to express and alter their feelings and their relationships. This nexus of emotions, meanings, and behavior was articulated by the monk as he talked to Lilu about the conflict with her friends, prior to his insistence that they eat together. As Lilu reported this conversation,

> The monk says everyday that as teachers of Sunday school it is not good to be angry like this. It is not a good example for the children. He asked me, "Why did those feelings happen?" I said, "I tried to talk to them, but since they are avoiding me, how can I?" Then he said, "You have to speak, because those who lost will not speak." He said that before the sports meet, they wanted to be champions. But I said that I also wanted to become a champion. He said, "That was in their minds, too. And that was not achieved."

"Irishiyava?" Inoka asked her. "Like that." Lilu said.

In looking at this conflict as it unfolded over time, we see that these girls first related as equals, with all that the friendship model entails. Then, Lilu was given special recognition and responsibilities over the other girls by their seniors in the hierarchy system in which they all participated and within which they were structural equals. Lilu wanted to take this opportunity to display and compare her talents and efforts. However, her aggression, pride, and desire could not be fully expressed and could not be accommodated within the model of friendship. Lilu's efforts to put herself and her house forward seem to have been experienced by the other girls as an insult and a rejection, a violation of their relationship. In return, they rejected Lilu and their relationship with her. Lilu felt and understood this as a loss that was not worth whatever enjoyment there was in her own success, reverberating with and reinforcing this lesson learned in childhood. With the assistance of the monk who was equally senior to all of the girls, both at school and at the temple, the girls were able to reestablish their equality and their commitment to their relationship of unguarded sharing.

As Lilu and her friends worked through this conflict and resolution, they drew on models of feelings and relationships they had learned earlier in their lives. As they did so, they were further developing their internal understanding of these models and further binding up their emotions into them. In this ongoing process of internalization, there are cascading interactions between emotions, understandings, and behaviors. This is not only a process of cognition but of powerful emotions that are elicited and enacted in these social interactions.

Lilu felt, alternately, proud and aggressive; rejected, hurt, and alone; relieved and reunited but mistrustful, as she said in later interviews. Her friends, for their part, felt rejected, hurt, shamed, envious, vengeful, powerful, stubborn, magnanimous, reunited, and mistrustful. Their interactions and the meanings and emotions entailed in them were not prescribed but were actively and improvisationally played out by the people involved, moment to moment.

In the next vignette, not only are the conscious experiences of envy, rivalry, anger, betrayal, and other emotions at play, but so are hypocognized and unconscious feelings. In this, as in the previous vignette, people worked to make sense of their feelings by drawing on cultural models of relationships and emotion. According to these models, envy and a destructive kind of desire can only occur between those who should be equal but are not. In the case of Lilu and her friends, I emphasized how these models facilitated the participants' expression, recognition, and resolution of conflicts, both internal and social. In this next case, however, in which the conflict is between a mother and a daughter, the same cultural models about envy and equality blot out the articulation of certain kinds of distress and suggest more culturally legible misrecognitions.

Conflict II: Susanthika, Her Mother, and Problems of Envy

Susanthika was another of the A-level girls at the school in Viligama. She lived in a village not far away, with her father and younger sister. When I first met her, Susanthika was eagerly awaiting her mother's return from Saudi Arabia. Like many women in Sri Lanka, her mother had been working in the Middle East as a housemaid to earn money for her family back home.[10] Susanthika's mother had been gone since Susanthika was eight years old, leaving her with the primary responsibility for raising her then three-year-old sister and running the household, all while she continued in school herself.

Susanthika had been full of hope that her mother's return would mean freedom from domestic tasks, freedom to study and score well on her A-level exams, freedom to pursue a career and maybe travel some day. However, when her mother, Anusha, did return, she showed little interest in taking up an active role in the household, involving herself in visiting with family and friends and in trying to arrange a marriage for Susanthika, so that she might return to her life in the Middle East. The prospect of an upcoming marriage and no end to domestic responsibilities left the normally vivacious Susanthika despondent—moping around her house, not attending school, or even changing out of her bedclothes on many days.

One day toward the end of an interview with Anusha, she asked me what I thought was the trouble with her daughter. Since I had been spending a fair amount of time with the girls at the school and had also been interviewing Susanthika one-on-one for some time, I had a pretty good idea of what the trouble was. However, not wanting to say anything that would betray Susanthika's confidence, I just said that I had noticed that Susanthika seemed like she might be having some kind of worries, something that was evident to everyone who knew her.

I asked Anusha if she had talked to Susanthika about this matter. Anusha said she had:

> I asked her, "What is the problem? If you have any difficulties, tell me. Or maybe there is something else, maybe a love affair which you haven't told me about but is still in your heart?" She said, "No, mother. There's nothing like that." But later Susanthika said that, maybe because of how well she had done with her mother, maybe her father's elder brother had said something to stop her schooling, because his own daughter did not do well. She said that the uncle's family may not be happy to see how well Susanthika has done, unlike their own daughter.

According to Anusha, Susanthika had suggested that her trouble was actually the result of a curse of some sort that this uncle had made against Susanthika. The curse was intended to interfere with Susanthika's school work, since the uncle was envious of her success which his own daughter did not share. Additionally, Anusha indicated that Susanthika recognized that she owed her success to her mother, Anusha.

After the tape-recorded part of that interview was over, Anusha returned to these concerns, asking what Inoka and I thought she should do about Susanthika. Inoka, speaking from her experience of having successfully prepared for her own A-level examinations, emphasized how important it was to allow Susanthika the time and freedom from household responsibilities to study for her exams, something that we knew Susanthika was distressed about. Although Anusha seemed to take this advice from Inoka seriously, she was convinced that Susanthika's uncle had arranged some sort of sorcery (*huniyam*) against Susanthika because he was envious of her success in school, her beauty, her skills in managing a home and children at such a young age—attributes his own daughter fell short of by comparison. In an interview conducted seven weeks later, Anusha was still focused on this theme of envy-inspired sorcery as the cause of her family's troubles, saying that she had consulted a diviner who told her that Susanthika's father's younger brother's wife was doing sorcery on them because of her envy. In these explanations, Anusha expressed no recognition of any nonmagical basis for Susanthika's distress.

In the story around these suspicions, envy plays at least two roles: it features centrally in the cultural model of sorcery, rivalry, and harm that Anusha employed, and it is evident in the less cognized, less articulated, but nonetheless powerful, emotional experiences Anusha and Susantika were having in relation to each other. Let me start by exploring the cultural model of sorcery and envy as Anusha applied it to Susanthika's distress.

Anusha's Conscious Use of the Cultural Model of Envy

Anusha first went abroad in 1990, leaving her husband with eight-year-old Susanthika and her three-year old daughter. Since then, she had only returned twice for brief visits. Susanthika's father, who did mechanical repair and odd jobs, usually lived at home with them, although he often worked long hours and occasionally was away for days or even weeks when he got jobs away from the village. Although there was a grandmother and an aunt who helped them at the beginning, Susanthika was left largely in charge of the house and family. It was she who managed the household money and purchases, prepared the meals, fetched the water, disciplined her sister, and cared for her when she was sick. Throughout this, Susanthika managed to excel in school, continuing into her Advanced-level schooling and looking forward to her exams.

Because of her success in managing all of these responsibilities so well, others have, according to Anusha, become envious of Susanthika. While Susanthika never spoke to me about the possibility that she was the target of sorcery, and on the contrary was dismissive of such beliefs, she too saw that others were envious of her. When I asked Susanthika if she had any enemies, she listed only two—both of them her father's brothers. She said that one of her father's elder brothers hated her because she took in his daughter after the girl's elopement. He and his family blame Susanthika for her role in this scandal and have threatened to disrupt any marriage proposal that comes her way so that she too will have to elope, a sort of envy in advance because Susanthika has prospects that his daughter no longer does. Susanthika professed not to be scared by this threat, but she did seem angry, saying "Now when I even think of that, my heart burns." Susanthika was also convinced that one of her father's younger brothers hates her, because she is more successful at school than his own children.

> My father's younger brother became my enemy because their children had no work to do at home. The father and mother did all their work, helped them in everything. But they could not pass the math part of the exam. And without math, they can't sit for the Advanced Level exam. Now I am studying for my A-level exam. Yet with so many difficulties. I have to help my younger sister in her work, help father, do the domestic work at home, and after all, I also have to go to school for my education. So they are envious. Somehow they want to see my downfall.

Later, when I again asked her if she was afraid of these uncles, she said that she was not afraid, but was angry, tempering this by adding, "There is a saying: Show loving kindness (*maitri*) to the people who hate (*waira*) you."

Susanthika and Anusha both agreed that these uncles and their families were envious of Susanthika and her mother. However, it was Anusha who made this envy the foundation for accusations of sorcery. She, more than Susanthika, was predisposed to find the explanation of envy-inspired sorcery particularly compelling. In general, Anusha was often preoccupied with issues of status and display, secrets and schemes. Having been married off to a man she considered beneath her as a disruption to and punishment for a love affair in her youth, she always felt that she was looked down on by her own brothers. During her visits to their village, she always brought gifts and worked hard to impress them with her success, simultaneously working to gain their respect, to show that she had made it without them, and to exact a little revenge by showing that she was better off than they were. In other words, she was deeply involved in the ideas, emotions, and behaviors around envy and its connections with hierarchy and equality. Additionally, she subscribed to the set of cultural beliefs about the efficacy of sorcery, divination, and the spirit world which made envy-inspired curses possible. And she was involved with secrets and schemes herself, leading her to assume these were activities in which others also engaged.

As we saw in the earlier vignettes in this chapter, envy is understood to occur between close, structural equals when one has advantages that the other does not. In this case, Susanthika had opportunities and successes that her cousins did not; by extension, her parents had a more successful daughter than their siblings did. This was how Anusha saw it—she had a beautiful, successful daughter and her brother did not, so he envied her. Within this cultural logic, envy of a structural equal leads to hatred and a wish to destroy the thing desired. In this case, what was envied and thus at risk was Susanthika's marriage prospects, her academic success, and Susanthika herself. One means of effecting this destruction intentionally but secretly is through sorcery.

Less Cognized Workings of Envy and Other Distress

In addition to this conscious use of cultural understandings around envy, desire, hierarchy, and equality, there are less conscious motivations that lead Anusha to assign the cause of Susanthika's distress to the sorcery of her uncles and their wives—and there are additional reasons why envy was so salient here. Susanthika is conflicted about her mother, about her own childhood, and about her future. Sometimes she sees her mother as having sacrificed in order to provide for her family as a good mother should in the widely held cultural model. In other ways, though, her mother has failed to recognize and provide what

Susanthika needs, failures that are ongoing and made more stark by her mother's actions since she returned to Sri Lanka. In my view, this conflict about her mother, along with the disappointment, frustration, and resulting anger she feels, have led to Susanthika's current distress. I would also argue that on some level Anusha knows this. She feels the weight of her daughter's disappointment and blame as directed at her, and it is this that she displaces onto the uncles through the cultural understandings around envy.

In order to examine this interpretation that Anusha is displacing the cause for her daughter's suffering from herself onto the envious uncles and transforming Susanthika's anger at her into the uncle's anger at Susanthika, it is helpful to look at things from Susanthika's perspective. In this way, we can come to understand more about Susanthika's frustrations and disappointments, the suffering they have led to, and her conflicted anger at her mother that this has produced. We can also see how the practice of disavowing one's own desires, with the expectation that senior people will identify and meet one's actual needs, leaves juniors vulnerable and potentially conflicted.

SUSANTHIKA'S ASSESSMENT OF THE PAST. Since she was eight years old, Susanthika has had the responsibilities of a Sinhala mother. Susanthika's assessment of her experience of running the house from such a young age is mixed. On the one hand, she is proud of how well she has handled these responsibilities, but on the other, she continually pines for freedom from those responsibilities.

SUSANTHIKA: Even myself, I could not believe how I did those things.
INOKA: Did you not suffer?
S: I suffered when I compare myself to friends of mine. I had no freedoms, which is very sad.

On the one hand, Susanthika is proud that others admire her accomplishments, noting that her teachers, her neighbors, and even her mother are impressed with all she has been able to do. At one point she says, "There is a teacher at the school who says he is proud of me because I do my school work while also keeping up with the housework. He always says that I have a male's strength—not always, but sometimes he says that." At another time, Susanthika says of her neighbors, "They say that I am good. There is another girl who lives nearby and when her mother was away, she had not behaved well. So me, people admire. Mother says that she is proud of me."

On the other hand, she says that her childhood was not good and repeatedly talks about her lack of freedom. She says of her childhood, "It was very hard. The lost freedom. I had to carry a mother's role at home." Not only did her responsibilities at home deny her the freedoms of childhood, they also interfered with her performance at school.

Because of my work load, it made me busy so that I could not get through the O-level exam with the high marks needed to go to a school outside of the village. Earlier, until grade 5, I was in 2nd or 3rd place. But once mother left, I dropped to 15th, 10th. So I was weak in education to some extent. Now, when mother returns in grade 12 again, I will be in a considerable position in education.

Here she correlates her drop in performance at school with her mother's absence. Anticipating her mother's return, she repeatedly talked about her expectation that, with her mother at home, she would be free to concentrate on her studies and get the grades she would need to find a good job and the independence she wished for.

In the days following her mother's return, Susanthika was elated, feeling a huge weight lifted off of her. She said that she used to feel angry with her mother when she was away, but now that she had returned the anger was gone. Asked how that change happened, Susanthika said, "I think that mother's being away must have made me angry. Now that I have freedom, the anger must have gone." She went on to say, "The weight on my shoulders is completely gone away, so there is relief for my mind."

In these interviews, it was clear that her relief and hopefulness at her mother's return was closely tied up in her thoughts of her suffering while her mother was away. At another point, we asked how she felt now that her mother had returned. She said she felt relieved, but immediately shifted to talking about the asthma that had afflicted her while her mother was away.

Susanthika was ambivalent about her mother being gone for so long. She sometimes portrayed her mother as a martyr, emphasizing the sacrifices she made for her family. In response to a question about what her mother said about her time abroad, Susanthika said, "Sometimes mother says, 'I suffered a lot because of you.'" Susanthika said repeatedly that it was economic necessity that made her mother be away for so long. This was part of the family rhetoric and a key piece of the cultural model that says a good parent provides for her children.

Susanthika felt the weight of this sacrifice, but she also used it to argue for why her mother should now stay home: "What I feel is that mother went abroad and took the trouble to earn—not for herself but for the children. So it is our duty now to do our share to help them out. It is our responsibility as we grow older." She went on to lay out a vision of the future in which her mother stayed home and Susanthika was free from household responsibilities, something she justified by claiming it was her mother's due:

I am not old enough to get married yet. After just three months, I will finish my exams. I don't intend to go to university, but I do wish to do very well on them. What I am thinking is that I will get a good job and do my share for our mother and father. To tell the truth, she went all these years to do other people's work as a servant—now it is our duty to help them out.

While Susanthika at times bought into the economic necessity justification for her mother's absence in the past, she did not feel that it justified the return to the Middle East that her mother was now contemplating. Anusha said that it was because of the money that she must go back to the Middle East, but that did not quite make sense to Susanthika. Here she was trying to work this out: "Mother said she was going. We don't think she should, but she does. When my father is around, she says that she has to go because of us. But my father earns around 500 rupees per day—that is enough if used properly. Mother has a lot of expenditures, that's what I think." Then she went on to talk about her mother spending money frivolously, taking presents to people in her natal village when she goes on her frequent visits there and spending money consulting astrologers, which Susanthika does not believe in. In an interview two months later, Susanthika's assertions about this had become stronger. I asked her why her mother was going away and she said,

> Now, in terms of money, I think our situation is better than what it was. Now father gets work daily. He earns thousands per day. So, I see that financially we are in a good position. There is enough money. But mother, after earning money abroad, has now become so greedy for money that she wants to collect more and more money. So there is no end to that.

At other times, Susanthika disregarded the economic justifications altogether, indirectly blaming her mother for abandoning her. She had said several times that she did not think it was good for women to go abroad and work. I had trouble understanding whether she thought that going abroad was bad or being a servant was bad, since she had once said that she herself dreamt of going abroad to work but not as a servant. She clarified that what was bad about working abroad was mothers leaving their children and moving away. Though still speaking generally and exempting her own family from the evaluations, she explained about the terrible consequences for children when their mothers go away:

> Then the family will be separated. But our family did not get separated. There was no room for that. Because father stood steady, we stood steady. Because of that reason. But comparing with other families—they are mostly separated. The main reason that happens is that, when fathers go out to work, there is no one to look after the children. No one to see to their meals. Study—how do they study? There is no one for that, either.

When they fall down, no one is there to help them. No one is there to love them. Then what will the children do? They will go out in search of love outside of the home. So then the family will be ruined. So I don't think a mother should consider working abroad. Instead, the mother must stay at home to build up the family.

She clarified further: "What is bad in it is that when a mother goes, there is no one to do the housework. The children become utterly helpless. There. I see something wrong in it."

This theme of needing love and her own mother not being there to love her came up in different ways. In one interview, we asked Susanthika if she thought she would raise a baby in the way her mother had raised her or if she would have a different system. She responded adamantly: "I will never be like my mother." We asked what the changes would be and she said: "If a baby is born to me someday, I will be very close to the baby. That's all. Definitely a mother must love her baby. It is a must. The first love, the foremost love, a baby will get from its mother. If you don't get that love, how can you love another?"

In an earlier interview, when Inoka asked Susanthika whether she thought she would become a mother someday, Susanthika responded with ambivalence about whether she herself was loved:

SUSANTHIKA: I want to be a good mother. I have heard the child who does not get love goes on a wrong path. I don't believe that, but I will give love and warmth.
INOKA: Do you have love?
S: Yes. I can't tell this or this is love. But I see other people hugging their children. I think that is love. My father did everything for us. I think that must be love.

Fortunately for Susanthika, her father was there to love her, even if this does not seem to have fully replaced her mother's love. In what almost sounds like an allegory for their family system, Susanthika reported the following, when asked whether she had been breastfed: "I drank milk from my mother. But mother didn't have much milk. Father had to buy condensed milk to feed us. So he brought a large amount of condensed milk to feed and raise us." While the talk about her mother's shortcomings centered on her absence, it is likely that her mother was never fully engaged with Susanthika, and even less so with her younger child.

SUSANTHIKA'S HOPES FOR THE FUTURE. Susanthika often spoke with us about her dreams of going to Europe or the United States and escaping her obligations in Sri Lanka. If that did not work out, at least she hoped to find a respectable job in a nice office as a secretary or bookkeeper. Uninterested in marriage for the time being, she continually talked about looking forward to a time when she could be free of household responsibilities and could pursue her own life. These plans had the quality of day dreams rather than specific, focused desires of the sort that I have argued that children are led to disavow. What she wished for was to be rescued.

In the weeks before her mother's arrival, Susanthika was full of jubilant expectancy. Now she would finally be released from her job as mother of the household. She would be free! The timing was perfect, she felt: She would be free to concentrate on her exams, would be able to do well, and then would be able to get a job, a job she would be free to take not having to mind the home. When I asked her, a week or so before her mother's arrival, if she thought she would be shy with her mother at first, she exclaimed "*A po!*" Not at all! As soon as she saw her mother, she said, she would be so happy she would run up and bite her on the cheek, an act which may capture the mixture of need, anger, possessiveness, and love that Susanthika felt toward her mother.

Soon after her mother's return, however, it became obvious that her mother had different ideas about Susanthika's future, plans that would not involve a release from domestic chores. In the months following her arrival, Anusha spent much of her time visiting with friends and relatives, impressing on them how well she had done for herself. These trips to her natal village and entertaining visitors at her own house left Susanthika still responsible for much of the household work and child care responsibilities.

The failure of her mother to take on her full responsibilities at home was not only Anusha's doing. In fact, there seemed to be some tension about who was the mother to the younger child, who had been only three when her mother had left. One day, Inoka asked Susanthika, "So if she saw you as her mother, when your mother came, whom does your little sister love more?" Susanthika answered, "I think me. Even if my mother shouts at her a bit, little sister still talks back. I think she loves me more." When Susanthika gave her instructions, the girl listened and followed them. Given the model of ranked relationships described in the last chapter and the emotional commitments of love tied into it, the lack of submission and respect for her mother indicated that the sister loved her mother less than she loved Susanthika, to whom she was obedient.

Although Susanthika's mother may have been envious of the love and respect shown to Susanthika and of her continued position of authority in the home, Anusha also made moves to emphasize her equality with Susanthika. In contrast to the ranked role of mother and daughter in the hierarchy model, Anusha frequently talked about how she and Susanthika are "like friends," a common assertion among grown mothers and daughters in the village. But Anusha took this further, talking at length about it and describing repeatedly how they were often mistaken for sisters.

It is unclear, and I will take this up below, whether Anusha was trying to craft an equal, friendship-like relationship with Susanthika or whether she was trying to claim for herself the youth and freedom that were more appropriate to Susanthika's age. In our interviews, Anusha often asked us to guess her age but was cagey about revealing it. At one point, she insisted she was as young as twenty-nine. This denial of age is in contrast to the cultural norm by which most women were glad to claim seniority by age (except, if the comparison should ever arise, with respect to their husbands).

At another point, there was a conflict between mother and daughter over what to call Inoka and me. Susanthika had known us first and called us both *akka*, elder sister. For Inoka, an unmarried woman in her late twenties, this was appropriate. While I was closer to her mother's age, calling me *akka* reflected the kind of relationship which Susanthika and I had established, as it did with Lilu and her friends. However, Anusha called both Inoka and me *nangi*, little sister, rather than *duwa*, daughter, as she did with Susanthika's friends. Although this was common in our relationships with mothers and daughters in Viligama, it clearly annoyed Susanthika. One day at their house, the tension thick between them anyway, Susanthika challenged her mother on this, asking why she called Inoka *nangi* when she should call her *duwa*. Although Anusha dismissed this, it was clear to me that Susanthika found her mother' pretension to being younger than she was ridiculous. She also, I believe, felt it as part of a bid to take away something from Susanthika that Susanthika thought should be hers—in this case, our friendship.

These assertions and efforts of Anusha have complicated intersections with the culturally elaborated models of envy, hierarchy, and equality and with less-cognized but still evident experiences of envy. When she simultaneously positioned herself as Susanthika's equal and tried to claim what might rightfully belong to Susanthika, Anusha's feelings of rivalry with and envy of her own daughter began to reveal themselves. Perhaps this is why Susanthika overtly challenged her mother's appropriation of our friendship and attempted to force her to assume a generationally senior role. Perhaps this is also why Susanthika felt able to do these things, scolding her mother in such a shaming and disrespectful way.

Even within the clearly marked-out hierarchy of mother and daughter, there were sources of envy between Anusha and Susanthika, although these were less recognizable using the standard cultural model of envy, leaving them hypocognized." From the outside, it was clear to me that Susanthika had many attributes that her mother did not and that Anusha longed for. All of the stories of Anusha's childhood centered around people misunderstanding and disapproving of her. This misunderstanding and disapproval culminated in her parents' presumably unfounded belief that she was no longer a virgin, and resulted in her hasty marriage to a man she considered too old and too poor for her. Anusha was still engaged in trying to redeem herself in the eyes of her natal village and gain their approval. Susanthika, by contrast, had the respect of her parents, her relatives, and her village. Anusha's intelligence was unrecognized and her interest in school was thwarted by her early marriage. Susanthika had been allowed to finish her schooling and all noted how bright she was. Anusha is very impressed with Susanthika's beauty and the interest she was sure to garner from suitors. Anusha herself very much wanted to be young, sexually active, and desirable. Although neither mother nor daughter articulated these inequities, it was hard to imagine that Anusha did not, on some level and in some moments, feel a kind of hypocognized envy toward Susanthika.

At the same time, there is good reason to imagine that Susanthika felt envious of her mother, although again this was likely to be hypocognized. Susanthika wanted to have a professional career, to travel, and to escape domestic responsibilities. But Anusha, who had the authority to make decisions that Susanthika did not, instead was trying to marry Susanthika off, thereby subverting Susanthika's desires while simultaneously gaining for herself those very things that Susanthika wanted: employment, independence, travel, and freedom from responsibilities at home.

The issue of Susanthika's marriage arose as soon as her mother arrived back from Saudi Arabia. Immediately, Anusha began making overtures toward finding Susanthika a husband. However, Susanthika said she was not ready for this and would refuse if it came to that. In an interview only weeks after her mother arrived, Inoka and I asked Susanthika what she thought about the prospect of marriage:

SUSANTHIKA: So far I haven't considered about it. But mother sent my photograph to find a suitor for me. But, I haven't considered it. Two times earlier, marriage proposals were brought to my parents. But I did not like those proposals.
INOKA: Why?
S: I think that I don't need that so soon.
BAMBI: Do you ever want that?
S: No. Maybe later, it may be needed, but not now.

We went on to ask why her mother was in such a hurry to find her a match. She said, "I don't know why. I only know that the photo was sent out. My parents said nothing, so I can't say why." When asked what she would do if they did get a proposal and tried to force her to marry, she said bluntly, "I would not agree at all."

Within several weeks, her mother was making progress on her plans to arrange a marriage for Susanthika and had begun to talk of returning to the Middle East to earn dowries for Susanthika and her sister. Although none of this was directly told to Susanthika, she heard her mother telling her father about it. Little by little, Susanthika's resolve to resist her mother's attempts were diminishing. She very much wanted to let her mother be the mother and so to trust her judgment. Susanthika began to go along with Anusha's decisions in trying to find a suitable marriage proposal, although she still hoped that she would be able to postpone an actual wedding. Susanthika was in the midst of working this out during the following exchange:

INOKA: What does the potential suitor do?

SUSANTHIKA: He has a shop, and he does some other things.

I: Without knowing everything, how do you know that your mother wants this?

S: He's my mother's cousin, no?

I: Have they brought a formal proposal?

S: He is from my mother's village, so they are saying he is good. My mother said that she wants to give me in marriage as soon as possible, but that she will find out a lot about him before doing anything.

I: You have not seen him yet.

S: I haven't seen him, but I haven't even thought about it yet. When I do see him, I don't know what I will feel. So when I see him, I'll come and tell you then. It is my mother who will want to do it quickly.

I: Your mother wants to do it quickly?

S: I can't say if that's it, but from the day she returned, she has been saying that she wants to do something about my marriage. It has not been a month even since the day she came back. I feel sometimes that I am a trouble to the house.

I: Does that mean that now—if your mother is leaving soon—then as soon as your exams are over, if he is good, you will marry him?

S: No. I wouldn't like that to happen. I say that because, while my parents might feel he is good, a marriage means the two should have a mutual understanding. So, if I feel he is good, he will have to wait for about four years.

I: Four years?

S: Yes.

I: And your mother?

S: Mother will also have to wait. I will tell that person to wait too. If he won't, then I will tell him to go away.

BAMBI: But will your mother have to go back again because of your little sister?

I: So that means, your mother is getting ready to go find your dowry, no? So once you marry, if your sister has to get married, then she will have to go abroad again?

S: She might not go again. That means, this time, she wants to go and put money in our accounts. When that happens, I have my sister and myself.

Then everything will be okay. Now, it is also okay. But she must be feeling it is not, so that is why she wants to go.

In this excerpt, Susanthika waffles between, on the one hand, her desire to have some of the freedom she's been dreaming about and, on the other, her trust in and obligation to her mother and her wish to be taken care of by her. As she talks, she tries to craft a reality that she can hang onto, one in which her mother is going to stay at home and her future husband will wait. But she is pulled by her feeling that she is a burden to her mother, that there is something not right at home, something that is not right about her—as when she says "I feel sometimes that I am a trouble to the house."

In this passage, Susanthika seems disoriented in her feelings about her mother and her future, in contrast to her earlier declarations that now that her mother is home, she is free. This shift reflects the general change I saw in Susanthika as the months of her mother's residency wore on. Before her mother came, Susanthika was upbeat, determined, and playful. She talked about and behaved as if she felt capable, confident, and secure, even if she also felt overworked. When her mother first arrived, she continued to feel optimistic about her opportunity for freedom from housework and her chance to study and do well on her upcoming exams. But a month later, the reality of her continuing obligations was settling in, and she began to see that there were new obligations on the horizon as her mother worked to set up a marriage for her. She was ambivalent about these new obligations and about her mother. She began skipping school and moping around the house, always complaining of feeling *kammali* (bored/lazy/lethargic) and often of feeling unwell. When I asked her how her studies were going, she seemed to find them pointless. Her dreams of a professional life away from her home were looking increasingly impossible as her mother determined to lock her into a life of domestic obligation while she herself went back to her professional independence, all the while claiming that it was in Susanthika's best interest.

These conflicts, disappointments, and frustrations, along with a feeling of envy that was not easily processed through the cultural understandings of *irishiyava*, produced what looked like depression.[12] Three months after her mother's return, I asked Susanthika what she thought about when she was alone. Laughing a little throughout as people tended to do in Sri Lanka when talking about upsetting things, Susanthika had this to say:

> Now life is lonely I feel. I think—then I start to think, I think that I did not get the love. At times I think that. Then at times I think that I am good at studies, generally. But I could not study to the extent I expected. I regret that very much. Now I feel very sad about that. I think about that too. "Life is . . . what?" I think. An awful feeling is there. To end the life.

There are many things to happen in the future. Now there is a very lonely feeling in my mind.

The conflicts and the loss in her life have produced a profound sadness and hopelessness, feelings so strong that she occasionally considers ending her life.

Analysis

Susanthika is clearly suffering. Her mother knows this. On some level, I believe, Anusha has the sense that she is somehow to blame. But that is not tolerable. So Anusha rallies the cultural models at her disposal to displace the fault from herself onto Susanthika's uncles. She draws on her cultural model of envy, and the related models of hierarchy and of desire. However, these cultural models were not chosen randomly. In Susanthika's troubles, in Anusha's own experience, and in their relationship with each other, issues of envy, hierarchy, and competing desires are highly salient. While their particular issues do not map perfectly onto the cultural models, they resonate with them.

Susanthika is envious, as well as disappointed, tired, and realistically discouraged—although the envy is only partially realized. Even so, as I have said, I believe that Anusha knows this and she feels the weight of Susanthika's rightful but not culturally explicable envy. As she displaces her own responsibility for Susanthika's troubles onto the uncles, Anusha also displaces Susanthika's envy onto the uncles. In this reworking, Anusha's brothers are said to be envious of her instead of this envy coming from her daughter. In this psychodynamic displacement, she also reworks the dynamics so that she and Susanthika are on the same side, with the uncles' envy threatening them both as a unit. In doing this, Anusha can be the hero and save Susanthika from the damage that on some level she knows that she herself has caused. Susanthika may be complicit in this reworking, as she—at least according to Anusha—suggested the uncles' envy as the cause of their shared troubles. In any case, pitting the envious uncles against mother and daughter furthers Susanthika's fantasy of being taken care of by her mother. In addition, all of the envy that Anusha herself feels toward Susanthika—envy for her successes, for her position in the family Anusha left behind, and for the opportunities ahead of her—Anusha projects onto the uncles. In doing so, she disavows her own feelings of envy, while simultaneously articulating them as she speaks through the uncles about all of the things that are enviable about Susanthika.

In this vignette, we see the model of envy being used in two overlapping ways. There is the conscious and overt use to which Anusha puts it when she attributes Susanthika's troubles to an envious uncle's sorcery, drawing on the related model of hierarchy which says that people at the same level should be the same, and if they are not the envious person might retaliate. Simultaneously, we see a less conscious mobilization of the understandings of envy that draw on the same model of hierarchical relationships, but to different ends. In this case, the conflict again involves people not playing their proper roles in the hierarchy. And again, understandings of envy are mobilized to make sense of the problem. However, here the models of envy and hierarchy are used to make sense of and protect Anusha, Susanthika, and their relationship from the undercurrents of blame, anger, envy, betrayal, and loss swirling between them. Because it is not possible for those of different hierarchical positions to envy one another, the feeling of envy must not belong to them. In this way, the cultural models of envy and hierarchy can be used unconsciously to disavow the destructive feelings between the women and displace them on a more culturally sensible and emotionally tolerable foe.

While both women seem to be drawing on the same models of envy and hierarchy and both women recognize the destructive power of desire, they seem to deal with their own desires in quite different ways, fueling this conflict. For reasons that are not at all clear from this study, Anusha does not seem to have developed the same habits of disavowing desire that I described in Chapter 3. Her desires seemed clear, focused, and forceful. Susanthika's expressions of desire were more in keeping with others I observed in Sri Lanka. Throughout our conversations, Susanthika talked about what she wanted. However, as I noted above, these desires were typically vague, unfocused, often unrealistic wishes. When she was faced with real possibilities—such as the marriage to her mother's cousin—she backed off, disavowing any interest in the suitor but not showing any commitment to resist, suggesting instead a willingness to comply eventually with her parents' wishes. Susanthika's main desire seemed to be to get to take what she saw as her proper place as a child in the hierarchy of the home, a place she had been pushed out of so early. She wanted her mother to take up her role as wife and mother, freeing Susanthika from that role and allowing her instead to be a good daughter, studying diligently and avoiding romantic relationships for now. She wanted her mother to take care of her, to be a good superior, to recognize what was best for Susanthika and to give it to her, without putting her own desires ahead of Susanthika's. In the final interviews, as Susantika struggled between her wish to be free of domestic responsibilities and her mother's plans to marry her off, she was starting to reframe her mother's plans as caretaking with the potential to affirm their relationship as that of a proper mother and daughter.

The dynamic that I am describing in which people use the cultural models they have available to interpret what is happening in ways that help them simultaneously deal with and avoid intolerable feelings is one that major figures in psychodynamic anthropology have all talked about, although they each use different terms. In Melford Spiro's (1997) terms, we could say that the model of envy provides a "culturally constituted defense mechanism" in which Anusha uses the ideas about sorcery and envious peers to project and displace the envy and blame that troubles her. In Robert Levy's (1984) terms, we could say that Anusha has a "primary appraisal" that there are feelings of envy between her and Susanthika. She then uses the cultural models she has of envy and sorcery, hierarchy and peer relations to interpret these initial appraisals, generating "secondary appraisals" that say that the uncle must be the envious one, leading her to certain courses of action and of feeling. In this conceptualization of Levy's—which is very much in line with the analysis I have laid out—while the cultural models available to Anusha enable some recognitions, they help others to go "hypocognized," so that she is not even able to call what she and Susanthika feel for each other "envy." Gananath Obeyesekere (1981, 1990) offers a different set of terms to talk about similar dynamics. Using his terms, we could say that the "cultural idiom" of sorcery gets picked up by Anusha who uses it like a "personal symbol" that is meaningful to those around her, but that she selects to express her own deeply felt, idiosyncratic meanings, feelings, and experiences. By doing this, Anusha is able to transform both her inner experience and her relationship with her daughter. In each of these anthropologists' conceptualizations, it is clear that as Anusha and Susanthika think about, feel, and act within their relationship, they draw on cultural resources to develop and transform their inner worlds in an ongoing and dynamic process.

Using Culture

In these different scenarios, the women involved mobilized their shared cultural models to make sense of each other, themselves, their relationships, and the conflicts within them. They drew on the understanding that potentially destructive feelings of envy are likely to occur between peers who should be the same but are not, an understanding that is rooted in the kinds of childhood experiences and lessons described in previous chapters. In the conflict between Lilu and the other girls at school, the participants' expectations about friendship and hierarchy—and the tensions inherent in these models—led to the kinds of feeling of envy that the cultural model of envy predicted and helped the girls work through. In the difficulties between Susanthika and her mother, these models of envy and relationships were also used to interpret and work through difficult feelings and conflicting desires. However, this time the envy that was felt and feared was not predicted or made sense of directly through the dominant cultural models. Instead, the cultural models at hand helped obfuscate threatening feelings of envy between mother and daughter, while simultaneously offering ways to displace those feelings and rework the relationship.

In these conflicts, we see that "culture" is not just a set of representations and symbols received but also a process in which people are actively engaged as they seek to understand, feel about, and create their worlds. While shared cultural models shape the way that people see relationships, fostering certain interpretations and feelings, they do not dictate how relationships will be conducted, not do they preclude the possibility of other feelings and responses. Within the Sri Lankan model of hierarchy, inequalities between people of different rank are treated in such a way that envy does not really make sense. However, by the same model of hierarchy, peer relationships are both idealized and fertile ground for envy—perhaps more fertile for the ubiquitous inequities that hierarchy justifies. At the same time, this model makes accusations of envy a useful tool for people to interpret and negotiate possible inequities in these peer relationships. This is something we see in the conflict between Lilu and her friends. But that is not to say that something that looks like envy cannot be felt in explicitly ranked relationships—as I am suggesting is the case between Susanthika and her mother. In that case, they use the cultural models of envy and hierarchy just as actively to make sense of themselves and their relationships, models that do not oblige them to recognize their painful feelings and allow them instead to displace and reinterpret those feelings as they work to build the kind of relationship they want and need. I would suggest that when Anusha and Susanthika use cultural models to occlude, misrecognize, and redirect emotions and interpretations, this is just as active a process—though perhaps less conscious—as it is when Lilu, the head monk, and the other students at school use the models of envy and hierarchy to work through their conflict.

In this chapter, I have illustrated how people actively use the working models and entailed emotions that they have derived in their earliest relationships to interpret and negotiate relationships as they grow up. In the next chapter, I will present situations in which these models of relationships learned and used in intimate relationships are transferred into other institutions and settings. In these new settings, these cultural models continue to be used actively and creatively, serving as templates for interpretation and interaction, but the models are also potentially changed by those interactions.

6

Engaging with Hierarchy
outside the Home

Education and Efforts at Change

Children bring the lessons they are learning at home into each new context they enter. The experiences that have in these new contexts—their interactions, the sense that they make of them, the strategies they undertake, the feelings that they have—add to the internal working models they are assembling. These new experiences may reinforce what they have learned at home, carving the models deeper. The new experiences may add specificity or new pieces to the models. These new experiences may also contradict, undermine, or provide alternatives to earlier models.

In the previous chapter, I examined how young women in Viligama drew on the lessons about desire and hierarchy that they had learned earlier in their childhood as they worked through interpersonal conflicts involving feelings of envy, anger, desire, betrayal, and frustration. In this current chapter, I examine how these models of relationships emerge in actions in a wider social field, focusing especially on education. In doing this, I demonstrate how understanding the hierarchy model, in particular, helps make sense of actions, interpretations, and feelings in these new contexts.

I am arguing that the cultural models and habits of feeling that are learned in childhood are activated and drawn on in similar situations encountered subsequently. However, I am not arguing that these childhood lessons lead smoothly and inevitably to produce uniform social participation. Rather, as I have discussed in the previous chapters, these models entail various strategies for action and response that people may take up, even as they use the models to interpret, act, and feel that there is a need for change. Further, these models that I have been describing are not the only ones available to people in Viligama. Alternative models and goals may suggest new plans for action. In implementing these new plans, however, the fundamental models learned early in life may pop up in ways that complicate that new plan. As grown people take up these efforts at change, and especially as they shape social institutions that touch children's lives, they may change the contexts in which the next round of young people are being socialized, thereby changing what those children are learning.

In this chapter, I begin by describing some of the ways that the model of hierarchy emerges in relationships outside of the home, focusing on the domain of education as well as healing and employment. I then introduce ways that this model of hierarchy might be changed through individual efforts or at a policy level, focusing on Sri Lanka's recent educational reform policies. These reforms challenge the older ways hierarchical relationships were enacted in schools. This has led teachers to alter their ways of relating to students in order to accommodate the new policy. At the same time, it has led them to alter their implementation of the policy in order to accommodate their own understandings of hierarchy. As teachers do this, they set up new ways for children to experience hierarchy and themselves. In all of these examples, I demonstrate how the cultural model of hierarchy emerges, arguing that understanding this model and how people actively engage with it is essential to understanding the ways relationships and efforts at change unfold. As in earlier chapters, I begin with one of the early field experiences that surprised me, making what I expected to be familiar strange and calling my attention to the importance of the particular shape of Sinhala hierarchy in contexts beyond the family.

Students and Teachers

When I first came to Sri Lanka, the school system did not seem to me remarkably different from what I was familiar with in the United States. Sure, the students wore uniforms—plain white in the village school, with special colors and ties in the private and national schools in town. The schedule was a little different from that in the United States, with the school year starting in January rather than September. And there were several big exams—a scholarship exam in the fifth grade, the Ordinary-level exam in the eleventh, and the Advance-level exam in the thirteenth—that determined what school a student could attend next. However, much of the rest of schooling looked the same. Children began formal education at five or six, progressing through one grade each year. They went each weekday morning and returned each afternoon, with days off for holidays and school breaks. Each school contained classrooms with small desks or work tables for the students, a larger desk for the teacher, and a blackboard at the front. In each classroom was a group of students of the same age and grade level, led by a teacher who had been trained and hired to teach them. Teachers determined what students did and students followed their instructions,

listening to the lessons in class, reading and writing, doing equations and taking tests, bringing in the homework they had been assigned. Teachers evaluated
this work and assigned grades to students.

University education also looked basically the same as it did in the United
States. After finishing secondary school, students who did well on their exams
could be admitted to one of the government-run universities or to one of the
private colleges or vocationally oriented training programs, although spots
in any of these programs were very limited. The system at the university was
based on the British model, with major comprehensive exams at the end of each
school year, rather than the US semester model. But still, university students
chose majors and went to different classes, each of which was taught by a faculty
lecturer. On these coeducational campuses, there were playing fields and librar-
ies and cafeterias (called canteens). Students were expected to study hard, but,
as in the United States, social activities, clubs, political action, and romantic
relationships often became even more important.

Having spent so much time in schools and universities myself, I felt at
home in these surroundings. Traveling to consult with professors at Peradeniya University, visiting the government school in Viligama, chatting with
my son's preschool teachers in Kandy—this all felt comfortable and predictable. However, there were deeper, more subtle differences I missed at first.[1]
These deeper differences had to do with how teachers and students related,
interactions that I came to see were patterned by the expectations about relating to hierarchical figures learned at home—something that appears to be true
both in Sri Lanka and in the United States [2]

This difference in cultural patterns of relating was brought to my attention during an interview with Shanthi, a young woman in Viligama who
was attending university, and whom I introduced in Chapter 4. In my first
interview with her, conducted in English at her request, I was trying to ask
about gender differences in university classrooms. In doing so, I was taking
for granted certain assumptions about how classrooms work. Luckily, Shanthi
corrected me.

BAMBI: If the professor asks a question of the students, do both the girls and the
    boys act the same? What do they do? Do they both raise their—
SHANTHI: Actually, our professors, they don't ask any questions.
B: No?
S: No! They—they feel it is important can't ask any questions.
B: What if you don't understand something?
S: You can't do it.
B: You just listen?
S: Yes.
B: So how is a normal university class? You arrive, you sit down—

s: It's mostly lecturers in our country.

B: How is it though? I have not gone so you have to tell me.

s: Any student don't ask any questions—all are lectures. They just go and read books sometimes, like that.

B: Do you find it easy to learn that way?

s: No because I can't—you can't understand some lecturers, but you can't—you can't ask questions about it.

B: Is there time to ask after the class?

s: Anyone don't.

B: Why?

s: I don't know, because—because from our school time, teachers don't like ask anything from them so we don't ask anything.

B: From the teacher?

s: We afraid, we afraid, so—

B: Mmm.

s: We afraid, so we don't go.

B: Do you think if you went to a teacher's office, a professor's office, and ask a question—would he be angry with you? Would he think you were stupid?

s: They don't like.

B: Why?

s: Angry—because Sri Lankan people, our people don't like ask any questions from them.

B: Mmm. Because it's a trouble? Or because—I don't know—why wouldn't they like that?

s: Because they don't want repeat again, so—

B: They think that you would just make them say the same thing again and it's a trouble for them to do that?

s: They think their teaching is not good if we ask anything.

B: Ah, so it's a criticism! You're saying they didn't do a good job.

s: Yes.

In this interview, I had assumed that I knew about how universities worked. I assumed that there would be interaction between students and instructors during class, including questions asking and hand raising, and I thought this might be one of the places that gender differences in the classroom would emerge. I knew gender norms differed between the United States and Sri Lanka, but I had not really thought about how student-teacher interactions might vary. When Shanthi interrupted me to point out that professors do not ask students to participate, she caught me up short. She made me realize that I was asking the wrong question. This is, of course, one of the main benefits of unstructured interviews. There was something going on here that I had not expected or even known to ask about.

What Shanthi reported was very much in line with the model of hierarchical relationships learned in Viligama's homes that I described in Chapter 4 (see Table 4.3). Shanthi said that the professors did not solicit the opinions or perspectives of students. She said that students should take the information that they are given without asking questions or presenting their own particular needs. The students, she says, are afraid of their teachers, an amplification of the emotional disposition well-socialized adolescents feel toward their parents. The professors, Shanthi believed, would be angry if a student violated these expectations, taking a question as an accusation that they had not already provided all that the student needed, that they were not good teachers. Shanthi explained that students had learned this through their earliest experiences in school—experiences I will describe later in the chapter and that parents expect will foster the respect and fear for superiors that children began learning at home. Further, Shanthi indicated that she saw this way of relating as particularly Sri Lankan.

Shanthi was using the Sinhala model of hierarchy she had internalized through her experiences with it to understand the feelings and behaviors of others and to explain decisions she made about her own behavior. But there are also differences between the model of hierarchy as it worked between parents and children and as it worked between teachers and students. In both cases, the senior person is expected to know what the junior person needs without the junior verbalizing their own thoughts and preferences. However, professors do not know students as well as parents might know their children, so are not as attuned to the subtle signs of the young person's needs, nor would I imagine they have the same level of individual care for their students that parents have for their own children. When Shanthi talks about this dynamic with her professors, she is not just observing but also objecting, if only implicitly. This frustration she seems to feel may account for the fact that this was the only time during our first interview when Shanthi dropped her self-consciousness over her English usage and spoke rapidly and with feeling. The potential for difficulty, misunderstanding, and frustration is something I saw in different kinds of hierarchical relationships, particularly as they were enacted beyond the intimacy of the family, which is something I explore later in this chapter.

The Hierarchy Model in Education

As children enter the education system, they bring with them expectations about relationships that they are developing at home. The hierarchy model they are internalizing emerges in relationships between students and teachers as the model is repeatedly enacted. This is true not only for the students, who are still developing their own working models of relationships, but for the teachers as well, teachers whose own models for relationships are well developed and intricately connected with all sorts of other models about the world and about themselves.

Until recently, teachers in Sri Lanka have taught primarily by telling students facts that the students memorize and are tested on—although this may be changing with the educational reforms I discuss later in this chapter.[3] Even at the university level, printed materials are hard to come by, so students have relied upon direct instruction from their lecturers. Interaction between students or between students and their teachers has not been commonly part of instruction. Teachers have told students what they need to know. Students have neither asked questions nor are they asked questions, except to test what they have learned. Students have not typically been encouraged to build on the ideas introduced in class, to apply what they are learning to their own realm of experience, or to contribute related material that they may have gotten elsewhere to a class discussion. Instead, they have been expected to memorize the information given by the teachers and to perform the written tasks required of them carefully and accurately.

In its general outlines, this is what Paulo Freire (1970) has called "the banking concept of education" seen in schools all over the world, in which a teacher deposits knowledge into the meekly waiting child. Freire argues, as do I, that this style of education orients the student to hierarchy; however, Freire is critical of these relationships. He does not value the hierarchies that are created or the ways of being that students are expected to take on, as parents in Viligama valued these. Further, people in Viligama generally have seen these relationships as beneficent rather than oppressive.

The ways that teachers and students have typically interacted in Sri Lanka echo the ways that parents and children interact, drawing and building on a general cultural model of hierarchy. The kinds of behavior expected of good students exemplify the passivity and compliance required of the "good subordinate" in the hierarchy model. Their teachers perform the "good superior" role by knowing what the students need to know and by providing it. As in family relationships, respect and compliance are exchanged for caretaking. This respect for teachers is shown by distance and deference, behaviors that are more consistently displayed as a person matures and has more fully internalized the hierarchy model.

By the time a student like Shanthi enters the university, something only about 2 percent of students have the opportunity to do,[4] they have not only learned the hierarchy model as it is manifest in their relationship with their parents but they have also learned how it applies to relationships with teachers. It not only patterns behavior but entails certain emotional commitments. It is something that people can use to think with, interpreting each other's behavior and intuiting each other's thoughts and feelings.

When students do not meet the expectations of their role, teachers have recourses similar to those of parents: they can ignore the behavior or they can correct the child. However, unlike parents, teachers are expected to be strict with students. Parents often told me that they expected their children to learn a fuller degree of respect and fear for seniors through their interactions with teachers, and parents encouraged their children to fear their teachers. In the Viligama school when I first visited it, if a student misbehaved and was unresponsive to the subtler marks of disapproval, teachers and administers regularly shamed the children through verbal reprimands or hit the students with a paddle. Corporal punishment was roundly held to be necessary and appropriate in the school setting.

If students felt that their needs were not being met, they might display their hurt and need in indirect ways, as they would at home, hoping that the superiors would recognize their need and meet it. However, such strategies are less useful in this kind of more professional relationship in which the affective ties are more tenuous. Instead, students might opt to use the exit strategy and leave the relationship, supplementing their education with assistance from outside tutors, trying to switch schools, skipping school, or quitting all together.

A third type of cultural strategy for subordinates who feel their needs are not being met emerges more fully in this domain than it did in the family. This strategy involves retaliation. This retaliation, however, is often enacted against a perceived rival, a structural equal who seemed to be getting what the aggrieved student deserved, rather than at the superior directly. One of the most common interpretations that students and their parents gave of perceived slights by teachers was that some other student was unfairly gaining privilege, thus usurping what these students felt should be theirs. By blaming the more privileged peer, not only could a direct conflict with the more powerful person be avoided but the perception of that superior's goodness and legitimacy could also be maintained. Further, as we saw in the conflict between the students in the last chapter, in a system in which there is direct competition for and comparison of limited goods such as marks, admissions, and leadership positions, envy and retaliation against peers is common and commonly feared. Teachers and administrators are talked about as if they *could* provide what a particular student desires, but do not because someone else is taking it instead. This understanding leads to feelings of envy and justifications for retaliation, as seen in the conflict between Lilu and her friends.

Understanding the model of hierarchy that students and teachers bring to their interactions helps make sense of the ways those interactions unfold and the emotional valences they seem to have. But this is not the only context in which it is helpful to understand this cultural model.

Hierarchy in Related Contexts: Health and Work

The working model of hierarchy that children in Viligama learn through their early interactions with caretakers serves as a template that is activated, reinforced, and developed in similar relationships across various domains of social life. A child who learns to wait patiently while a seemingly omniscient and omnipotent parent recognizes and fulfills the child's needs as that parent sees fit, and who finds this relationship at least minimally satisfying, brings these expectations and attitudes to subsequent hierarchically ranked relationships. This is the case not only for contexts they enter while still children, such as schools, but also for ranked relationships in which they participate over their life course—be that in the context of employment, religion, politics, or medicine. Relationships between an expert with resources and someone petitioning for aid, in particular, activate this cultural model of hierarchy with its attendant associations of dependency and care.[5] However, any ranked relationship—which might be based on age, gender, wealth, caste, education, moral reputation, employment, family history, and so on—may draw on features of this model.

Relationships between patients and healers in Sri Lanka are one type in which this model of rank and dependency can be seen. Whether they work within the Western medical tradition, the ayurvedic tradition, indigenous herbal medicine, or more spiritually oriented healing practices, healers in Sri Lanka are in the superior position. Accordingly, healers determine the needs of their patients, with little to no input from the patients themselves. In the clinical encounters I observed across many of these healing contexts in Sri Lanka, only limited information was exchanged. The opinions, observations, and understanding of the subordinate were treated as irrelevant by both the patient and the healer. Medical doctors whom I interviewed, whether trained abroad or in Sri Lanka, described their process of diagnosis emphasizing their own observations, experience, and readings from instruments but did not mention, for instance, taking a detailed history from patients. When people brought their suffering and illnesses to a *devale* (deity temple) instead, the priestesses whom I observed—or rather the divine beings who spoke through these priestesses while they were in possession trances—began by telling the supplicants what their problem was and asking only for the supplicants to say whether it was right or not, calling them child (*putaa*) all the while and putting their hand on the supplicants' head.[6] Similarly, I was told that traditional snakebite healers prescribe remedies based on the time and direction from which the messenger arrives to tell them of the bite, while astrologers diagnose and determine treatment based on time and place of birth.[7] Patients are then expected to follow the provider's advice without question.

When patients I knew in Viligama were unsatisfied with a doctor or a course of treatment that did not seem to be working, they did not return to their doctor to try to work out a more effective treatment. Instead, they switched providers, using a strategy suggested by the model of hierarchy learned at home. The emotional tone that accompanied those exits from the relationship was also consistent with the hierarchy model I observed in other domains: the healers under whose care a patient did not recover were said be cheats, liars, imposters. Conversely, the providers under whose care a patient did recover were said to be good, wise, and powerful. Whether or not healers could correctly identify and provide for their patients' needs was what defined them as legitimate or illegitimate. As the model of hierarchy is used by participants in these clinical interactions, it is reenforced, concretized, and elaborated in ways particular to its enactment in this setting.

Similarly, encounters between employees and employers resonate with this model of hierarchy. In Caitrin Lynch's ethnography of women who work in Sri Lanka's village-based garment factories in the Kandy area, she observes that sometimes workers did not like the harsh ways in which some managers spoke to them, and some even quit over these objections. However, she "never heard of anyone expressing these concerns to management, although they were continually discussed [among the workers] in hushed tones within the factories or quite candidly elsewhere" (2007: 4). Just as in hierarchically ranked relationships in other domains, juniors did not articulate their perspectives and opinions to their superiors. If superiors did not behave as juniors believed they should, those workers could quit, using one of the strategies available to juniors by exiting the relationship. On other occasions, Lynch reported, workers might demonstrate their feelings of mistreatment by slowing down work production. This had the effect of retaliation against managers who scolded too severely, which is another strategy juniors in hierarchical relationships in Sri Lanka often take, while still showing themselves to be properly deferential to their seniors. Workers described their slowdown not as conscious protest, but as an involuntary result of the feeling produced by the scolding itself. Lynch reports:

> I saw many cases of harsh scolding but also many where managers spoke about problems to workers gently, quietly, and, it seemed, kindly. Workers frequently explained to me that the latter approach was more effective than the former. One said, "If they speak nicely and ask for the target amount, then the worker, feeling good about it, will somehow try to give her amount. If they speak in an unpleasant manner, frequently the target lessens even more." One worker explained that because there is a close relationship between the mind and body, when a worker's "feeling are

pounded" it becomes difficult to work. From being insulted the worker becomes physically uncomfortable, ailments increase, and she becomes less productive. "But if the sirs and supervisors speak well and lovingly, no matter how difficult it is to work, it is not a big deal. We can do the job happily." (2007: 214–215)

Sandya Hewamanne also conducted ethnographic research among women who worked in Sri Lanka's garment factories, although the factories that were the setting of her study were in the free trade zone (FTZ) outside of Colombo, the nation's urban center. Hewamanne, too, reported that managers who spoke kindly to workers, positioning themselves as father-figures, were more likely to gain workers' compliance. She observed, "Workers usually found it hard to disobey and disrespect anybody who was older than they and this discomfort was more pronounced regarding older men in authority positions" (2008: 71–72). As in Lynch's research, Hewamanne observed strategies of silent protests against perceived mistreatment, as when the workers began surreptitiously throwing away the cutlery their Japanese managers insisted they use to eat their lunches, until management relented and let them eat with their fingers as they preferred (64). Along with these strategies that are in keeping with the hierarchy model learned in Viligama homes, Hewamanne also reports more explicit, verbal, and sometimes even physical, conflicts between managers and workers. That workers in these FTZ factories may be more likely to speak up to managers could reflect regional differences within Sri Lanka, as people in the Kandy area are reputed to be less harsh and outspoken than those in the south. More likely, this difference reflects new ways of relating developed in this particular context, changes to the unusual ways of relating within hierarchy that are part of socialization within these FTZ factories. Describing an incident in which a factory worker returned a slap to her immediate supervisor who had slapped her, Hewamanne says, "My research notes on Line C were replete with entries like this one which showed that the women were not meek victims of supervisors' aggression but responded to dehumanizing working conditions with action and words. . . . When new workers chose to be silent, others urged them to speak up or they themselves took up the fight with [the managers]" (68). In addition to being altered by its use in new contexts, the model of hierarchy learned at home may butt up against other models of behaving, other goals and agendas, or may be changed intentionally, as I develop below.

Still, the model of hierarchy as legitimated by care has a strong pull, even in the face of antagonistic relations between management and workers. Hewamanne reports, for instance, that one particular manager "actively promoted this image [of being like a father] by his words and his concern for protecting workers. The affection many workers had for him effectively prevented their criticism targeting managers and directors" (2008: 71). Lynch also observed that workers said that "owners really cared about the workers" and that the worker "felt they owed the owners their loyalty because they provided them with jobs." In turn, Lynch says that "workers also tried to leverage these personal connections for specific advantages" (2007: 211). In both Lynch's and Hewamanne's accounts, workers emphasized care and the ability to provide what was needed as legitimating managers' authority and their own voluntary deference. At the same time, both Hewamanne and Lynch document ways that managers and workers drew on this model to advance their own interests.

The cultural model of hierarchy I have been describing does not dictate how people will behave, what sense they will make of things, or how they will feel—nor does any other cultural model. Rather, individuals use these models to interpret their worlds, to figure out how to act, and to predict what other people might do. This particular model, given its foundation in early childhood experience and its activation in so many domains of social life, is something that people in Viligama use a lot. Each time they do, the model is reinforced and communicated anew. Seeing how this model emerges across domains of social life indicates how robust the model is, how deeply it is internalized through early interaction, how it might be adapted to new contexts, and how useful it is in understanding interactions in these new contexts.

Alternative Models

This one cultural model is not, however, the only source of ideas and strategies for engaging in relationships, does not contain all of the values that people care about, nor does it get people to all of the goals they want to pursue. During my fieldwork, some people I met were critical of the dominant cultural model of hierarchy and sought to change aspects of it—mothers who talked of being friends with their children, a doctor who wanted more communication with his patients, educators who wanted students to be more active learners. In trying to make these changes, they drew on other values and models.

This is not necessarily a case of old and new values, old and new ways of interaction, although it sometimes is. There is a strong egalitarian thread in Sri Lanka that weaves through many people's stories and relationships, as well as through history and politics, as Tamara Gunasekera 1994 points out. This value stands apart from the more obvious value placed on hierarchy and status, although it is emphasized in the friendship relationships discussed in the previous chapter, relationships that expect equality and mutuality. Openness and the sharing of secrets were also supposed to be part of these friendships. Talk, verbal expressiveness, and word play were things that people in Viligama enjoyed, and activities that they saw as particularly Sinhala. Initiative and creativity were also valued, especially in economic pursuits, although they were not particularly fostered among the subordinates in hierarchical relationships. Although self-awareness and individual responsibility are not encouraged within the model of hierarchy I have been describing, they are highly valued in the religious teachings and practice of Buddhism (Gombrich and Obeyesekere, 1988). Further, negotiation and compromise have played a role, if sometimes only a temporary or aspirational one, in the political arena. This can be seen, for instance, in various efforts at crafting a resolution to Sri Lanka's civil war, even though each of these negotiations ultimately failed and the war finally ended instead in a brutal defeat. These more egalitarian values, while not supported and sometimes directly contradicted by the experience of hierarchy, are clearly part of the Sinhala cultural repertoire.

People I spoke with in Sri Lanka drew on these and other ideas as they worked to find ways to relate across rank that were different from those prescribed by the usual cultural model of hierarchy. At the same time, it is striking how much the standard cultural model of hierarchy continues to pattern interaction, feeling, and meaning making, even as people consciously critique it. One example surfaced in an interview I conducted (in English) with a middle-aged doctor who had been educated in England. This doctor, who headed a well-established private clinic near Viligama that served a poorer clientele, was critical of the type of doctor-patient interaction typical in Sri Lanka. Even as he described his efforts to make changes to the norms that limit doctor-patient communication, he drew heavily on other aspects of the standard model of hierarchy in his description of his interactions with patients.

DOCTOR: Actually, now for patients, I am like a—for small children I am like a father to them. Ok? So when they grow up they feel they should get advice from me, no? . . . If they come for a problem to discuss here—if I have about twenty, thirty patients in front of me, but I never see them—I see the problem of that patient. That is the important thing.

BAMBI: What is the general procedure then when someone comes here? Do they just wait and come directly in to speak with you? What do you speak with them about? What happens when you—

D: Yeah actually, when the patient comes, I ask—if he's Sinhala—"*Mokakda asanipe?*" [what is the sickness?]. In that way. So they tell. The complaints there are, what they have seen. So, I listen very carefully. And after that only, I do the diagnosing things. Ok? Using stethoscope or any other thing. So I tell them this is the kind of disease that you have. And I explain everything— what they have. In Sri Lanka, you know, some doctors, they think the patient, they don't have any claim to know about this disease. Or the drugs which the doctor is prescribing. Ok? But that is not the real thing. They have enough responsibility to know that, what is the disease that patient is suffering—that person, the particular patient is suffering—what kind of drugs that we are issuing from our counter—that is the thing that they should know. Here some doctors think that that is not a thing that they should know.

This doctor clearly sees himself as appropriately determining what is in the best interests of his patients and providing that to them, positioning himself as a father to them. However, he also believes, unlike many of his peers, that patients' reports of their illness experiences may be helpful in diagnosis. He believes that patients should know about their illness and that doctors should give them more information. It was not clear where these different ideas of his had come from—whether from his experiences in medical school in the UK, his own personal history, or his clinical experience. Whatever their origins, he worked to put these alternative ideas into action with his patients, listening to them carefully and trying to explain their conditions to them. As he blends innovations into the standard Sri Lankan model of hierarchy in his interactions in the clinic, he alters both his and his patients' experiences of this type of relationship.

As people change the ways they behave within hierarchical relationships, they change the experiences through which they and others are building their own working models of relationships, others, and themselves. This can have a particularly powerful effect on children who are just beginning to build their own models and dispositions through interaction with important others. This is especially so when it is a parent who is using a different model.

Kumari was one such parent. She objected to the limited information exchanged between parents and children because of some of her difficulties with her own parents, and so she was working to change the way she interacted with her son. Kumari had left home in late adolescence to marry a boyfriend whom her father had forbidden her to see, a situation I described in Chapter 4. Both Kumari and her father regretted their estrangement and how the conflict had been handled. It is for this reason, Kumari said, that she wanted to build a more open relationship with her own children. Although she generally acted in and talked about her relationship with her eight-year old son in ways similar to other parents, solidly grounded in the usual Sinhala hierarchy model, she also avowed that she wanted to have an honest relationship with her son in which he would not be afraid of her and would speak his mind, hoping that they would be "like friends." This difference in the kind of relationship she wanted led to differences in how she interacted with her son, interactions that appear to have led her son to internalize a different model for interacting with authority figures than that of most other children I knew in Viligama.

Not surprisingly, my interviews with her son were by far the most successful of those I conducted with children in Sri Lanka. In my early play-interviews with children, I had tried to build rapport using the same taken-for-granted techniques that had worked for me in the United States, as I described in Chapter 1: I would ask children about what they liked and did not like, what their favorite things were, and so on. To most children in Viligama, this preference talk was perplexing, especially coming from someone clearly so senior to them. Within the model of hierarchy these children were internalizing, it was incomprehensible that a superior would be asking for their opinions. Further, given the cultural lessons they were learning about the unsuitability of expressing desires described in Chapter 3, they were not practiced at or comfortable discussing their own particular ones. Unlike the American children with whom I had worked, the children I knew in Viligama did not have a well-developed patter about their preferences and were less comfortable sharing their imagination or their observations with an adult. Kumari's son, however, was quite different. A bit shy at first and still unsure about how to participate in the preference talk, once he warmed up he talked about his thoughts and unselfconsciously acted out in the doll house elaborate stories of his daily activities, freely weaving in fantasy elements as he went along. Raised by a mother who intentionally altered her enactments of their hierarchical relationship to foster the kind of self-expression and open communication that might more often be part of a friendship in Viligama, this child was prepared to participate with me in a different way than the children of the other mothers were.

The kinds of improvisational, creative efforts to change the ways that people of different rank relate to each other—efforts such as those undertaken by this mother and this doctor—are just part of the ways that individuals live out and make sense of their lives. Such actions may, over time and in interaction with others, lead to more widespread alterations in the cultural models and feelings that people hold in Viligama. However, there are more systematic efforts to change how juniors and seniors relate that have the potential to create more generalized changes in the kinds of models that people hold and the ways that children are socialized.

Sri Lanka's New Educational Reforms: Intended and Unintended Changes

At the outset of this chapter, I described how students and teachers interacted in ways that were consistent with the model of hierarchy learned at home, embellishing key pieces of the working model that participants internalized. Beginning in the late 1990s, however, Sri Lanka's Ministry of Education began working to implement educational reforms that entail new ways for teachers to interact with children. In what follows, I begin with an overview of education in Sri Lanka and some of the reforms that impact relationships in the classroom. I then describe ways that school teachers in Viligama are taking up these policies, blending the directives of the new reforms with the models of relationships and personhood that they already hold. The ways that these teachers draw on these old and new models of hierarchy in their interactions with students alters the contexts in which children are developing their own cultural models of hierarchy and their own senses of themselves.

Education in Sri Lanka

Education has deep and robust roots in Sri Lanka. It is central to national identity and pride, as evidenced by national history narratives and oft-quoted literacy rates of over 90 percent. School attendance is compulsory between the ages of six and fourteen, and schooling is supported by the government through the university level. However, education is not only a governmental concern. It is prized and admired among the people I knew at all levels of Sri Lankan society and is considered important for both boys and girls.

People in Viligama, along with more middle-class parents I knew in the city, worried about getting their children into good schools and making sure they did well on their exams—exams that determined not only whether they would pass onto the next stage of their education but also which schools they would be able to attend and where. When parents could afford it, they enrolled their children in preschool programs—referred to as "Montessori" schools—and paid for private tutorial classes to supplement regular schooling. Mothers spent many hours escorting young children to and from school and sitting up late at night with them working on projects by oil lamp. Offerings were made at shrines to gods to ensure success on exams, and sorcery against successful students was feared and suspected.

Education was seen as a virtue in itself, as well as a path to a good job and financial security. Beyond this, parents looked to schools to do more than just teach academic skills and provide practical job preparation and credentialing. They counted on schooling in general and teachers in particular to play a crucial role in the socialization of their children and the inculcation of central values and sensitivities regarding hierarchy and moral personhood. When I asked mothers and others how it is that children develop the sense of *lajja-baya* (shame-fear) which is critical to appropriate social behavior, especially toward seniors and especially for girls, they often said that it was at school that they developed this—although, as I have described in earlier chapters, this was something children also learned at home. Parents said that when children started school, they would be impressed, intimidated, and frightened by teachers, whose authority was backed up by the possibility of meting out public humiliation and corporal punishment. When I asked how it is that children learn to treat their parents more formally as they grow up, they often said they learned this at school, as well. For instance, when I asked whether mothers instructed their children to bow to them, I was usually told that that this was something learned at school, although children certainly witnessed and participated in this at home, as well. Indeed, when my own child went to a "Montessori" school in the town, he was taught to bow along with the other three- and four-year-olds, in preparation for the New Year's festivities at the school. When the parents arrived for these festivities, each child—save my own American child, who greeted us with hugs instead—solemnly knelt on the ground in front of his or her parents, deeply bowing to each and touching their feet as they had been coached by the teachers. This was something that obviously moved and delighted the parents. Parents' expectation of the role that schooling would play in the socialization of their children rested on expectations about the kinds of experiences children would have at school, the ways that teachers would be with them, and the ways children would interact with their peers—as well as the kinds of lessons they would be taught and the forms these lessons would take.

Educational Reforms

However, the school system is not a fixed institution. Over the past decade, Sri Lankan education policy makers at the national level have worked to implement substantial changes in the ways that teachers teach and students learn throughout the country's public schools.[8] In 1991, the National Education Commission (NEC) was established. This commission was charged with reforming and restructuring Sri Lanka's education system in order to address what had been identified as critical problems facing Sri Lanka, including problems of unemployment, youth unrest, and poverty (Little 2010). In order to do this, the NEC developed a set of strategies to address two primary goals articulated in Ministry of Education publications:[9]

1. To provide a system of education that would equip students with the necessary knowledge, skills and attitudes, to empower them and make them employable and productive citizens of Sri Lanka.
2. Create a generation of young people with correct values compassion and care towards fellow citizens and who will be able to live with tolerance towards one another. (Moe 2009)

These reforms, supported and informed by wealthier donor countries and international education schemes, aimed to build capacities and orientations in children thought to make them more successful in a global economy and more peaceful citizens in a country that had been torn by violent insurrections and civil war.

The new curriculum was introduced to government schools through massive teacher training programs, beginning with the first grade in 1999, just as

I first arrived in Sri Lanka to begin my research. One of the centerpieces of the curricular reforms was a shift away from what had been the standard teacher-centered approach to more student-centered learning. The first recommendation regarding primary education issued by the Presidential Task Force in the National Education Commission's 1997 report stated, "Education will be child centered, not teacher centered. The emphasis will be on developing the child's mind, skills, attitudes and abilities" (NEC 1997). Sri Lanka's Ministry of Education outlined the criteria for a "child friendly school" as one in which children have rights, where all are included equally, regardless of gender, socioeconomic background or ability, where "corporal and psychological punishment are not practiced and preventative measures and responses to bullying are in place" (MOE 2008: 5), and where "the classroom atmosphere is inclusive, stress-free, democratic and conducive for learning" (7). Students and teachers should "interact easily and feel at ease to share their views and opinions," and students should "participat[e] in classroom-based decision making process" (7). Instruction should take place through "child centered teaching methodologies" (8). A more recent edition of the national policy guidelines explains the purpose of this approach:

> Years 1 to 5 constituting the primary stage of education is a formative period in the life of the child when the foundation is laid for physical, mental, emotional and social development. These beginning years of a child's schooling will be made pleasant and memorable. The freedom for pupils to discover things for themselves, to discuss things among themselves when necessary, freedom to move about and express their thoughts and ideas is conducive to the development of a growing child's individuality, creativity and cooperative ability. The child should also be disciplined to the extent that he can concentrate his attention for a significant period of time on a task in hand. (NEC 2010: 10)

This plan for educating children aims to create a very different kind of school experience for children—and a very different kind of child—from what teachers and parents had expected in the past. What the effects of these different experience will be on the kind of people these children become is yet to be seen, along with how those results will be judged by their elders. However, one of the things that we can see now is how teachers are taking up and implementing these ideas. In order explore this, I will describe the way that children now start school at the first grade under the new reforms, drawing on my observations in Viligama's government school, which serves children in the surrounding area from the first grade through the Ordinary level (eleventh grade), and continuing through the Advanced level (thirteenth grade) in the arts. I then describe some of my own observations and the teachers' perspectives regarding this new approach to schooling, which the school had begun implementing in the primary grades. These teachers were drawing on, shifting, reinscribing, and potentially altering central cultural models in ways that are not straightforwardly predictable from the articulated agenda of the state-sponsored reforms.

Sellam Gedara

Because parents had so often pointed to the transition to school as playing a critical role in the socialization of their children, I went to Viligama in January of 2006 in order to observe exactly what was happening as children entered this new domain. I expected to see an abrupt transition from a home where children experienced a nurturing kind of hierarchy and where their demands were often, if ambivalently, indulged to a school environment with strict and intimidating teachers, where respect was explicitly demanded and rote memorization insisted upon. Instead, I found that, as instructed under the new educational reforms, the school had intentionally crafted a gradual, "child-friendly" introduction to formal schooling for their beginning first graders.

Instead of starting right away with lessons and books and white uniforms, the first few weeks were designated as a *Sellam Gedara*—literally, "The Play House"—for the new students. School had already officially started in the older grades, but these new students began more slowly. During these first few days, they came to their new classroom in their regular clothes, spent a half day playing, rather than having explicit instruction, and then went home after lunch. This continued for over two weeks and was capped off with two mornings of ceremonies. In the first ceremony, the new students were formally welcomed with flowers, performances, and speeches by older students and teachers. In the second, a *pirith* was held in which a Buddhist monk chanted and offered blessings. Only after this would school officially begin for the first grade, complete with uniforms and lessons—although these lessons would still be activity-focused, emphasizing the hands-on group work promoted by the new curriculum.

The purpose of this Sellam Gedara period, according to the teachers, was twofold. One of the goals they mentioned was to give the teachers time to assess the students and their individual levels and needs—and indeed, this is the official goal of this period as stated by the National Education Commission (1997).[10] The other goal—the one that teachers emphasized—was that this warm introduction would make children like school.

Mixing Old and New Models

Although this new introduction to school and the goals it was crafted to pursue were in contrast to earlier educational strategies and my own expectations, when I talked to the teachers about their approach and observed their interactions with students and parents, a more complicated picture of continuities and shifts emerged. I want to highlight three areas in which teachers blended pieces of existing cultural models of relationships and personhood with the directives of the new reforms. This is evident in teachers' conception of their own roles, their techniques for correcting students' behavior, and their promotion of student interaction during instructional activities.

"NOW TEACHERS ARE LIKE MOTHERS." One of the things teachers in the primary grades—all of whom were women—consistently told me was that now teachers were like mothers. The first grade teacher explained: "Nowadays, students are not afraid of the teachers. Now the teachers are like mothers. The teachers treat them as a mother would. They hang on the teacher's saree." She seemed to see these as positive changes. She explained, "The children come to school after studying with their parents, no? So we must give love, care, and affection like their mothers. As they are around five years old, we must attend to them like mothers do. Therefore, we attend to them, call them *duwa* (daughter) and *putaa* (son). Then the students won't feel any difference and will become very close to us." The third-grade teacher explained that this was part of the changes in their teaching methods: "Now it is completely different. In those days, the teacher had a cane in her hand. But I do not. I never use a cane. You may remember that girl called me *Ammi* (mother)?"—something that I had indeed noticed. The third grade teacher explained, "I think the image of 'teacher' may have entered her mind as like a mother."

Previously, I discussed the role that parents expected teachers to play in teaching their children to fear and respect superiors, something that would add to the model children were learning at home. In the early version of the model learned at home, good parents know what is good for their children and provide it—kindly, confidently, and lovingly, but without consulting the child or justifying their actions. Good children wait patiently and uncomplainingly, taking what they are given—returning to the parent deference, obedience, admiration, and love. But when children enter school, parents say that they will learn to be more deferent, and properly *lajja-baya* to seniors in general—including their parents—through their interaction with these imposing, stricter figures.

So it is interesting to me that these teachers are explicitly rejecting their role as distant and authoritative over their students, saying instead that they are like mothers—that they act out of care, empathy, and love as well as a knowledge of what is best for children. In doing this, teachers work to maintain the legitimacy of their seniority by comparing themselves with mothers, even as they give up the kind of strict disciplinarian aspects of their role that had previously been key to their authority. Saying that they are acting "like mothers" shores up their moral seniority and legitimates the shift in their behavior.

Importantly, though, this shift in teachers' behavior and children's experience of school may not serve the same role in children's socialization as it did in the past, given that it alters children's experiences of authority and seniority by removing the associated fear and distance. At a minimum, it makes the transition between the home style of hierarchical authority and the stricter school style of authority more gradual, compared to the abrupt juxtaposition children experienced in the past. There was some indication from the teachers of the upper grades that teachers become less affectionate and more strict as students get older, and my own observations of higher-grade classrooms corroborated this. However, this may change as the reforms are incorporated more fully in the upper grades.

Nevertheless, there is still much to impress and intimidate children in these first few days at school. The pageantry of the opening ceremony alone and the religious blessings that followed it could not help but impress the importance of this new context upon children and clearly distinguish it from the home.

ADVISING RATHER THAN HITTING. Related to this shift in emotional orientation to "loving" the students as mothers were shifts in the strategies teachers used to shape children's behavior. The first-grade teacher said that, when she was a child, the teachers hit students for any kind of wrongdoing, even small children. But no longer. So what do they do with students who behave badly now? "We must advise them," she said. "But even if they don't listen to us, we do not hit them. In those days we hit them with a cane. So now we advise them. If they do any wrongs, we advise them not to do that, and we show them the result of that bad behavior. We always try to bring them to a good level by advising." She said: "If we become harsh with the mischievous ones, they will come to hate school. So we have to speak to them lovingly and touch them tenderly and make suggestions to do work and play."

This strategy of verbally "advising" young children to teach good behavior is in contrast to the general philosophy of the reforms, which hold that children learn more from their active experience than they do by being told about something. Over all, the primary grade teachers enthusiastically endorsed the "guided play" (NEC 1997: 11) that is recommended as the principal learning mode for first and second graders, and other new curricular activities, crediting them for keeping children's attention and interest. Despite their endorsement of a curriculum that explicitly propounds the superiority of activity-oriented, child-centered learning over teacher-dispensed learning, teachers did not seem to extend this teaching strategy to discipline matters, instead emphasizing the effectiveness of "advising." As we have seen in other contexts, people in Viligama often thought that this type of advising (without explaining) by respected, caring others—especially seniors—would make people substantially change their behavior, putting them onto the right track."[11] In emphasizing instruction about how to behave properly rather than having children figure out their own ways, teachers defaulted to familiar aspects of the old model of hierarchy in their interactions with their students, rather than drawing on the recommendation of the new reforms.

These disconnects between the edicts of the state reforms and the talk of the teachers suggest that what is happening is neither a simple replication of an older system of authority nor a full adoption of a new model handed to them by a Westward-looking school system. Rather, it is an emergent one that teachers and others are assembling using pieces of both the existent and reform models.

PEER GROUPS OF EQUALS. Another area in which teachers have made substantial changes in their teaching, while still tailoring their implementation of the reforms in light of their understandings of hierarchy, is in the kinds of relationships they foster between students. The new reforms emphasize the importance of group learning activities as opposed to the old teacher-led instruction and rote learning. The reforms recommend active learning strategies as a way to promote individual learning, as well as group cooperation. As quoted above, the proponents of the reforms at the national level say, "The freedom for pupils to discover things for themselves, to discuss things among themselves when necessary, freedom to move about and express their thoughts and ideas is conducive to the development of a growing child's individuality, creativity and cooperative ability" (NEC 2010: 10). They say that the activities should "enhance the children's abilities to do logical thinking, face challenging situations, respond quickly, accept both defeat and victory, concentrate attention, and to remember details" (NEC 2010: 24). In addition, these "co-curricular activities" in which children work together are designed to "help to develop qualities of leadership, team work, ideas of cooperation, organizational and practical skills, concern for others and a sense of justice and fair play" (NEC 1997: 25).

All of the teachers and administrators I spoke with heartily endorsed this approach. The first- and second-grade teachers especially liked the approach, finding it much more suited to the little children's capabilities than their prior techniques had been. However, when teachers talked about the purpose of the children working in groups on these activities, they put a different spin on it from what was contained in the official documents. What the teachers emphasized in their talk with me was not how these activities fostered each child's individuality and creativity, even as they learned to get along with a diverse set of other creative, individual children. Rather, they talked about how well these activities worked to bring all of the students to the same level, so that—by making them help each other—no student moved past another and no one lagged behind. This concern resonates with an aspect of the model of hierarchy I have seen so robustly elsewhere: everyone at an equal rank—especially those in close contact—must be the same as each other. If not, there will be trouble—perhaps the kind of trouble that erupted between Lilu and her friends in the previous chapter.

Prior to the introduction of the educational reforms, students in a classroom were equalized under the strong authority of the teacher—and although opportunities for competition, rivalries, and jealousies presented themselves, these were defended against, negotiated, and were troubling to the students. Under this new system, students are equalized not by a harsh authority but by the mandate to work together until all produced equal work. As teachers organize these activities for children, they do so in ways that make sense in terms of their existing model of hierarchical and peer relationships. In this we see a new technique introduced by the reforms used to serve an old purpose—though quite possibly to altered effect.

Changing Models/Changing Socialization

In these three areas—teachers' roles, behavior management strategies, and peer relations—we see that the process of implementing these state-driven reforms is not a simple one of adoption or rejection. Teachers revise both the way they use the hierarchy model that underpinned the old teaching approach and the agenda of the new reforms, using their own best judgment to put these reforms into action and educate their students. In doing so, they sometimes draw on the old models in new ways—seeing themselves as mothers, a different but cognate role in the hierarchy model. They adopt one mandate of the reforms—abolishing corporal punishment—but continue to rely on strategies like "advising" that are rooted in a theory of the mind and a model of relations that are at odds with the approach advocated by the reforms. They take up other reform strategies with enthusiasm—the group activities—but use them to pursue a goal the makes sense within their existing ideas about social relations.

As teachers draw on the various ideas, strategies, and goals that are available to them—drawing some from robust cultural models, some from new educational policy, others from more idiosyncratic experiences of their own—they help create the context in which children develop. Along with the actions of parents and others, those of teachers shape the setting for the experiences that children have, experiences through which those children derive and amend their own cultural models, their own sense of social relations and how to participate in them, and their own sense of themselves and their capacities.

It is hard to know what the effects of these innovations will be. The ways that teachers combine the new reforms with the older model of hierarchy may have the effect of preserving that older model with little effect from the new ideas about students' self-expression. On the other hand, the new ways that teachers are drawing on this older model of hierarchy may change it. The conversion of the teacher role to one more like the mother role, alone, may alter the cultural model of hierarchy that children in Viligama are expected to develop. By preventing children from confronting the more distant and exacting authority of the teacher, children may not have the opportunity to learn about important aspects of hierarchy.

As I observed the first graders entering the classroom during the first few days of school, the mothers, fathers, and grandmothers who had brought them lingered in the room, hovered anxiously around the doorway, peered in through the wire mesh across the large windows. Throughout the morning, the mother of a little boy who was crying silently but inconsolably kept scooting back into the classroom to be near him. The teachers told me later that they thought the mother should have just left, but they knew how difficult it was for her. It was difficult for mothers to hear their children cry and not give in. The teachers, working under this new sense of themselves as also like mothers, did not stop the mother of the crying boy from continually entering the classroom to tend to her son, as teachers in the past might have.

I have argued in Chapter 3 that parents' indulgence plays a key role in prompting children to disavow their own desires and learn not to ask. But for those children who do not learn those early lessons fully, schooling was expected to reinforce it in other ways. For children who did not come to disavow their desires through their experiences at home, the stricter figure of the teacher would teach self-control in other ways. Important social lessons have redundant mechanisms and opportunities to ensure that they are learned. But if teachers now are like mothers, some of these opportunities and the lessons that are being offered may be shifting. While the national education reforms explicitly aim to change the ways that children are being shaped, the implementation of those reforms within this complex field of cultural models and choice making may lead to changes the reformers did not anticipate.

Changing Contexts

In this chapter, I have been arguing that children bring the lessons they have learned at home into new contexts and new relationships that they enter. This is particularly true for lessons that are evoked as broadly as is the model of hierarchy. It is also particularly true for lessons that are as deeply felt and as central to who a person is as are the lessons about desire and attachment, lessons rooted in the earliest interactions that children have. Understanding what these early lessons are helps make sense of cultural patterns in subsequent interactions, as I have demonstrated in this discussion of the ways that juniors and seniors interact in everyday encounters at work, in clinics, and in classrooms.

To say that the model of hierarchy is evoked in these contexts and that it patterns interaction in them is not, however, to say that events play out in singular, consistent ways. People use this model to make sense of their relationships, to know how they are supposed to act and what they can expect from others. They use it to interpret other people's actions and guess at their feelings and intentions. They use it to interpret their own feelings and figure out what to do if things are not going as they would like. Working within this model can lead to the kind of smooth and peaceful interactions that people in Viligama value. However, sometimes working within the expectations for hierarchical interactions leaves people unsatisfied, misunderstood, their own needs thwarted. When it does, the model itself suggests options to try to do something about this state of affairs.

Change can come from working within this model of hierarchy. But change can come from other avenues as well. Certainly the model of hierarchy I have been describing is not the only source of ideas, values, or plans for action. People I knew in Viligama were sometimes critical of the ways that people interacted across rank—and sometimes this critique led to new ways of acting. This happened on the individual level, as with the doctor who wanted a more open exchange of information with his patients and the mother who wanted more open communication with her son. This also happens in more systematic ways, as with the new educational reforms.

Interacting differently within hierarchies, however, does not change the full model of hierarchy—nor does it necessarily change the model in predictable ways. As people work to enact alternative values, they continue to draw on other, more taken-for-granted pieces of the hierarchy model, more deeply engrained ways of being and feeling. Existing models continue to emerge and to shape interaction in ways that may be in contrast with more explicit plans for change. New actions may have broader effects on the old models than people anticipated or even wanted. Actions that people undertake, in turn, shape the experiences that those around them are having and, thereby, shape the ideas and feelings these other people hold. When these other people are young and these experiences are frequent or emotionally salient, they have a greater chance of shaping the models of the world and of themselves that those children are developing. This might lead to individual variation. Or it might lead to more widespread culture changes.

In the final chapter, I will continue this discussion of how culture is transmitted, endures, and changes through people's everyday interactions.

7

Culturing People

I began this book with two contrasting ways that children and caretakers interacted in Viligama. In one, a little girl screamed for what she wanted and those
around her gave in to her demands, no matter how unreasonable. In the other,
she sat on her mother's lap, quietly and contentedly accepting the bits of food
her mother placed in her mouth. Although these are quite different ways of
interacting—especially in their emotional tone—the lessons that children learn
through them are not incompatible. In the first, the little girl learns that her
own desires are not to be trusted, that asserting them is likely to ruin the very
things she cares most about, especially her relationships with those around her.
In the second, she learns that it is much more pleasant to accept what she is
given by her caretakers, rather than try to direct their behavior and control her
world herself. She learns that if she waits passively, she will not only receive
things that are suitable for her but that she will also be approved of by those she
cares about most.

Important lessons like these build on children's innate needs and developing capacities, as well as whatever inborn temperamental dispositions they
have. However, these lessons also shape those needs, capacities, development,
and temperament in fundamental ways. Human infants are born prematurely,
relative to other animals. This means that much of our earliest development
takes place in a social world. Because the particular social worlds in which
infants develop vary, that development is necessarily shaped in varied ways.

Human development requires the incorporation of social learning, of
culture. At the same time, cultural transmission takes advantage of particular features of human development. The need to be cared for and the capacity to become emotionally attached to caretakers are two of those features
of human development that culture takes advantage of to hook people into

particular relationships and to shape the ways that they participate in those relationships—not only as children but later in life as well. Each culture group plays on the human attachment system to shape the ways that its children feel about others and themselves, and to shape the ways those children behave in relationships with others—including, eventually, their own children. As I have argued in Chapter 4, this is evident in the culturally patterned ways that caretakers and children interact in Sri Lanka, the United States and elsewhere, leading to cultural patterning in other sorts of interactions as well.

Another place where cultural patterning plays on children's developing capacities involves what has been identified as "*the five to seven year shift*" (Sameroff and Haith 1996). This apparently universal shift in children's cognitive capacities around this age corresponds with shifting expectations and roles for children in this age bracket, although, as Thomas Weisner (1996) and Barbara Rogoff (1996) have argued, those expectations and roles vary across cultures. This is the age when children in many places, including Sri Lanka, begin formal schooling. It is also the age at which people in Viligama expect that children's "understanding" will begin to develop, as I discussed in Chapters 3 and 4. Not until around ten did people expect this social understanding would be fully developed. Rogoff and her colleagues (1980) have suggested that the period between ages eight and ten may actually be the more important shift in development, with the period between ages five and seven being the time during which social practices prepare children for this shift. As Rogoff (1996) concludes, there are important and comparable shifts in development at many ages; she argues that these shifts are not shifts *in* the child, but in the ways that child is treated within a particular community—and it is these changing ways by which children participate in their communities that shape any particular child's development. Weisner (1996) talks about such developmental transitions as offering solutions as well as posing problems for particular communities to accomplish the tasks they have before them—tasks such as the universally important one of caring for young of different ages. Taking an ecocultural approach, Weisner examines how children's increasing abilities to decenter and self-regulate around the age of five might have been selected for in our evolution as a species, since it would have offered an advantage in assisting in care for younger members. He then considers how various societies might use and shape these emerging capacities in different ways. Weisner, along with some other developmental psychologists and psychological anthropologists, argues that how communities involve children in daily activities not only responds to the child's development, it shapes it. Thus, the shape of children's development varies from community to community, as do their daily activities, but these activities may capitalize on an underlying species-wide shift in children's capacities around this age.

Perhaps the most fundamental human capacity that is mobilized in enculturation—and one that Sarah Hrdy argues is also a product of natural selection—is our capacity for empathy. Hrdy places the development of inter-subjectivity between infants and their mothers at the heart of what it is to be human and how we became so. In these interactions between children and their caretakers, children develop "the capacity and eagerness to share in the emotional states and experiences of other individuals" (2009: 2). This capacity opens infants up to being shaped by those around them in profound ways. The emotions of others can clue them in to what to pay attention to and how to interpret it. I have specifically argued that this is key to how children in Viligama come to mistrust their own desires, and later to mistrust the desires of others. I have also argued that it is part of how they learn to feel shame, as their experience of their parents' shame sensitizes them to social norms and disapproval. But this ability to sense what others are feeling and the tendency to feel it, too, is crucial to how and why children take up the cultural lessons offered by their interactions with important others.

A caretaker's own capacity for empathy is also key to producing the circumstances in which children are socialized. In Viligama, parents use their ability to read the subtle cues from their infants to identify accurately what it is their children need, and they are moved to want to provide it as they feel their children's distress as their own. In addition, this capacity for empathy lays the groundwork for adults' more subtle, psychodynamically complex motivations to act in ways that socialize their children in a culturally patterned manner. This is what I have argued may be the case with Rashika's mother's vicarious enjoyment of her daughter's assertion of will and desire in ways that she herself gave up long ago.

Mothers and others are motivated to produce socializing experiences for their children by the explicit ethnotheories about parenting that they hold (Harkness and Super 1996), ethnotheories that are situated in particular socio-economic conditions but are not determined by them (Gottlieb 2004, Lareau 2003, Scheper-Hughes 1992, Seymour 1999). Parents' ideas are only one source of their actions, which take place moment to moment, creating the circumstances in which children are socialized. Caretakers act out of their own complex set of models of the world, models that they developed as children and that have been variously elaborated, altered, or reinforced over their lifetime. Adults who were socialized to disavow their own desire are alarmed by their children's flagrant demonstrations of desire, desires that they have also learned through more explicit cultural doctrines are morally suspect and socially damaging. Parents whose own model of hierarchical relationships says that superiors know what is best for their juniors and should provide it do not think to ask their children which vegetables they want for dinner or how they want their hair cut or whether they would like to have a big girl ceremony. They simply provide these things as they see best, almost inadvertently communicating this model to their children.

However, as I have also shown, parents sometimes fall short of caring for their children in ways that they think they should, ways that their children think they should, or ways that cultural norms would dictate. Parents in Viligama, as elsewhere, are faced with competing pulls on their time and resources, resources that are often insufficient to provide everything that they would like for their children. They must prioritize their efforts, working to meet some needs over others, choices that in turn shape children's experience. This was evident, for instance, in Susanthika's mother's choice to provide for her children by leaving them when they were young to work abroad, discussed in Chapter 5. It was evident, too, in her more recent efforts to find Susanthika a husband, rather than allowing her to concentrate on preparing for her exams, as the girl had hoped. Parents may also fall short in other ways as they work to balance the goal of providing for their children with other kinds of goals—as when Susanthika's mother worked to impress her relatives and to arrange for her return to the life she valued abroad, rather than taking up an active role in the household with her children. Still other caretakers may change some of the ways they interact with their children intentionally, consciously working to change aspects of how children participated in hierarchical relationships—something we saw in the previous chapter with Kumari's efforts to create more open communication with her son or the teachers' efforts to change how they disciplined children.

Central cultural lessons are not taught just once or in just one way, however—nor are they up to one parent alone to teach. If they were, given the contingencies of the world as it is lived out, they would not be likely to continue to be important cultural lessons. The ideas about desire and hierarchy I have been describing are part of central cultural models. If children somehow miss these lessons—or if their caretakers fail to provide them—there are ample other opportunities to learn them. If Rashika's older brother, Sampath, had somehow missed the lessons about the dangers of his own desires when he was a toddler, he would have many further opportunities to learn that desires are dangerous and destructive when he is made to indulge his little sister, sitting by helplessly as her uncontrolled desires break his toys, eat up his dessert, or divert the attention of his mother and father. If his parents did not insist he indulge younger children, other people would insist that he did—as I witnessed a visiting aunt do when Sampath started to object to his younger cousins' destruction of an art project he had been very proud of.[1] If he still misses these lessons, he will have new opportunities and new ways to learn them at school, as he negotiates relationships with his teachers and his peers. The lessons about desire and about hierarchy that he is learning though these experiences are reinforced each time they are evoked, not only in childhood but also in adulthood, as he is introduced to related theories about envy, desire, and how relationships work. As children grow and throughout the life course, important lessons they learned earlier are reinforced and supplemented, often from new perspectives.

Culture is durable, but it is also dynamic. Options for changing social arrangements are built into cultural models—such as the one for hierarchy I have been describing—and the models themselves may be changed. Indeed, the same properties of cultural models that lend them durability also allow for them to be changed. This is what Claudia Strauss and Naomi Quinn (1997) argue in *A Cognitive Theory of Cultural Meaning.* In it, they say that the nature of cognitive schemas, as connections developed in the mind through experience and use, lead to what they call the "centripetal" tendencies of culture to be motivating and durable in a person, as well as across a group, over generations, and in different areas of social life. These same features of cognitive schemas also lead to what they call the "centrifugal" tendencies of culture, so that it sometimes does not motivate people; can change over time, within a person, or across generations; can be unevenly shared across a group; or may apply only in limited circumstances. Early, repeated, emotionally charged, and shared experiences lead to widely held and well ingrained cultural models. Each time a schema is used to make sense of a situation, its validity is reinforced. However, changes to patterns of experience for a person or a group can lead to changes in those schemas, as can conscious reflection.

Similarly, the view I am advocating for how culture is transmitted to children—in Viligama and elsewhere—contains the possibility for both continuity and change. Culture is transmitted to children through emotionally charged everyday interactions with others. During these everyday experiences, children are developing understandings about how the world works, how they can participate in it, and what they can expect from those around them. They are also are developing their own sense of themselves, the feelings, wishes, conflicts, and anxieties they will have to manage, and their own—usually unconscious—strategies for doing so. Caretakers generate the physical and emotional circumstances in which children are developing these and suggest ways for children to interpret their experiences. Caretakers do this through their conscious decisions and planning, their habitual ways of behaving in general and toward children in particular, their moment-to-moment responses to the contingencies of everyday life, and their own emotional states and psychodynamic processes. As a result, culture is not just transmitted but also created and recreated in these encounters, producing intergenerational and social patterns as well as variability and the potential for change.

This way of understanding the process of cultural transmission through emotionally charged everyday interactions continues the work of anthropologists conducting culture and personality studies in the first half of the twentieth century, while it also draws on the work of more contemporary anthropologists and other lines of theory and research. Early anthropologists like Margaret Mead, Ruth Benedict, and Edward Sapir asked how personality is culturally patterned. Beginning with their work and continuing in the work of Beatrice and John Whiting (1975), Robert LeVine (1966), Jean Briggs (1970), and others, anthropologists have asked how people are shaped in cultural ways and have looked to child rearing to see that process in action. This approach differs dramatically from that of most developmental psychologists in that it does not assume that the ways that children develop in contemporary Euro-American societies is the only or best way for children to develop.[2] Instead, anthropological approaches look for how children are raised in societies around the world in order to understand more about the range of human potential as well as the processes through which that potential is shaped in particular ways. The view of cultural transmission that I am advocating takes a similar approach, examining how it is that child rearing is actually done in a particular community in order to see how it is that people develop in culturally patterned ways.

There are, however, new pieces, corrections, and clarifications that I am advocating be added to our methods and our theories about enculturation and the cultural patterning of individuals, along with new ways of combining the approaches of particular researchers. Like Mead (1975 [1930]), we must look to the actual ways that people interact with children and the messages these interactions convey, allowing for individual differences in how these practices are carried out. Like Benedict (1934, 1946), we can look for links between patterns in childrearing, adult social practices, and larger institutions, although we must be mindful to base these connections on careful ethnography, to recognize diversity, contradiction, and change, and to recognize that culture is not simply personality writ large. Like Sapir (2002), as well as Irving Hallowell (2010 [1937]) and Anthony Wallace (1970 [1961]), we must attend to individual variation and internal diversity as well as cultural patterns. In addition, we must attend to unconscious, psychodynamic patterns that child rearing practices set up and how those reverberate through adult life (Carstairs 1958, Chodorow 1978, Du Bois 1960 [1944], Erikson 1950, Freud 1981[1930], Levy 1973, Obeyesekere 1981 and 1990, Spiro 1997), without expecting that psychoanalytic theory as it has developed in the West has captured the full range of psychodynamic possibilities, without reducing the rich cultural worlds people produce to mere neurotic projections, and without focusing too exclusively on any particular kind of experience.

The comparative approach implicit in some anthropological studies and explicit in others is indispensible if we are to understand cultural variation. We must be careful, however, not to remove particular actions from the cultural context in which those actions become meaningful. Researchers who have undertaken to quantify and compare child rearing experiences have found disappointing results in terms of answering the questions they started with, especially in relation to rich ethnographic accounts (e.g. Whiting and Whiting 1975, Straus 1957). Further, by determining ahead of time which actions to pay attention to, the researcher has predetermined which actions will be meaningful, often even assuming what they will mean in any particular context. This is one reason this line of research has fallen out of favor.

Individual child care behaviors may look similar across different cultural contexts; however, it is only within those contexts that they take on and convey their particular meanings. Actions are only meaningful within the web of other actions, meanings, and feelings in which they occur. Children in the United States, for instance, are sometimes required to eat what they are served, which is something I have said is true for children in Viligama. However, the experiences of those encounters are likely to be quite different for children in the United States than they are for children in Viligama. Children in the United States may be required to eat their lima beans, but they are usually expected to eat them by themselves, from their own plate, perhaps sitting at a dinner table shared by their parents and siblings, perhaps grumbling while they do.[3] Being expected to eat what one is served in this US context conveys very different lessons about hierarchy, autonomy, authority, and care than it does in Viligama, where children are fed directly from their mother's hand, from the same plate as their brothers and sisters, after senior people have been fed, and before their mother eats. Further, these actions take on particular shades of meaning in the context of any particular family, on any particular day. In order to understand the import of a behavior, we must look at it in context.

When I describe how children in Viligama learn to stop screaming for things even though their parents regularly give in to their demands, friends in the United States often remark that maybe they should try this strategy to get their own kids to stop asking for things. But I strongly suspect this would not work. The entire context that supports the interpretation that desire is dangerous, the repetition of and resonance with other experiences of receiving, and the emotional tone that accompanies these experiences of indulgence in Viligama and makes this lesson stick would all be missing. Further, this is not a way of being that most of the people who make such comments actually value. These US parents want their children to express themselves and cultivate their preferences, to learn to speak up for themselves and go after the things they want—they just don't want to have to engage in the time-consuming and exhausting techniques that American parents use to develop these characteristics in their children.

No particular parenting technique can be removed from one cultural setting and plopped into another, while still retaining all of its previous meanings. At the same time, what looks like the same parenting goal or particular lesson learned may not have the same implications in one setting that it does in another. Certain aspects of hierarchy in Viligama may look similar to hierarchy in Japan or in England, but the way those aspects connect to other cultural features makes all the difference.

How children are raised primes them to participate in a social world that their caretakers imagine. But childhood is not only preparation for the social world to come. Childhood is part of the social world. In my view, it is a mistake to think of what we learn as children as "precultural" preparation for the cultural beliefs we learn later (Spiro 1997). Although, as I have argued, the lessons we learn as children may prepare us to find certain subsequently encountered ideologies right and true and to engage in subsequent relationships in particular kinds of ways, we are learning cultural lessons throughout our lives. Further, the ways that adults deliver those lessons through everyday caregiving is necessarily shaped by their own cultural beliefs, values, and participation in institutions. To me, this is one of the most important differences between the way I conceptualize childhood and the way it was conceived of by early anthropologists like Abram Kardiner and Ralph Linton (1939) and later by John Whiting and Irvin Child (1953). In these earlier models, the "primary institutions," including the economy as well as the family and child-rearing practices, were seen as separable from and productive of "secondary institutions" or "projective systems," like art and religion. As the ethnography from Viligama demonstrates, these are all woven together; dividing them into spheres to consider separately keeps one from seeing the ways in which values and beliefs infuse and fundamentally shape what parents do with their children, how family members feel about each other, and how economic relations are carried out. Although LeVine (1980) has made the point that parents have different levels of priorities in their parenting goals, I would argue that the ways that parents work to ensure their children's basic survival and prepare them to participate economically are as shaped by and convey as many cultural values as their more intentional efforts to teach children such values. Culture is not an add-on to child care. Culture shapes the basics ways that child care is done, and it is conveyed through them.

Although it is essential that we look at child rearing, development, and the transmission of particular cultural lessons in the context in which they take place, we must be mindful that social groups are not bounded or internally consistent. People move in and out of Viligama, in and out of Sri Lanka. Ideas and practices also move across geographical boundaries, introducing and also acquiring new meanings and uses as they do. Even those ideas and practices that have long been part of the worlds of people who live in one particular place do not necessarily fit smoothly together. Cultures are certainly not coherent and sensible wholes, although the people that share them often experience them as such—or at least have found ways of dealing with the conflicts and inconsistencies.

One of these reasons for this perception of coherence—both for the participant in a life world and for the observer—is that major cultural models a person holds often share pieces with other models, overlapping and interconnecting. Accordingly, these interconnected models are mutually implicated and reinforced in use. This is the case, for instance, with the cultural model of hierarchy I have described. This cultural model overlaps with many other models, such as that for envy. The model of envy draws on the model of desire people have learned as children. That model of desire connects with ideas about receiving, ideas which in turn are used in understanding hierarchy. In addition, these models are acted out, adapted, and reinforced in important relationships and countless daily interactions, giving those interactions a similarity while reinforcing the sensibleness and compatibility of the models.

At the same time, there are conflicts, alternatives, disconnects, and discontents produced by these models, as I have also demonstrated. Further, individuals do not all have identical experiences, and so do not hold identical sets of cultural models, and do not have identical ways of being or acting in the world. This is true within a single family and even truer across a society segmented by class, rural/urban divides, gender, ethnicity, religious worldview, education, and so on. The cultural learning and the ways that learning is put to use in Viligama that I have described represent only a tiny portion of what people learn and what they use to make a life, although I do think these are some of the most important pieces. These models and their applications are likely to differ across groups in Sri Lanka, let alone the region and its diaspora. However, many of the basic ideas about hierarchy and desire do resonate with similar models that people connected with this region hold.

At the opening of this chapter, I said that the lessons a child learned from experiences of getting what she wanted when she screamed for it and of passively receiving what she needed without saying anything were not incompatible. The reason they are not incompatible is not by design or because cultures function as seamless wholes. It is because this little girl is actively making sense of both sets of experiences—as she does with everything else she learns—using them both as she builds her internal understandings and expectations of the world around her, of how to interact with others, and of herself. This is not to say that we cannot contain contradictions—we all do, and usually without even noticing or being bothered by this. But these styles of interaction involve many of the same schemas—schemas for mother, for desire, for receiving, for being a good person. Each of these experiences builds upon earlier ones, creating complex and well-entrenched working models. Because these experiences are so frequent and so common, those around her also have an impetus to derive similar lessons and fit them together in similar ways. Her mother, too, participates in these encounters actively and improvisationally, drawing on her own understandings of the world that she has assembled in similar early experiences. As this mother participates with her daughter, she has renewed chances to refine, intensify, build on, or change these models of her own and how the pieces fit together.

It is not only ideas and cognitive models that people are actively learning and using and modifying through their culturally patterned experience. They are also developing, using, and modifying a whole range of emotional associations and psychodynamic practices. They are learning, as we have seen, to disavow desires, to experience themselves as separate from others in particular kinds of ways, and to project their own envy onto someone else. If we want to understand why people behave as they do, we need to pay attention to and theorize these kinds of largely unconscious psychodynamic processes. This is especially vital if we are to understand how people in general and children in particular are shaped by their social experience—and how they are shaped in culturally concordant ways.

In order to understand this process, we must look closely at what is happening in those social interactions, attentive to the emotional register as well as the ideas and actions. Briggs's 1998 examination of the daily "dramas" through which Inuit children derive cultural lessons and establish culturally patterned emotional worlds stands as a model for this kind of examination. This and other close examinations of the emotionally rich exchanges children have in ordinary interactions (e.g., Barlow 2010, Pelka 2010, Rae-Espinoza 2010, Sirota 2010, Trawick 1992) demonstrate how parents' natural-feeling behavior conveys deep and deeply felt cultural lessons to children. In making sense of these daily dramas, children are actively—sometimes painfully—engaged, although not necessarily consciously. While generally less concerned with the psychodynamic lessons children are learning, those who study the ways that children are socialized into particular language communities (e.g., Fung 1999, Heath 1986, Miller 1986, Schieffelin and Ochs 1986) and practical knowledge (e.g., Rogoff and Lave 1984) also offer evidence for the usefulness of looking closely at everyday interaction. These and similar studies of everyday childrearing as it actually happens demonstrate the simultaneous importance and interplay of structure and agency, of cultural patterning and variation. This approach is part of a more general move within anthropology to examine the everyday (Bowen and Early 1993, Mines and Lamb 2002), as well as to recognize the importance of practice (Bourdieu 1977, also see Lester 2005) and of experience (Csordas 1994, Luhrmann 1989 and 2012). It is in daily life as it plays out moment to moment that people actively make sense of their world and communicate that to each other.

One of the most important aspects of the view of enculturation I am advocating has to do with the role of the children themselves. Children are active
in their own development of culture and in their use of it. Especially in recent
years, anthropologists have recognized that children are active cultural players
in their own right and their perspectives are worth attending to (e.g., Bluebond-
Langner 1978, Clark 2003, Huberman 2013, Lanclos 2003, Lancy 2008, Montgomery 2009). The circumstances of the experiences children have are shaped by the
adults around them, but children are active participants in these experiences.
How they interact shapes their own experiences as well as the experiences of
others. But it is not just children's actions that shape the lessons they take from
their interactions. It is the ways that they interpret these interactions, how
they feel about them, and how they connect these ideas and feelings to other
ideas and feelings they are developing. This active sense-making and emotional
strategizing—all of which occurs largely outside of conscious awareness—shapes
the internal worlds of children, the cultural models they hold, and the ways they
approach subsequent interactions. Further, it is not helpful to think of these
children in isolation. The enculturation process and culturally shaped development happens in interaction with other people. So it is the interaction that we
must examine, rather than just the child. As we do so, we must attend to the
emotions circulating during these interactions, which are as important in what
is conveyed and how it is taken up as any explicit proposition or procedure.
These emotional registers of interactions convey essential information, as they
attach cultural models to notions of a child's own basic goodness or badness
(Quinn 2005b) and arouse anxieties and other emotions, suggesting particularly culturally patterned habits of managing them.

There is no such thing as failed socialization or an unsocialized child. All of
us are necessarily shaped by our experiences with others throughout our lifetime. These experiences and what we make of them shape our perception and
understanding of the world, our emotional life, and our behavior. These experiences may be in greater or lesser accord with those of others in our social group.
The ways we take them up may be more or less in sync with cultural expectations or social demands. Disconnects may emerge because our experiences have
been anomalous or because the social context has changed. Caretakers generally
work to prepare children for the world they expect them to enter; however, that
world may have changed by the time those children have grown up. Whether
or not we are shaped in ways that seem suitable to the current circumstances
in which we find ourselves, we are shaped nonetheless. We have all been and
continue to be shaped by our experiences, especially those experiences with
emotionally important others, especially—but not only—when we were young.

In this book, I have presented some of the interactions I observed in Sinhala families in one village in Sri Lanka, the patterns that emerged in those

interactions, and how people used them as models for future interactions. I have shown how those models also entail ways to manage conflict and advocate for change. I have also shown how the models themselves might be changed, as people choose new courses of action, changing their own experiences and those of the people around them. The effects of such experiences may be especially powerful for children, altering the foundational models those children take up. I offer these observations and this interpretation as a model for thinking about what culture is, how it is transmitted, how it might change, and why its role in child development is vital to take seriously.

NOTES

CHAPTER 1 INTRODUCTION

1. "Viligama" is a pseudonym, as are the names I use for the people that live there. However, I have left the names of those who provided professional assistance and mentor-
   ship unchanged: Inoka Baththanage, Indika Ratnayake, Kalinga Tudor Silva, and Loku
   Menike.
2. The national census for 2001, conducted during my first field stay in Sri Lanka, reported
   a population of 110,049 for the Kandy municipal area (DCS-SL 2001d) and 1,279,028 for
   the city of Kandy District (DCS-SL 2001a). Within the Kandy district, 74.1 percent of
   people identified their ethnicity as Sinhala (DCS-SL 2001b) and 73.3 percent identified
   as Buddhist (DCS-SL 2001c). The estimated population for the nation as a whole for
   the same year was 18,797,257 (DCS-SL 2001a).
3. The information about the household construction, amenities, employment, and
   education came from a survey conducted just before my arrival in the village by the
   Grama Niladhari, the local government administrator, who generously shared his
   findings with me.
4. See Quinn 2005a on "finding culture in talk."
5. I borrow the distinction between "informant" and "respondent" from Levy and Hollan
   1998: 335.
6. See Levy 1973, Levy and Hollan 1998, Levy and Wellenkamp 1989, Parish 1996.
7. Although these interviews were unstructured, I used a variety of tools to raise new topics and to generate comparable material across participants, including Robert Levy's
   "Check Sheet of Topics from Psychodynamic Interviews" (1973: 509–511) and several
   standardized psychological assessment tools and projective tests that I adapted for
   my purposes. Although these tests did not produce quantitatively useful results, they
   prompted fruitful discussions.
8. My own Sinhala skills, while adequate by then for ordinary interactions, were not suf-
   ficiently sophisticated that I could do the kind of intensive, psychologically attuned
   interviewing I had in mind. Since I interviewed most participants in Sinhala, I initially
   recruited my Sinhala teacher, Indika, and then later Inoka, to assist me; they would
   translate as needed, sometimes intervening to frame a question more strategically or
   to alert me to a nuance I was missing.
9. Part of what made those later visits particularly productive for me was the absence
   of my own son, whose frequent presence during earlier fieldwork complicated what I
   was observing. Although having my son with me in the field certainly helped place me
   into a recognized social role, it made doing fieldwork more complex. The differences
   in my ways of parenting, while generative of useful conversation with my Sri Lankan
   neighbors, could also be taken as critique. Further, I sometimes found myself torn

between attending to what was going on around me and attending to my son, a situation in which many mothers find themselves.

10. For an overview of these resources in the psychoanalytic and object relations traditions, see the works by Anthony Elliot (2002) and Lavina Gomez (1997), respectively.

11. For a discussion of cross-culture challenges to attachment theory, see Quinn and Mageo 2013.

12. That these processes remain vague for social theorists is a point Kulick and Schieffelin (2004) make as they argue for the value of language socialization studies in demonstrating how certain kinds of subject positions, performativities, and habituses are developed.

13. See, for instance, Mead's *Growing Up in New Guinea* (1975 [1930]) and *Sex and Temperament* (1963 [1935]), Benedict's *Chrysanthemum and the Sword* (1946), and Sapir's collected lectures in *The Psychology of Culture* (2002).

14. For incisive commentary on the history and disparagement of culture and personality studies, see Robert LeVine 2001, 2010.

15. Bateson and Mead's 1952 film *Bathing in Three Cultures* (2005) provides an excellent example of attention to everyday, ordinary interactions as well as some of the limits of that early work. For further discussion of ordinary interactions as sites of socialization and connections to contemporary strands of anthropology, see Barlow and Chapin 2010a.

CHAPTER 2   SRI LANKA: SETTING THE ETHNOGRAPHIC CONTEXT

1. Since the mid-1980s, there has been a proliferation of writing about the violence that has dominated Sri Lankan national and local politics since Independence. Policy makers, scholars, clinicians, and journalists have described the civil violence of the last forty years, seeking its roots in history and looking for ways to end it (see Committee for Rational Development 1984, de Silva 1986, Jeganathan 1998, Kakar 1996, McGowan 1992, Peiris 2009). Anthropologists have made significant and diverse contributions to the understanding of the cultural factors that have led to the violence in Sri Lanka over the past decades (e.g., Daniel 1996, Kapferer 1988, McGilvray 2008, Spencer 1990, Tambiah 1986 and 1992, Thiranagama 2011, Winslow and Woost 2004), as they have to the consideration of the social registers of violence more generally (Antze and Lambek 1996, Cole 2001, Das and Nandy 1985, Feldman 1991, Kirmayer 1996, Linger 1992, Nordstrom 1992, Scheper-Hughes 1992).

2. See Chandraprema 1991, Gunaratna 1990, T. Gunasekara 1999, P. Gunasekera 1998, Peiris 1999.

3. Much of the material in this section borrows from the "Sri Lanka" entry in *Countries and Their Cultures* (Chapin and Silva 2001) that I co-authored with Kalinga Tudor Silva.

4. See the edited volume by Spencer (1990) for a discussion of the role of history in the conflict.

5. For an overview of Sri Lankan history, see Peebles 2006.

6. The preliminary report from the first islandwide census to be conducted in thirty years, which took place in February and March of 2012, put the population at 20,277,597 (DCS-SL 2012: 29).

7. The national census conducted in 2001, during the time of my first field stay in Sri Lanka, estimated the total population at 18,797,257 (DCS-SL 2001a). However, due to the civil war in the north and the east of the country, the census did not actually cover those areas and so used other records to estimate the total population. That 2001

census, which is the most recent reporting of population by ethnicity at the time of writing, reported the Sinhala population among the 16,929,689 people in the south to be 13,876,245 (DCS-SL 2001b), which comes to 73.8 percent of the total estimated population of the island.

8. The 2001 census excluded the areas of the island dominated by the Tamil population and the ethnicity breakdown from the 2012 census conducted after the war is not available at time of writing. Dennis McGilvray (2008: 7), who conducted extensive fieldwork in the conflict zone in the east, reported that Sri Lankan Tamils made up 12 percent of the total population.

9. The 2001 census reports the "Indian Tamil" population at 5.1 percent (DCS-SL 2001b), whereas McGilvray estimated the Up-country Tamil population to be 6 percent (2008: 8). For an ethnographic account of Up-country Tamil identity and politics, see Daniel Bass (2012).

10. See McGilvray 2008.

11. According to the 2001 Sri Lankan census (DCS-SL 2001b).

12. These statistics are drawn from the Sri Lankan Department of Census and Statistics (DCS-SL 2001c).

13. For an introduction to Buddhism, see Rahula 1974; for an introduction to Buddhism in Sri Lanka, see Berkwitz 2012; for deeper explorations of Buddhist practices in Sri Lanka, see Abeyesekera 2002, Bond 1988, de Silva 1981, Gombrich 1971, Gombrich and Obeyesekere 1988, Samuels 2010, Seneviratne 1999, and Tambiah 1992.

14. Figures for income reported by Sri Lanka's Department of Census and Statistics report, "Household Income and Expenditure Survey 2002" (DCS-SL 2002).

15. These statistics come from the Sri Lankan government's "Sri Lanka 2006–7: Demographic and Health Survey" (DCS-SL 2011b).

16. Sri Lankan government, "Sri Lanka 2006–7: Demographic and Health Survey" (DCS-SL 2011b). The US figures are for 2007 and come from the Center for Disease Control's "National Vital Statistics Report" (Mathews and MacDorman 2011). The figures for India are for 2005, reported by the Indian government's Central Bureau of Health Intelligence, India (2007).

17. For a classic overview of caste in Sinhala society, see Ryan 1953. See also a range of close ethnographic studies of how caste plays out and is being reconfigured in particular communities in Sri Lanka (e.g., Gamburd 2000, McGilvray 1982, Reed 2010).

18. See de Silva 1981.

19. For a nuanced demonstration of the relatively higher status of potter women in Sri Lanka as compared with India and its relation to caste, see Winslow 1994.

20. For two excellent ethnographic studies of women workers in the garment industry, see Lynch 2007 and Hewamanne 2008.

21. See Gamburd's (2000) intimate portrait of women's experiences with working abroad.

22. In 2010, Sri Lanka's Ministry of Education reported that in grades 1–13, there were 1,988,917 girls enrolled at government schools and 59,380 enrolled in private schools for a total of 2,048,297 girls attending school; at the same time, 1,951,155 boys attended government schools, 57,982 attended private schools, and 62,091 attended pirivenas run by the monasteries, for a total of 2,071,228 boys attending school (MOE 2010).

23. That the Sinhalese family structure is distinct from that which is common in the rest of South Asia offers the opportunity for productive regional comparisons, such as Obeyesekere 1984 has produced and McGilvray 1988 has critiqued. For descriptions of joint family practices as they play out in India, see Kolenda 1987 and Seymour 1999. The literature on the dynamics and psychological implications of the joint family

common in India, such as Good 1991, Kakar 1981, Kurtz 1992, Misri 1985, and Trawick 1992, also provide promising points of comparison.

24. For statistical evidence, see the Economic and Social Commission for Asia and the Pacific 1997. For ethnographic evidence and discussion of this, see Arachchige-Don 1994, Baker 1998, Obeyesekere 1984, Ryan 1958, Yalman 1971. Other ethnographies demonstrate the default centrality of the nuclear family with extended family the back up (e.g., Gamburd 2000, Samuels 2010).

25. For variation in this pattern, see Alexander 1982, Baker 1998, Obeyesekere 1984, and Yalman 1971.

26. In Yalman's 1971 analysis, he argues that there are consistent principles that form an underlying and enduring structure of kinship in this area encoded in the language and reflected in a variety of practices across Sri Lanka and parts of south India. These principles insist on caste endogamy, make bride price shameful, and entail the ideal of cross-cousin marriage that preserves the small, self-sufficient, in-marrying family group which is a model of what he calls the "micro-caste." He argues that these principles can be pushed in different directions, creating a variety of structures from matrilineal-matrifocal to patrilineal-patrifocal without violating the general form. Trawick 1992 extends this analysis regarding cross-cousin practices in south India, proposing that these cross-cousin matches may have as much to do with felt relationships and the establishment of certain longings as they do with rules and structures.

27. The average age for marriage of women, according to Sri Lanka's Department of Census and Statistics, has stayed at twenty-five for the years 1992–2006 in the Kandy district and twenty-four to twenty-five islandwide. The average age of marriage for men in the Kandy area over the same period was twenty-nine, with the national average fluctuating between twenty-eight and twenty-nine (DCS-SL 2013).

28. There is a small but growing literature that attends to the intimate and everyday lives of women in Sri Lanka (Gamburd 2000, Hewamanne 2008, Lynch 2007, Marecek 1998, Winslow 1980) and elsewhere in South Asia (Huberman 2013, Lamb 2000, Mines and Lamb 2002, Trawick 1992). This contemporary work on women and children's lives in Sri Lanka complements more general ethnographies that are helpful in establishing the patterns and general shape of life among Sinhala families (e.g., Alexander 1982, Arachchige-Don 1994, Baker 1998, Knox 1989 [1681], and Ryan 1958,).

29. See Goonesekere 1996 and Risseeuw 1996 regarding relations of the sexes in the precolonial period.

30. A notable exception, Obeyesekere (1981, 1984, 1990) has regularly linked child care practices to effects on adult personality in his work, although he does not generally describe the general cultural patterns of child care. When he has (1984), he has been taken to task for not basing this on systematic observation (McGilvray 1988). Murray Straus (1954, 1957; Straus and Straus 1957) also worked to link specific childrearing tasks to specific personality formations in among Sinhala people, but was not satisfied with the results. More recently, there have been two important ethnographies examining lives of Sri Lankan children, although these have each focused on children who are in unusual circumstances: Trawick, *Enemy Lines* (2007) and Samuels, *Attracting the Heart* (2010).

31. This pattern of periodic nighttime waking seems to have been around a long time in Sri Lanka. The late seventeenth-century recordings of Knox (1989 [1681]) report "Chingulays" (Sinhalas) of all ages getting up during the night, women tending to a fire and children warming themselves by it. He goes on to say, "They are so little given to sleep, that they do rise many times in the night to eat *Beatel* and to take *Tobacco*.

Which done they lay them down, and sing songs until they fall a sleep again" (262, italics in original).

32. In the analysis by Senarath et al. (2010) of data collected as part of the *Sri Lanka Demographic and Health Survey* in 2000, the year in which I began my fieldwork in Viligama, they found that, of the 1,127 children sampled from all but the most war-torn areas of the island who were under the age of two at the time of the study, 99.7 percent had been breastfed at some point. By the end of the first year, 85.7 percent were still being breastfed and, by the end of their second, 65.7 percent were. Van den Berg and Ball 2008 found similar results in intensive, semi-structured interviews about breastfeeding and nutrition collected in 2002 from sixty mothers of children between six months and four years old in Kandy and other parts of the island. All of those sixty mothers reported beginning breastfeeding as soon as their babies were born and continuing, on average, until the child was nearly three years old, although many gave other fluids as well. Solid foods such as liquefied fruits, vegetables, or rice were introduced by most mothers around four months old. Even so, most continued to breastfeed, as well, until their children reached a median age of 2.9 years, with one mother stopping as early as eight months old and another continuing past the child's third birthday.

33. Van den Berg and Ball 2008 reported that all sixty of the mothers slept in the same room with their child, and most (82 percent) in the same bed. This enabled frequent nursing throughout the night, an average of five times per night for babies under one year old, declining to two and a half times per night for one- and two-year-olds.

34. The average age the women in the van den Berg and Ball 2008 study reported having been weaned fully from their own mothers was at 2.8 years old, with a fifth of them saying they continued past their fourth birthday and a few until six, seven, or even eight years old.

35. The live birth rate for 1988–1993 was 2.26, as reported by De Silva 1994.

CHAPTER 3   SOCIALIZING DESIRE: DEMANDING
TODDLERS AND SELF-RESTRAINED CHILDREN

1. This chapter builds on an earlier article entitled "'We Have to Give': Sinhala Mothers' Responses to Children's Expressions of Desire" that was part of an *Ethos* special issue on "Mothering as Everyday Practice" (Chapin 2010).

2. This long-existing US cultural concern with "spoiling" has emerged in relation to anxieties about social change and the current generation of young people, articulated in such books as Maggie Mamen's "The Pampered Child" (2006).

3. Contrast this with US goals for the management of desires by mature children, who will ideally be able to rationally articulate their desires, accept delay or refusal, and negotiate reasonable compromises, while being "assertive without being hostile, and in control of his or her impulses" (Schmitt 2005: 309). Although there is much discussion and concern in the United States over how adults—be they parents or advertisers—may try to manipulate children into wanting different things, they are aiming to capture children's desire, to direct and recruit it to serve their purposes (Seiter 1998), not to eliminate it, as I am arguing is the desired outcome for Sinhala children.

4. Quinn herself discusses how this case "seriously complicates" and extends her analysis of these universals of childrearing (2010: 447).

5. Although this may look like a Batesonian "double bind," these are not "unresolvable sequences of experiences" (Bateson 1972: 206). Rather, these are exactly sequences *to*

be resolved as the maturing child comes to prioritize the correctly interpreted messages the mothers' emotional responses communicate and to escape, through disavowal, the conflict between those messages and the child's own wishes.

6. That a mother's physical gesture might suggest a psychodynamic move by a child was suggested to me by Naomi Quinn in a personal communication.

7. As Allen Johnson (1998) suggests by his analysis of disavowal and repression in light of a folktale told by Brazilian peasants, we might look for culturally sanctioned arenas for the indulgence of the normally disavowed desires, what some would call "projective systems." Maybe this is part of what is so appealing about certain giving and receiving events in Sri Lanka where people eat food from gods (as *prasad*) or from strangers (as *dana* during Poson) with great pleasure. It may be part of the way alcohol is used as a license for emotional outbursts of violence, tears, and sexual indulgence. And it may be part of the popularity of gods and goddesses who indulge their appetites, such as Kataragama, who is considered lusty and amoral, or even Kali who, in her demon form, craves blood and demands sacrifices.

8. I am indebted to Inoka Baththanage for pointing out the connection between ideas about envy and these fears having to do with food.

9. As discussed in the introduction, this description is not meant to convey the orthodox Buddhist view, but rather the ideas circulating in the talk of the people I worked with in Sri Lanka.

10. In Bryce Ryan's 1958 ethnography of a *Sinhalese Village* in the lowlands of the southwest coast of Sri Lanka, he observed that those *perethayas* who "do not yield to the power of the almsgiving ceremony . . . are likely to be those who were greedy, overly fond of their wives and children, or simply those who loved life too much" (113).

11. A brief study I undertook in the United States, interviewing US-born mid-life converts to Buddhism, provides an informative contrast by showing how this noble truth is understood in a different cultural context. Those whom I interviewed in the United States explained that desire caused suffering because, no matter how many of one's desires were fulfilled, this would never be satisfying, either because there would always be more things to want or because material objects were not the sources of true happiness.

12. Yalman observes in his earlier ethnography of a Sinhala village that it is the establishment of a separate hearth that defines the basic unity of the *ge* or family, which ideally "consists of a wife, unmarried children, and a husband" (1971: 102). He also says that the establishment of this separate hearth marks the turning point of "a casual affair" into a "more permanent relationship" (103) and that a woman feeding a man unrelated by blood gives people the idea that she is having sex with him (115).

13. *Prasad* is the remains from supplicants' gifts to the gods that are returned to people, considered clean for all to eat since it comes from and contains the essence of the deity, much as the leftover food from humans contains their saliva and so puts a bit of the first eater into subsequent ones.

14. Discussions of the complexities of gifts are woven throughout the history of anthropology and the anthropology of South Asia. One ethnographic account that is particularly relevant to my analysis is Gloria Raheja's analysis of ritual giving in a north Indian village, in which she explicates the ways that customary rights to give and obligations to receive act out and justify the dominance of the central caste. Through these ritual gifts (*dan*), those in a dominant position rid themselves of inauspiciousness, sin, and pollution by transferring it to those obliged to receive these gifts that are also spoken of as "'poison' (*vis*)" (1988: 32).

15. For an examination of the significance of a mother's identification with her demanding child under quite different social, economic, and cultural conditions, see Scheper-Hughes (1990). In the desperately poor neighborhood in Brazil that she describes, she says that sick or hungry babies remind mothers of their own unsatisfied needs, leading the mother to reject or deny the needs of her child (1990: 561).

CHAPTER 4   SHAPING ATTACHMENTS:
LEARNING HIERARCHY AT HOME

1. Alan Fiske (1991) has argued that there are four basic relationship models that people all over the world use; however, he makes it clear that people can and do switch between these models, even in interactions among the same set of people.

2. A similar contradiction about who leads weaning is reflected in the findings van den Berg and Ball reported from mothers in Sri Lanka, saying "The majority of breast-feeding mothers (34/46, 74%) favoured mother-initiated weaning of their child. The remainder favoured child-initiated weaning. Mothers reported that public health personnel had regularly recommended breastfeeding for at least 2 years or *until the child 'doesn't accept the breast anymore'*" (2008: 233, emphasis mine).

3. The teachers at one of the preschools in town expressed dismay to a fellow foreign researcher whose child was still wearing diapers at nearly three years old. Apparently finding it incomprehensible that these parents would put diapers on such an old child, the teachers approached the mother to find out if there was something wrong with the child.

4. This period starting around five during which people in Viligama expected that children would develop "understanding" correlates with *The Five to Seven Shift* (Sameroff and Haith 1996) that developmental psychologists identify as a key transition in children's development, something I will take up in the final chapter.

5. *Lajja* is a concept and term that has close cognates and similar importance throughout South Asia. It has been the subject of much literature and research, including ethnographic accounts such as Parish's 1994 work on *lajya* in Nepal, as well as Shweder's 2003 work in Orissa, India.

6. Barlow (2010) notes a comparable pattern among the Murik in Papua New Guinea, in which children's primary mother figures provide comfort rather than scolding when children misbehave while onlookers play a more critical role—although in that setting, the distribution of responsibilities is differently parsed and assigned than it is in Viligama.

7. For a comparative description of these first menstruation rituals in different ethnic groups in Sri Lanka and the concepts of womanhood they convey, see Winslow 1980.

8. At the time I conducted fieldwork in Viligama, half of people who were married said their marriages were arranged by proposal and half were love matches. Within the 71 households surveyed on a single day in Viligama in 2001, the residents reported 43 arranged "proposal" marriages, 43 "love-match" marriages. This includes one "love-match" that was an informal, common-law marriage and one "proposal" marriage of a widow in her nineties about which the respondents were guessing. Excluded are three marriages of older family members about which the respondents did not know. This represents the full set of households surveyed, an addition to the partial results reported in my dissertation (Chapin 2003).

9. See Chapter 2 for a fuller discussion of marriage and residency patterns in Viligama and around the island.

10. Not only do individuals have the right to refuse a marriage proposal, but women and men both have the right to leave unhappy marriages, even if it is considered scandalous and shameful to exercise this right—especially for women.

11. Given the care-giving relationship between spouses—although this is complicated and not fully one-directional, as discussed in Chapter 2—it could be argued that both women also entered the new charge of their husbands.

12. This model of a caring hierarchy I am describing for Viligama shares a family resemblance with valued forms of hierarchy throughout the region. See Marrow's description of hierarchy in north Indian families (2011).

13. For a comprehensive review of attachment theory, see Cassidy and Shaver 2008.

14. Quinn and Mageo 2013 provide a thorough review of these critiques and introduce further challenges, including my own, which I am reprising here (Chapin 2013). In addition, see LeVine 2004, and Weisner 2005.

15. Although key theorists, including Bowlby, who was British, and Ainsworth, who was Canadian, have come from other countries, the foundational research has primarily been conducted in the United States, along with studies in Western Europe and English-speaking countries. For notable exceptions, see Ainsworth's early work in Uganda (1967) and Ijzendoorn and Sagi-Schwartz's review of non-Western uses of attachment theory (2008).

16. The Strange Situation experiment was developed initially by Ainsworth out of her more naturalistic observations in order to present the kinds of stressors which would allow observation and assess of the quality of a child's attachment to the mother. For an overview of this experiment and the patterns it produced, see Weinfield et al. 2008.

17. In their review of the cross-cultural research on attachment, attachment theorists Ijzendoorn and Sagi-Schwartz conclude that "the studies are remarkably consistent with the theory. Attachment theory may therefore claim cross-cultural validity" (2008: 910), this despite the considerable variation in practices and patterns recorded in the studies they review.

18. For important examples of ethnographic observations that offer critiques of attachment theory, see Harwood et al. 1995, Keller and Harwood 2009, LeVine and Norman 2001, Morelli and Rothbaum 2007, Quinn and Mageo 2013, and Rothbaum et al. 2000.

19. For a particularly nice example of the encouragement for children to "use their words" in the United States, see Tobin et al.'s (1989) film of preschools in Japan, China, and the United States.

20. See Allen 2008 for a discussion of attachment in adolescence that entails these features.

CHAPTER 5   MAKING SENSE OF ENVY: DESIRES
AND RELATIONSHIPS IN CONFLICT

1. Although *irishiyava* is usually translated by the English term "jealousy," the strict meaning of which it also can convey, the usual meaning of the Sinhala term as my informants used it was to describe situations closer the English term envy. Of course, in contemporary US usage, the term "jealousy" also includes both envy and the more strictly defined jealousy, in which one feels or fears that someone else is taking away some rightful belonging, especially a person. The basic root meaning of envy might be put in Wierzbiecka's universal vocabulary (1992) like this: "When I see that you have something that I do not have, and I want that thing, I have this feeling."

2. In Sabini and Silver's discussion of envy, they borrow Heider's definition of envy as something a person feels "when he wants what someone else has just because that person has it. According to Hieider, this feeling, in part, derives from an 'ought force'—people who are similar should have similar outcomes" (Sabini and Silver 1982: 16). This definition is in keeping with the Sinhala concept of *irishiyava*, particularly in the ways it is activated between structural equals.

3. Sabini and Silver (1982: 16) distinguish between this use of the confession of envy as a compliment from its use as a moral violation. While this is a common way to convey a compliment in the United States, I never heard Sri Lankans use envy this way.

4. Parallel cousins are the children of same-sex siblings. Cross-cousins are the children of opposite-sex siblings.

5. This is in keeping with Lindy Warrell's 1990 analysis of networks of leaders and followers in a Sinhala village. It is also similar to Pocock's 1991 observations about the workings of envy-inspired *najar* ("the evil eye") in Gujarat, India.

6. This fits with caste regulations about eating and the contamination of food in which substance is transferred from person to person by their leftovers. As mentioned in Chapter 2, I found people in Viligama hesitant to talk about caste and to downplay its significance. However, the practices around cooking and food sharing are in keeping with the more overt caste structures and prohibitions found in other South Asian communities, such as those described by Parish among the Newar of Nepal (1994: 149–156).

7. Spiritual merit is earned by good works done during one's life, but it can continue to be accrued after death through the transfer of merit from good works done by others on behalf of the deceased.

8. In general, people in Viligama disliked eating leftovers. However, the leftover food of monks or from a temple was something people enjoyed.

9. That the girls would not feed each other directly may be simply a reflection of their hesitance about reconciling at that point. However, it may also be that this nonritual hand feeding the monk proposed felt too private to share publically or too intimate to do with someone not a lover or a parental figure. It may also be that the turn taking required for one to feed and then the other would have meant that someone had to put themselves in the junior position first, a subordination none of the girls was prepared to enact.

10. Many women from this area and all over Sri Lanka worked in the Middle East and elsewhere, typically as housemaids. Like Susanthika's mother, these migrant women were usually married and left children behind in the care of fathers and other relatives. For more information on Sri Lankan women who worked abroad and the effects on their families and communities, see Gamburd's 2000 study of a village on the island's southwestern coast. See also her 2004 analysis of the ways that remittances are used and talked about as having certain kinds of agency, and the intersections with envy, relationships, emotion, and aspiration.

11. Robert Levy (1973, 1984) uses the term "hypocognized" to describe those appraisals, perceptions, and emotions that are un- or under-elaborated with cultural models, so that they are difficult for people to identify, think about, or process explicitly. This is in contrast to those appraisals, perceptions, and emotions he calls "hypercognized," which are highly elaborated with cultural ideas and models, allowing them to be interpreted and processed in culturally scripted ways.

12. Although I am not arguing that Susanthika's primary problem was clinical depression, she did meet the diagnostic criteria for this disorder as established by American

Psychiatric Association (DSM-IV) during the period following her mother's return. She had both an "abnormal depressed mood" and "an abnormal loss of all interest and pleasure most of the day, nearly every day, for at least two weeks." In addition, she had a lack of appetite, slept much of the day, complained of fatigue and trouble concentrating, and spoke of suicide, all of which can be seen as additional symptoms of depression.

CHAPTER 6   ENGAGING WITH HIERARCHY OUTSIDE THE HOME: EDUCATION AND EFFORTS AT CHANGE

1. Ethnographers of education in other societies have similarly documented ways that deep, local cultural patterns shape what seems, on the surface, to be the same system of formal schooling everywhere. At the same time, Anderson-Levitt argues, "However thin the shell of global schooling compared to its rich local cultural content . . . global schooling nonetheless must have an impact on childhood experiences and notions of childhood" (2005: 993). This interplay of local cultural models and the impacts of globally circulating ideas about schooling is something I explore later in this chapter.

2. That students' interactions with their teachers are shaped by their interactions with their parents is something that university faculty in the US occasionally comment on in hallway conversations and more formal presentations. They observe that "millennials," as members of the current generation of US college students are called, expect praise, individual attention, and caring from their professors that earlier generations of students would not have, expectations that are in line with changing parenting practices in the United States.

3. This description is based on my conversations with students and teachers at different educational levels in Sri Lanka, as well as my direct observations, especially in the village school in Viligama and at Peradeniya University. Not only may the ways of relating between students and teachers be changing, as I discuss later in the chapter, but there is likely to be both patterned and idiosyncratic diversity across schools and across individuals in the ways that teachers, students, and their families relate. Differences in access to resources, language, and social class are particularly likely to shape this variation.

4. While I was conducting fieldwork, approximately 30 percent of students finishing their Ordinary Level of Education (eleventh grade) went on to Advanced Level education; of those, 50 percent qualified for university education—but only 15 to 16 percent of those were admitted to Sri Lankan universities, something that has been pointed to as source of social problems (Nanayakkara 2004:27).

5. Lindy Warrell has identified the historic precedent and contemporary day-to-day manifestation of the protection::service aspect of this relationship in her analysis of Sinhala political hierarchies that she calls "retinue," a system of bonds between leaders and their followers in "interdependent relations characterized . . . by an asymmetry of protection and service . . . [that] gives form to social life" (1990: 28). She emphasizes the necessity of followers' service and respect to the status and social power of the leader.

6. For further information, see Chapin 2008.

7. The ethnographic film *A God for All Seasons* (Nairn and Obeyesekere 1990 [1987]) offers visual documentation of this style of encounter in which the petitioners' own perception of their affliction is not needed, but rather the skills of the experts are demonstrated in their ability to identify the needs of a supplicant correctly. In the film, the

worried parents of a missing boy consult an astrologer to help find their son. Instead of asking why they have come, the astrologer tells them why they are there, why the boy is missing, and advises them what to do.

8. For a comprehensive review of Sri Lanka's education reform efforts and their political context, see Angela Little's 2010 report for the Consortium for Research on Educational Access, Transitions and Equity.

9. I am quoting these goals for educational reforms from the web pages of Sri Lanka's Ministry of Education (MOE 2009), goals which are also included in documents summarizing Sri Lanka's educational policy from UNESCO-IBE 2011: 2 and the United States Department of Labor 2011: 1.

10. The NEC includes the following recommendations for how children will be introduced to school: "At the point of entry the teacher will engage children in a series of specially designed play items and activities, with a view to identifying each child's capabilities at entry, as early as possible. This will help the teacher to plan the learning, teaching process according to the needs of each child. Throughout the learning-teaching process children will be assessed continuously, placing emphasis on informal methods of assessment. Towards the end of each key stage, children will be assessed to determine their levels mastery of Essential Competencies, lists of which will be available to the teachers. This will enable teachers to assess the degree of success achieved and to take corrective measures, where necessary" (NEC 1997: 12).

11. For comparable strategies in India, see Jocelyn Marrow 2008.

CHAPTER 7   CULTURING PEOPLE

1. On this occasion, one of Sampath's aunts was visiting his house with two-year-old twins. When the twins where examining Sampath's art project, it began to come apart, and Sampath, age eight at the time, moved to stop them. The visiting aunt scooped up the boys and left in a huff, angry with Sampath's mother because of Sampath's reaction, saying that he was old enough to know better.

2. There are important exceptions to this tendency of developmental psychologists not to look at childrearing across cultures, including Michael Cole (1990), Suzanne Gaskins (2006), Patricia Greenfield (2004), Gilda Morelli (Morelli and Rothbaum 2007), and Barbara Rogoff (2003).

3. Cultural models of relationships and goals for childrearing alter over time, in the United States as in Sri Lanka. They also may vary across class and other lines, as Annette Lareau (2003), Adrie Kusserow (2004) and others have documented for the United States. However, as Kusserow makes clear, basic cultural themes—like "individualism" in the United States—may cut across these lines, even if they emerge in different ways.

REFERENCES

Abeysekara, Ananda. 2002. *Colors of the Robe: Religion, Identity, and Difference.* Columbia: University of South Carolina Press.

Ainsworth, Mary D. Salter. 1967. *Infancy in Uganda: Infant Care and the Growth of Love.* Baltimore: Johns Hopkins University Press.

Ainsworth, Mary D. Salter, and John Bowlby. 1991. "An Ethological Approach to Personality Development." *American Psychologist* 46(4): 333–341.

Alexander, Paul. 1982. *Sri Lankan Fisherman: Rural Capitalism and Peasant Society.* Canberra, Australia: Australian National University.

Allen, Joseph. 2008. "The Attachment System in Adolescence." In *Handbook of Attachment Theory, Research and Clinical Applications*, 2nd ed., edited by Jude Cassidy and Phillip R. Shaver, 419–435. New York: Guilford Press.

Anderson-Levitt, Kathryn M. 2005. "The Schoolyard Gate: Schooling and Childhood in Global Perspective." *Journal of Social History* 38(4): 987–1006.

Antze, Paul, and Michael Lambek. 1996. *Tense Past: Cultural Essays in Trauma and Memory.* New York: Routledge.

Arachchige-Don, Neville S. 1994. *Patterns of Community Structure in Colombo, Sri Lanka: An Investigation of Contemporary Urban Life in South Asia.* Lanham, MD: University Press of America.

Baker, Victoria J. 1998. *A Sinhalese Village in Sri Lanka: Coping with Uncertainty.* Fort Worth, TX: Harcourt Brace College Publishers.

Barlow, Kathleen. 2010. "Sharing Food, Sharing Values: Mothering and Empathy in Murik Society." *Ethos* Theme Issue: "Mothering as Everyday Practice," edited by Kathleen Barlow and Bambi L. Chapin, 38(4): 339–353.

Barlow, Kathleen, and Bambi L. Chapin. 2010a. "The Practice of Mothering: An Introduction." *Ethos* Theme Issue: "Mothering as Everyday Practice," edited by Kathleen Barlow and Bambi L. Chapin, 38(4): 324–338.

———, eds. 2010b. *Ethos* Theme Issue: "Mothering as Everyday Practice," 38(4).

Bass, Daniel. 2012. *Everyday Ethnicity in Sri Lanka: Up-Country Tamil Identity Politics.* New York: Routledge.

Bateson, Gregory. 1972. *Steps to an Ecology of Mind.* New York: Ballantine Books.

Bateson, Gregory, and Margaret Mead, producers. 2005 [1952]. *Bathing Babies in Three Cultures.* 9 min. New York: Institute for Intercultural Studies; University Park: Audio-Visual Services, Pennsylvania State University.

Benedict, Ruth. 1934. *Patterns of Culture.* Boston: Houghton Mifflin.

———. 1946. *The Chrysanthemum and the Sword: Patterns of Japanese Culture.* Boston: Houghton Mifflin.

Berkwitz, Stephen C. 2012. "Buddhism in Modern Sri Lanka." In *Buddhism in the Modern World*, edited by David L. McMahan, 29–47. London: Routledge.

Bluebond-Langner, Myra. 1978. *The Private Worlds of Dying Children*. Princeton, NJ: Princeton University Press.

Bond, George D. 1988. *The Buddhist Revival in Sri Lanka: Religious Tradition, Reinterpretation, and Response*. Columbia: University of South Carolina Press.

Bourdieu, Pierre. 1977. *Outline of a Theory of Practice*. Cambridge, UK: Cambridge University Press.

Bowen, Donna Lee, and Evelyn A. Early. 1993. *Everyday Life in the Muslim Middle East*. Bloomington: Indiana University Press.

Bowlby, John. 1982 [1969]. *Attachment*, 2nd ed. Vol. 1, *Attachment and Loss*. New York: Basic Books.

Briggs, Jean. 1970. *Never in Anger: Portrait of an Eskimo Family*. Cambridge, MA: Harvard University Press.

———. 1998. *Inuit Morality Play: The Emotional Education of a Three-Year-Old*. New Haven, CT: Yale University Press.

Burr, Rachel. 2006. *Vietnam's Children in a Changing World*. New Brunswick, NJ: Rutgers University Press.

Carstairs, G. Morris. 1958. *The Twice-Born: A Study of a Community of High-Caste Hindus*. Bloomington: Indiana University Press.

Cassidy, Jude, and Phillip R. Shaver, eds. 2008. *Handbook of Attachment Theory, Research and Clinical Applications*, 2nd ed. New York: The Guilford Press.

Central Bureau of Health Intelligence, India. 2007. "Mortality Statistics in India 2006—Status of Mortality Statistics Reporting in India: A Report, March 2007," edited by Ashok Kumar, D. K. Raut, Pratima Gupta, and Umed Singh. http://cbhidghs.nic.in/Mortality%20Statistics%20in%20India%202006.htm, accessed January 19, 2012.

Chandraprema, C. A. 1991. *Sri Lanka: the Years of Terror: The JVP Insurrection 1987–1989*. Colombo, Sri Lanka: Lake House Bookshop.

Chapin, Bambi L. 2003. "Hierarchy, Envy, and Spirit Possession: Case Studies of Internalization among Sinhala Women in Central Sri Lanka." Ph.D. dissertation, University of California, San Diego.

———. 2008. "Transforming Possession: Josephine and the Work of Culture." *Ethos* 36(2): 220–245.

———. 2010. "We Have to Give: Sinhala Mothers' Responses to Children's Expressions of Desire." *Ethos* Theme Issue: "Mothering as Everyday Practice," edited by Kathleen Barlow and Bambi L. Chapin, 38(4): 354–368.

———. 2013. "Attachment in Rural Sri Lanka: The Shape of Caregiver Sensitivity, Communication, and Autonomy." In *Attachment Reconsidered: Cultural Perspectives on a Western Theory*, edited by Naomi and Jeannette Marie Mageo, 143-163. New York: Palgrave Macmillan.

Chapin, Bambi L., and Kalinga Tudor Silva. 2001. "Sri Lanka." In *Countries and Their Cultures*. edited by Melvin Ember and Carol R. Ember, Vol. 4: 2086–2099. New York: Macmillan Reference USA.

Chodorow, Nancy. 1974. "Family Structure and Feminine Personality." In *Woman, Culture, and Society*, edited by Michelle Zimbalist Rosaldo and Louise Lamphere, 43–66. Stanford, CA: Stanford University Press.

———. 1978. *The Reproduction of Mothering: Psychoanalysis and the Sociology of Gender*. Berkeley: University of California Press.

Clark, Cindy Dell. 2003. *In Sickness and in Play: Children Coping with Chronic Illness*. New Brunswick, NJ: Rutgers University Press.

Cohler, Bertram, and Scott Geyer. 1982. "Psychological Autonomy and Interdependence within the Family." In *Normal Family Processes*, edited by F. Walsh, 196–228. New York: Guilford Press.

Cole, Jennifer. 2001. *Forget Colonialism?: Sacrifice and the Art of Memory in Madagascar.* Berkeley: University of California Press.

Cole, Michael. 1990. "Cognitive Development and Formal Schooling: The Evidence from Cross-Cultural Research." In *Vygotsky and Education,* edited by L. C. Moll, 89–110. Cambridge: Cambridge University Press.

Committee for Rational Development. 1984. *Sri Lanka, the Ethnic Conflict: Myths, Realities, and Perspectives.* New Delhi, India: Navrang.

Csordas, Thomas J. 1994. *Embodiment and Experience: The Existential Ground of Culture and Self.* Cambridge, UK: Cambridge University Press.

D'Andrade, Roy G. 1995. *The Development of Cognitive Anthropology.* Cambridge, UK: Cambridge University Press.

———. 2008. *A Study of Personal and Cultural Values: American, Japanese, and Vietnamese.* New York: Palgrave Macmillian.

Daniel, E. Valentine. 1996. *Charred Lullabies: Chapters in an Anthropography of Violence.* Princeton, NJ: Princeton University Press.

Das, Veena, and Ashis Nandy. 1985. "Violence, Victimhood, and the Language of Silence." *Contributions to Indian Sociology* 19(1): 177–195.

DCS-SL (Department of Census and Statistics, Sri Lanka). 2001a. "Census of Population and Housing 2001: Population by District, Sex, Sex Ratio and Population Density." http://www.statistics.gov.lk/PopHouSat/PDF/Population/p9p2%20Population%20by%20district%20,%20sex,%20sex%20ratio%20and%20population%20density.pdf, accessed July 19, 2012.

———. 2001b. "Census of Population and Housing 2001: Number and Percentage of Population by District and Ethnic Group." http://www.statistics.gov.lk/PopHouSat/PDF/Population/p9p8%20Ethnicity.pdf, accessed July 19, 2012.

———. 2001c. "Census of Population and Housing 2001: Number and Percentage of Population by District and Religion." http://www.statistics.gov.lk/PopHouSat/PDF/Population/p9p9%20Religion.pdf, accessed July 19, 2012.

———. 2001d. "Population by Ethnicity according to Urban Area (Provisional)." http://www.statistics.gov.lk/census2001/population/district/t002c.htm, accessed through http://web.archive.org/web/20070610120717/http://www.statistics.gov.lk/census2001/population/district/t002c.htm, July 26, 2012.

———. 2002. "'Household Income and Expenditure Survey 2002." http://www.statistics.gov.lk/HIES/HIES2002/HIES2002_DistrictLevel.pdf, accessed September 18, 2012.

———. 2011a. "Social Conditions of Sri Lanka," http://www.statistics.gov.lk/social/social%20conditions.pdf, accessed January 18, 2012.

———. 2011b. "Sri Lanka 2006–7: Demographic and Health Survey," http://www.statistics.gov.lk/social/DHS%20200607%20FinalReport.pdf, accessed January 18, 2012.

———. 2012. "Population of Sri Lanka by District." In Census of Population and Housing 2011: Enumeration Stage February–March 2012, Preliminary Report (Provisional), April 20, 2012. http://www.statistics.gov.lk/PopHouSat/CPH2011/index.php?fileName=CPH%202011_R1&gp=Activities&tpl=3, accessed July 26, 2012.

———. 2013. "Population and Housing." http://www.statistics.gov.lk/page.asp?page=Population%20and%20Housing, accessed November 7, 2013.

De Silva, Deema. 2002. *Life Cycle Rituals among the Sinhalese.* Dehiwala, Sri Lanka: Sridevi Printers.

De Silva, K. M. 1981. *A History of Sri Lanka.* London: C. Hurst.

———. 1986. *Managing Ethnic Tensions in Multi-Ethnic Societies: Sri Lanka, 1880-1985.* Lanham, MD: University Press of America.

De Silva, W. Indralal. 1994. "Ahead of Target: Achievement of Replacement Level Fertility in Sri Lanka before the Year 2000." *Asia-Pacific Population Journal* 9(4): 3–22.

DeLoache, Judy, and Alma Gottlieb. 2000. *A World of Babies: Imagined Childcare Guides for Seven Societies.* Cambridge, UK: Cambridge University Press.

Du Bois, Cora. 1960 [1944]. *The People of Alor.* Vol. 1. New York: Harper & Row.

Dumont, Louis. 1965. "The Functional Equivalent of the Individual in Caste Society." *Contributions to Indian Sociology* 8: 85–99.

Economic and Social Commission for Asia and the Pacific. 1997. *Women in Sri Lanka: A Country Profile.* New York: United Nations.

Elliot, Anthony. 2002. *Psychoanalytic Theory: An Introduction,* 2nd ed. Durham, NC: Duke University Press.

Erikson, Erik. 1950. "Hunter across the Prairie." In *Childhood and Society*, 98–140. New York: W. W. Norton.

Ewing, Katherine P. 1991. "Can Psychoanalytic Theories Explain the Pakistani Woman? Intrapsychic Anatomy and Interpersonal Engagement in the Extended Family." *Ethos* 19(2): 131–160.

Feldman, Allen. 1991. *Formations of Violence: The Narrative of the Body and Political Terror in Northern Ireland.* Chicago, IL: University of Chicago Press.

Fingarette, Herbert. 1969. *Self-Deception.* London: Routledge.

Fiske, Alan Page. 1991. *Structures of Social Life: The Four Elementary Forms of Human Relations.* New York: Free Press.

Fong, Vanessa L. 2004. *Only Hope: Coming of Age under China's One-Child Policy.* Stanford, CA: Stanford University Press

Freire, Paulo. 1970. *Pedagogy of the Oppressed.* New York: Herder and Herder.

Freud, Sigmund. 1981 [1930]. *Civilization and Its Discontents.* Translated by James Strachey. New York: W. W. Norton.

Fung, Heidi. 1999. "Becoming a Moral Child: The Socialization of Shame among Young Chinese Children." *Ethos* 27(2): 180–209.

Gamburd, Michele Ruth. 2000. *The Kitchen Spoon's Handle: Transnationalism and Sri Lanka's Migrant Housemaids.* Ithaca, NY: Cornell University Press.

———. 2004. "Money That Burns Like Oil: A Sri Lankan Cultural Logic of Morality and Agency." *Ethnology* 43(2): 167-84.

Gaskins, Suzanne. 2006. "Cultural Perspectives on Infant-Caregiver Interaction." In *The Roots of Human Sociality: Culture, Cognition, and Human Interaction*, edited by N. J. Enfield and S. Levinson, 279–298. Oxford, UK: Berg.

Geertz, Clifford. 1973. *The Interpretation of Cultures.* New York: Basic Books.

Gombrich, Richard F. 1971. *Precept and Practice: Traditional Buddhism in the Rural Highlands of Ceylon.* Oxford, UK: Clarendon Press.

Gombrich, Richard F., and Gananath Obeyesekere. 1988. *Buddhism Transformed: Religious Change in Sri Lanka.* Princeton, NJ: Princeton University Press.

Gomez, Lavinia. 1997. *An Introduction to Object Relations.* New York: New York University Press.

Good, Anthony. 1991. *The Female Bridegroom: A Comparative Study of Life-Crisis Rituals in South India and Sri Lanka.* Oxford, UK: Clarendon Press.

Goonesekere, Savitri. 1996. "Gender Relations in the Family: Law and Public Policy in Post-Colonial Sri Lanka." In *Shifting Circles of Support: Contextualizing Kinship and Gender in South Asia and Sub-Saharan Africa*, edited by Rajni Palriwala and Carla Risseeuw, 302–333. Walnut Creek, CA: AltaMira Press.

Gosh, Amitav. 1983. "The Relations of Envy in an Egyptian Village." *Ethnology* 22(3): 211–223.

Gottlieb, Alma. 2004. *The Afterlife Is Where We Come From: The Culture of Infancy in West Africa*. Chicago, IL: University of Chicago Press.

Greenfield, P. M. 2004. *Weaving Generations Together: Evolving Creativity in the Zinacantec Maya*. Santa Fe, NM: SAR Press.

Gunaratna, Rohan. 1990. *Sri Lanka, a Lost Revolution?: The Inside Story of the JVP*. Kandy, Sri Lanka: Institute of Fundamental Studies.

Gunasekara, Tisaranee. 1999. "Insurrectionary Violence in Sri Lanka: The Janatha Vimukthi Peramuna Insurgencies of 1971 and 1987–1989." In *Ethnic Studies Report*, edited by K. M. de Silva, Vol. 17, No. 1. Kandy, Sri Lanka: International Center for Ethnic Studies.

Gunasekara, Prins. 1998. *A Lost Generation: Sri Lanka in Crisis: The Untold Story*. Colombo, Sri Lanka: S. Godage and Brothers.

Gunasekara, Tamara. 1994. *Hierarchy and Egalitarianism: Caste, Class, and Power in Sinhalese Peasant Society*. London: Athlone Press.

Hallowell, Irving. 2010 [1937]. "Psychological Leads for Ethnological Field Workers." In *Psychological Anthropology: A Reader on Self in Culture*, edited by Robert A. LeVine, 30–32. West Sussex, UK: Wiley-Blackwell.

Harkness, Sara, and Charles M. Super, eds. 1996. *Parents' Cultural Belief Systems: Their Origins, Expressions, and Consequences*. New York: Guilford Press.

Harwood, Robin L., Joan G. Miller, and Nydia Lucca Irizarry. 1995. *Culture and Attachment: Perceptions of the Child in Context*. New York: Guilford Press.

Heath, Shirley Brice. 1986. "What No Bedtime Story Means: Narrative Skills at Home and School." In *Language Socialization across Cultures*, edited by Bambi B. Schieffelin and Elinor Ochs, 97–124. New York: Cambridge University Press.

Hewamanne, Sandya. 2008. *Stitching Identities in a Free Trade Zone: Gender and Politics in Sri Lanka*. Philadelphia: University of Pennsylvania Press.

Hrdy, Sarah Blaffer. 2009. *Mothers and Others: The Evolutionary Origins of Mutual Understanding*. Cambridge, MA: Harvard University Press.

Huberman, Jenny. 2013. *Ambivalent Encounters: Childhood, Tourism, and Social Change in Banaras, India*. New Brunswick, NJ: Rutgers University Press.

Ijzendoorn, Marinus H., and Abraham Sagi-Schwartz. 2008. "Cross-Cultural Patterns of Attachment: Universal and Contextual Dimensions." In *Handbook of Attachment Theory, Research and Clinical Applications*, 2nd ed., edited by Jude Cassidy and Phillip R. Shaver, 880–905. New York: Guilford Press.

Jeganathan, Pradeep. 1998. "'Violence' as an Analytical Problem: Sri Lankanist Anthropology after July '83." *Nethra: Journal of the International Centre for Ethnic Studies* 2(4): 7–47.

Johnson, Allen. 1998. "Repression: A Reexamination of the Concept as Applied to Folktales." *Ethos* 26(3): 295–313.

Kakar, Sudhir. 1981. *The Inner World: A Psycho-analytic Study of Childhood and Society in India*. Delhi, India: Oxford University Press.

———. 1996. *The Colors of Violence: Cultural Identities, Religion, and Conflict*. Chicago, IL: University of Chicago Press.

Kapferer, Bruce. 1988. *Legends of People, Myths of State: Violence, Intolerance, and Political Culture in Sri Lanka and Australia*. Washington, DC: Smithsonian Institute Press.

Kardiner, Abram, and Ralph Linton. 1939. *The Individual and His Society: The Psychodynamics of Primitive Social Organization*. New York: Columbia University Press.

Keller, Heidi. 2011. "Attachment as a Biocultural Construct: Taking Biology and Culture Seriously." Manuscript in circulation for the Lemelson/Society for Psychological Anthropology Conference "Rethinking Attachment and Separation in Cross-Cultural Perspective," Washington State University, Spokane, May 19–21.

Keller, Heidi, and Robin Harwood. 2009. "Culture and Developmental Pathways of Relationship Formation." In *Perspectives on Human Development, Family, and Culture*, edited by S. Bekman and A. Aksu-Koç, 157–177. Cambridge, UK: Cambridge University Press.

Kirmayer, Laurence J. 1996. "Landscapes of Memory: Trauma, Narrative, and Dissociation." In *Tense Past: Cultural Essays in Trauma and Memory*, edited by Paul Antze and Michael Lambek, 173–198. New York: Routledge.

Knox, Robert. 1989 [1681]. *An Historical Relation of the Island Ceylon*, 2nd ed. Dehiwala, Sri Lanka: Tisara Press.

Kobak, Roger, and Stephanie Madsen. 2008. "Disruptions in Attachment Bonds: Implications for Theory, Research, and Clinical Intervention." In *Handbook of Attachment Theory, Research and Clinical Applications*, 2nd ed., edited by Jude Cassidy and Phillip R. Shaver, 23–47. New York: Guilford Press.

Kolenda, Pauline. 1987. *Regional Difference in Family Structure in India*. Jaipur, India: Rawat Publications.

Kulick, Don, and Bambi B. Schieffelin. 2004. "Language Socialization." In *A Companion to Linguistic Anthropology*, edited by Alessandro Duranti, 349–368. Malden, MA: Blackwell.

Kurtz, Stanley N. 1992. *All the Mothers Are One: Hindu India and the Cultural Reshaping of Psychoanalysis*. New York: Columbia University Press.

Kusserow, Adrie. 2004. *American Individualisms: Child Rearing and Social Class in Three Neighborhoods*. New York: Palgrave Macmillan.

Lamb, Sarah. 2000. *White Saris and Sweet Mangoes: Aging, Gender, and Body in North India*. Berkeley: University of California Press.

Lanclos, Donna Michelle. 2003. *At Play in Belfast*. New Brunswick, NJ: Rutgers University Press.

Lancy, David. 2008. *The Anthropology of Childhood: Cherubs, Chattel, Changelings*. Cambridge, UK: Cambridge University Press.

Lancy, David F., and M. Annette Grove. 2010. "The Role of Adults in Children's Learning." In *The Anthropology of Learning in Childhood*, edited by David F. Lancy, John Bock, and Suzanne Gaskins, 145–179. Walnut Creek, CA: AltaMira Press.

Lareau, Annette. 2003. *Unequal Childhoods: Class, Race, and Family Life*. Berkeley: University of California Press.

Leach, Penelope. 2010. *The Essential First Year*. New York: DK Publishing.

Lester, Rebecca J. 2005. *Jesus in Our Wombs: Embodying Modernity in a Mexican Convent*. Berkeley: University of California Press.

LeVine, Robert A. 1966. *Dreams and Deeds: Achievement Motivation in Nigeria*. Chicago, IL: University of Chicago Press.

———. 1980. "A Cross-Cultural Perspective on Parenting." In *Parenting in a Multi-cultural Society*, edited by M. D. Fantini and R. Cardenas, 17–26. New York: Longman.

———. 2001. "Culture and Personality Studies, 1918–1960: Myth and History." *Journal of Personality* 69(6): 803–818.

———. 2004. "Challenging Expert Knowledge: Findings from an African Study of Infant Care and Development." In *Childhood and Adolescence: Cross-Cultural Perspectives and Applications*, edited by Uwe P. Gielen and Jaipaul Roopnarine, 149–165. Westport, CT: Praeger.

———. 2010. *Psychological Anthropology: A Reader on Self in Culture*. West Sussex, UK: Blackwell.

LeVine, Robert A., and Karin Norman. 2001. "The Infant's Acquisition of Culture: Early Attachment Reexamined in Anthropological Perspective." In *The Psychology of Cultural Experience*, edited by Carmella C. Moore and Holly F. Mathews, 83–104. Cambridge, UK: Cambridge University Press.

Levy, Robert I. 1973. *Tahitians: Mind and Experience in the Society Islands.* Chicago, IL: University of Chicago Press.

———. 1984. "Emotion, Knowing, and Culture." In *Culture Theory: Essays on Mind, Self, and Emotion*, edited by Richard Schweder and Robert LeVine, 214–237. Cambridge, UK: Cambridge University Press.

Levy, Robert I., and Douglas Hollan. 1998. "Person-Centered Interviewing and Observation." In *Handbook of Methods in Cultural Anthropology*, edited by H. Russell Bernard, 333–364. Walnut Creek, CA: AltaMira Press.

Levy, Robert I., and Jane C. Wellenkamp. 1989. "Methodology in the Anthropological Study of Emotion." In *The Measurement of Emotions*, edited by Robert Plutchik and Henry Kellerman. New York: Academic Press.

Linger, Daniel Touro. 1992. *Dangerous Encounters: Meanings of Violence in a Brazilian City.* Stanford, CA: Stanford University Press.

Little, Angela. 2010. "The Politics, Policies, and Progress of Basic Education in Sri Lanka." Research Monograph No. 38, June. Consortium for Educational Access, Transitions and Equity (CREATE), Centre for International Education, University of Sussex, Falmer, UK.

Luhrmann, Tanya M. 1989. *Persuasions of the Witch's Craft.* Cambridge, MA: Harvard University Press.

———. 2012. *When God Talks Back: Understanding the American Evangelical Relationship with God.* New York: Alfred A. Knopf.

Lutz, Catherine A., and Lila Abu-Lughod. 1990. *Language and the Politics of Emotion.* Paris: Cambridge University Press.

Lynch, Caitrin. 2007. *Juki Girls, Good Girls: Gender and Cultural Politics in Sri Lanka's Global Garment Industry.* Ithaca, NY: Cornell University Press.

Mamen, Maggie. 2006. *The Pampered Child.* London: Jessica Kingsley.

Marecek, Jeanne. 1998. "Culture, Gender, and Suicidal Behavior in Sri Lanka." *Suicide and Life-Threatening Behavior* 28(1): 69–81.

Marriot, McKim. 1976. "Interpreting Indian Sociology: A Monistic Alternative to Dumont's Dualism." *Journal of Asian Studies* 36: 189–195.

Marrow, Jocelyn. 2008. "Exhorting with Reason in Psychotherapy and with Love in the Family." In "Psychiatry, Modernity, and Family Values: Clenched Teeth Illness in North India." Ph.D. dissertation, University of Chicago.

———. 2011. "Promises from the Ideal North Indian Joint Family: The Psychodynamics of Paternalism and Patriarchy." Paper presented at the Society for Psychological Anthropology's biennial meetings, Santa Monica, CA.

Mathews, T. J., and Marian F. MacDorman. 2011. "Infant Mortality Statistics from the 2007 Period Linked Birth/Infant Death Data Set." In *National Vital Statistics Reports* 59(6). Hyattsville, MD: National Center for Health Statistics. http://www.cdc.gov/nchs/data/nvsr/nvsr59/nvsr59_06.pdf, accessed January 21. 2012.

McGilvray, Dennis B. 1982. *Caste Ideology and Interaction.* Cambridge, UK: Cambridge University Press.

———. 1988. "The 1987 Stirling Award Essay: Sex, Repression, and Sanskritization in Sri Lanka?" *Ethos* 16(2): 99–127.

———. 2008. *Crucible of Conflict: Tamil and Muslim Society on the East Coast of Sri Lanka.* Durham, NC: Duke University Press.

McGowan, William. 1992. *Only Man Is Vile: The Tragedy of Sri Lanka.* New York: Farrar Straus Giroux.

Mead, Margaret. 1928. *Coming of Age in Samoa: A Study of Sex in Primitive Societies.* New York: William Morrow.

———. 1963 [1935]. *Sex and Temperament in Three Primitive Societies.* New York: William Morrow.

———. 1975 [1930]. *Growing Up in New Guinea: A Comparative Study of Primitive Education.* New York: Morrow Quill Paperbacks.

Miller, Peggy. 1986. "Teasing as Language Socialization and Verbal Play in a White Working Class Community." In *Language Socialization across Cultures,* edited by Bambi B. Schieffelin and Elinor Ochs, 199–212. Cambridge, UK: Cambridge University Press.

Mines, Diane P., and Sarah Lamb, eds. 2002. *Everyday Life in South Asia.* Bloomington: Indiana University Press.

Minturn, Leigh, and John T. Hitchcock. 1963. "The Rajputs of Kalapur, India." In *Six Cultures: Studies in Childrearing,* edited by Beatrice B. Whiting, 207–361. New York: Wiley Press.

Misri, Urvashi. 1985. "Child and Childhood: A Conceptual Construction." *Contributions to Indian Sociology* 19(1): 115–132.

MOE (Ministry of Education, Sri Lanka). 2008. "Indicators of the Child Friendly School Initiative in Sri Lanka." http://www.moe.gov.lk/web/images/stories/branchnews/indicators_e.pdf, accessed July 11, 2012.

———. 2009. http://www.moe.gov.lk/Education_his_2.html, accessed November 19, 2009.

———. 2010. "Sri Lanka Education Information 2010." Prepared by Data Management Branch, Ministry of Education, using school census data. http://www.moe.gov.lk/web/images/stories/statistic/sri_lanka_education_information_2010.pdf, accessed July 26, 2012.

Montgomery, Heather. 2009. *An Introduction to Childhood: Anthropological Perspectives on Children's Lives.* West Sussex, UK: Blackwell.

Morelli, Gilda A., and Fred Rothbaum. 2007. "Situating the Child in Context: Attachment Relationships and Self-regulation in Different Cultures." In *Handbook of Psychology,* edited by Shinobu Kitayama and Dov Cohen, 500–527. New York: Guilford Press.

Mosier, Christine E., and Barbara Rogoff. 2003. "Privileged Treatment of Toddlers: Cultural Aspects of Individual Choice and Responsibility." *Developmental Psychology* 39(6): 1047–1060.

Nairn, Charlie, and Gananath Obeyesekere. 1990 [1987]. *Kataragama: A God for All Seasons.* Granada Films, producers. New York: Filmakers Library.

Nanayakkara, A.G.W. 2004. "Employment and Unemployment in Sri Lanka: Trends, Issues and Options." Colombo, Sri Lanka: Department of Census and Statistics Sri Lanka. http://www.statistics.gov.lk/samplesurvey/emp_unemp_in%20sri%20lanka.pdf, accessed July 12, 2012.

NEC (National Education Commission, Sri Lanka). 1997. "Presidential Task Force Report on Reforms in University Education." http://www.nec.gov.lk/web/images/pdf/policies/National_Policy_1997-I.pdf, accessed July 11, 2012.

———. 2010. "Action Oriented Strategy Towards a National Education Policy." http://www.nec.gov.lk/web/images/pdf/policies/National_Policy.pdf, accessed July 11, 2012.

Nordstrom, Carolyn. 1992. "Backyard Front." In *Paths to Domination, Resistance, and Terror,* 260–274. Berkeley: University of California Press.

Obeyesekere, Gananath. 1981. *Medusa's Hair: An Essay on Personal Symbols and Religious Experience.* Chicago, IL: University of Chicago Press.

———. 1984. *The Cult of the Goddess Pattini.* Chicago, IL: University of Chicago Press.

———. 1990. *The Work of Culture: Symbolic Transformation in Psychoanalysis and Anthropology.* Chicago, IL: University of Chicago Press.

Parish, Steven M. 1994. *Moral Knowing in a Hindu Sacred City: An Exploration of Mind, Emotion, and Self.* New York: Columbia University Press.

———. 1996. *Hierarchy and Its Discontents: Culture and the Politics of Consciousness in Caste Society.* Philadelphia: University of Pennsylvania Press.

Peebles, Patrick. 2006. *The History of Sri Lanka.* Westport, CT: Greenwood Press.

Peiris, Gerald H. 1999. "*Insurrection and Youth Unrest in Sri Lanka.*" In History and Politics: Millennial Perspectives – Essays in Honour of Kingsley de Silva, edited by Gerald Peiris and S.W.R. de A. Samarasinghe, 165–199. Colombo: Law and Society Trust.

———. 2009. *Insurrection Twilight of the Tigers: Peace Efforts and Power Struggles in Sri Lanka.* New Delhi: Oxford University Press.

Pelka, Suzanne. 2010. "Observing Multiple Mothering: A Case Study of Childrearing in a U.S. Lesbian-Led Family." *Ethos* Theme Issue: "Mothering as Everyday Practice," edited by Kathleen Barlow and Bambi L. Chapin, 38(4): 422–440.

Pocock, David F. 1991. "The Evil Eye." In *Religion in India*, edited by Triloki N. Madan, 50–62. Delhi, India: Oxford University Press.

Quinn, Naomi. 2005a. *Finding Culture in Talk: A Collection of Methods.* New York: Palgrave Macmillan.

———. 2005b. "Universals of Child Rearing." *Anthropological Theory* 5(4): 477–516.

———. 2010. "Good Ethnographies Make Good Theories." *Ethos* Theme Issue: "Mothering as Everyday Practice," edited by Kathleen Barlow and Bambi L. Chapin, 38(4): 441–448.

Quinn, Naomi, and Jeannette Mageo. 2013. *Attachment Reconsidered: Cultural Perspectives on a Western Theory.* New York: Palgrave Macmillan.

Rae-Espinoza, Heather. 2010. "Consent and Discipline in Ecuador: How to Avoid Raising an Antisocial Child." *Ethos* Theme Issue: "Mothering as Everyday Practice," edited by Kathleen Barlow and Bambi L. Chapin, 38(4): 369–387.

Raheja, Gloria Goodwin. 1988. *The Poison in the Gift: Ritual, Prestation, and the Dominant Caste in a North Indian Village.* Chicago, IL: University of Chicago Press.

Rahula, Walpola. 1974. *What the Buddha Taught.* New York: Grove.

Reed, Susan Anita. 2010. *Dance and the Nation: Performance, Ritual, and Politics in Sri Lanka.* Madison: University of Wisconsin Press.

Risseeuw, Carla. 1996. "State Formation and Transformation in Gender Relations and Kinship in Colonial Sri Lanka." In *Shifting Circles of Support: Contextualizing Kinship and Gender in South Asia and Sub-Saharan Africa*, edited by Rajni Palriwala and Carla Risseeuw, 79–109. Walnut Creek, CA: AltaMira Press.

Rogers, John D., Jonathan Spencer, and Jayadeva Uyangoda. 1998. "Sri Lanka: Political Violence and Ethnic Conflict." *American Psychologist* 53(7): 771–777

Rogoff, Barbara. 1996. "Developmental Transitions in Children's Participation in Sociocultural Activities." In *The Five to Seven Year Shift: The Age of Reason and Responsibility*, edited by Arnold J. Samerroff and Marshall M. Haith, 273–294. Chicago, IL: University of Chicago Press.

———. 2003. *The Cultural Nature of Human Development.* New York: Oxford University Press.

Rogoff, Barbara, and Jean Lave. 1984. *Everyday Cognition.* Cambridge, MA: Harvard University Press.

Rogoff, Barbara, N. Newcombe, N. Fox, and S. Ellis. 1980. "Transitions in Children's Roles and Capabilities." *International Journal of Psychology* 15:181–200.

Roland, Alan. 1988. *In Search of Self in India and Japan.* Princeton, NJ: Princeton University Press.

Rothbaum, Fred, John Weisz, Martha Pott, Kazuo Miyake, and Gilda Morelli. 2000. "Attachment and Culture: Security in the United States and Japan." *American Psychologist* 55(10): 1093–1104.

Ryan, Bryce F. 1953. *Caste in Modern Ceylon.* New Brunswick, NJ: Rutgers University Press.

———. 1958. *Sinhalese Village.* Coral Gables, FL: University of Miami Press.

Sabini, John, and Maury Silver. 1982. *Moralities of Everyday Life.* Oxford, UK: Oxford University Press.

Sameroff, Arnold J., and Marshall M. Haith, eds. 1996. *The Five to Seven Year Shift: The Age of Reason and Responsibility.* Chicago, IL: University of Chicago Press.

Samuels, Jeffrey. 2010. *Attracting the Heart: Social Relations and the Aesthetics of Emotion in Sri Lankan Monastic Culture.* Honolulu: University of Hawai'i Press.

Sapir, Edward. 2002. *The Psychology of Culture: A Course of Lectures.* Reconstructed and edited by Judith T. Irvine. Berlin: Mouton de Gruyter.

Scheper-Hughes, Nancy. 1990. "Mother Love and Child Death in Northeast Brazil." In *Cultural Psychology: Essays on Comparative Human Development,* edited by James Stigler, Richard Shweder, and Gilbert Herdt, 542–565. Cambridge, UK: Cambridge University Press.

———. 1992. *Death without Weeping: The Violence of Everyday Life in Brazil.* Berkeley: University of California Press.

Schieffelin, Bambi B., and Elinor Ochs, eds. 1986. *Language Socialization across Cultures.* Cambridge, UK: Cambridge University Press.

Schmitt, Barton D. 2005. *Your Child's Health.* New York: Bantam Books.

Schwartzman, Helen B. 2001. *Children and Anthropology: Perspectives for the 21st Century.* Westport, CT: Bergin and Garvey.

Sears, William, and Martha Sears. 2003. *The Baby Book: Everything You Need to Know about Your Baby from Birth to Age Two.* New York: Little, Brown.

Seiter, Ellen. 1998. "Children's Desires/Mothers Dilemmas: The Social Contexts of Consumption." In *The Children's Culture Reader,* edited by Henry Jenkins, 287–317. New York: New York University Press.

Senarath, Upul, Michael J. Dibley, S.S.P. Godakandage, Hiranya Jayawickrama, Aravinda Wickramasinghe, and Kingsley E. Agho for the South Asia Infant Feeding Research Network (SAIFRN). 2010. "Determinants of Infant and Young Child Feeding Practices in Sri Lanka: Secondary Data Analysis of Demographic and Health Survey 2000." *Food and Nutrition Bulletin* 31(2): 352–365.

Seneviratne, H. L. 1999. *The Work of Kings: The New Buddhism in Sri Lanka.* Chicago, IL: University of Chicago Press.

Seymour, Susan C. 1999. *Women, Family, and Childcare in India: A World in Transition.* New York: Cambridge University Press.

———. 2004. "Multiple Caretaking of Infants and Young Children: An Area in Critical Need of a Feminist Psychological Anthropology." *Ethos* Theme Issue: "Contributions to a Feminist Psychological Anthropology," edited by Katherine Frank, Wendy Luttrell, Ernestine McHugh, Naomi Quinn, Susan Seymour, and Claudia Strauss, 32(4): 538–556.

———. 2013. "'It Takes a Village to Raise a Child': Attachment Theory and Multiple Child Care in Alor, Indonesia and in North India." In *Attachment Reconsidered: Cultural Perspectives on a Western Theory,* edited by Naomi and Jeannette Marie Mageo, 115–139. New York: Palgrave Macmillan.

Shweder, Richard A. 2003. "Towards a Deep Cultural Psychology of Shame." *Social Research* 70(4): 1109–1130.

Shweder, Richard A., Lene Arnett Jensen, and William M. Goldstein. 1995. "Who Sleeps by Whom Revisited: A Method for Extracting the Moral Goods Implicit in Practice." In *Cultural Practices as Contexts for Development,* 21–39. San Francisco: Jossey-Bass.

Sirota, Karen Gainer. 2010. "Fun Morality Reconsidered: Mothering and the Relational Contours of Maternal–Child Play in U.S. Working Family Life." *Ethos* Theme Issue: "Mothering as Everyday Practice," edited by Kathleen Barlow and Bambi L. Chapin, 38(4): 388–405.

Spencer, Jonathan, ed. 1990. *Sri Lanka: History and Roots of the Conflict.* London: Routledge.

———. 1999 [1990]. *A Sinhala Village in a Time of Trouble: Politics and Change in Rural Sri Lanka,* 2nd ed. Oxford, UK: Oxford University Press.

Spiro, Melford E. 1997. *Gender Ideology and Psychological Reality: An Essay on Cultural Reproduction.* New Haven, CT: Yale University Press.

Spock, Benjamin. 2004. *Dr. Spock's Baby and Child Care,* 8th ed., revised by Robert Needlman. New York: Pocket Books.

Straus, Murray A. 1954. "Childhood Experience and Emotional Security in the Context of Sinhalese Social Organization." *Social Forces* 33: 152–160.

———. 1957. "Anal and Oral Frustration in Relation to Sinhalese Personality." *Sociometry* 20(1): 21–31.

Straus, Murray A., and Jacqueline H. Straus. 1957. "Personal Insecurity and Sinhalese Social Structure: Rorschach Evidence for Primary School Children." *Eastern Anthropologist* 10(2): 97–11.

Strauss, Claudia, and Naomi Quinn. 1997. *A Cognitive Theory of Cultural Meaning.* Cambridge, UK: Cambridge University Press.

Tambiah, S. J. 1986. *Sri Lanka: Ethnic Fratricide and the Dismantling of Democracy.* Chicago, IL: University of Chicago Press.

———. 1992. *Buddhism Betrayed? Religion, Politics, and Violence in Sri Lanka.* Chicago, IL: University of Chicago Press.

Thiranagama, Sharika. 2011. *In My Mother's House: Civil War in Sri Lanka.* Philadelphia: University of Pennsylvania Press.

Tobin, Joseph, David Wu, and Dana Davidson. 1989. *Preschool in Three Cultures: Japan, China, and the United States.* 58 min. Fourth Wave Productions.

Trawick, Margaret. 1992. *Notes on Love in a Tamil Family.* Berkeley: University of California Press.

———. 2007. *Enemy Lines: Warfare, Childhood, and Play in Batticaloa.* Berkeley: University of California Press.

UNESCO-IBE (United Nations Educational, Scientific and Cultural Organization—International Bureau of Education). 2011. "Sri Lanka." In *World Data on Education,* 7th ed., 2010/2011; updated version, July 2011. http://www.ibe.unesco.org/fileadmin/user_upload/Publications/WDE/2010/pdf-versions/Sri_Lanka.pdf, accessed July 11, 2012.

United States Department of Labor. 2010. "Sri Lanka: Report on Child Labour, Forced of Indentured Child Labour and Other Worst Forms of Child Labour, and Efforts Made to Eliminate Such Child Labour." (Original source: Special Police Investigation Unit, Child Protection Authority, Sri Lanka.) https://www.dol.gov/ilab/programs/ocft/FR20100224/SriLanka/SriLankaSubmission.pdf, accessed July 11, 2012.

Van den Berg, Martina, and Helen L Ball. 2008. "Practices, Advice, and Support Regarding Prolonged Breastfeeding: A Descriptive Study from Sri Lanka." *Journal of Reproductive and Infant Psychology* 26 (3): 229–243.

Wallace, Anthony F. C. 1970 [1961]. *Culture and Personality.* New York: Random House.

Warrell, Lindy. 1990. "Conflict and Hierarchy: Jealousy among the Sinhalese Buddhists." *South Asia* 13(1): 19–41.

Weinfield, Nancy S., L. Alan Sroufe, Byron Egeland, and Elizabeth Carlson. 2008. "Individual Differences in Infant-Caregiver Attachment: Conceptual and Empirical Aspects of

Security." In *Handbook of Attachment Theory, Research and Clinical Applications*, 2nd ed., edited by Jude Cassidy and Phillip R. Shaver, 78–101. New York: Guilford Press.

Weisner, Thomas S. 1996. "The 5 to 7 Transition as an Ecocultural Project." In *The Five to Seven Shift: The Age of Reason and Responsibility*, edited by Arnold J. Sameroff and Marshall M. Haith, 295–326. Chicago, IL: University of Chicago Press.

———. 2005. "Attachment as a Cultural and Ecological Problem with Pluralistic Solutions." *Human Development* 48: 89–94.

Whiting, Beatrice Blyth, and Carolyn Pope Edwards. 1988. *Children of Different Worlds: The Formation of Social Behavior*. Cambridge, MA: Harvard University Press.

Whiting, Beatrice Blyth, and John W. M. Whiting. 1975. *Children of Six Cultures: A Psycho-Cultural Analysis*. Cambridge, MA: Harvard University Press.

Whiting, John W. M., and Irvin L. Child. 1953. *Child Training and Personality: A Cross-Cultural Study*. New York: Yale University Press.

Wierzbiecka, Anna W. 1992. *Semantics, Culture, and Cognition: Universal Human Concepts in Culture-Specific Configurations*. New York: Oxford University Press.

Winslow, Deborah. 1980. "Rituals of First Menstruation in Sri Lanka." *Man* 15(4): 603–625.

———. 1994. "Status and Context: Sri Lankan Potter Women Reconsidered after Field Work in India." *Comparative Studies in Society and History* 36(1): 3–35.

Winslow, Deborah, and Michael D. Woost, eds. 2004. *Economy, Culture, and Civil War in Sri Lanka*. Bloomington: Indiana University Press.

Woolf, Alan D., Howard C. Shane, Margaret A. Kenna, and Kathleen Cahill Allison. 2001. *The Children's Hospital Guide to Your Child's Health and Development*. Boston: Perseus Publishing.

Yalman, Nur. 1971. *Under the Bo Tree: Studies in Caste, Kinship, and Marriage in the Interior of Ceylon*. Berkeley: University of California Press.

INDEX

Note to Index: An *n* following a page number indicates a note; a *t* following a page number indicates a table.

ABOUT THE AUTHOR

BAMBI L. CHAPIN is associate professor of anthropology in the Department of Sociology and Anthropology at the University of Maryland, Baltimore County.

CPSIA information can be obtained
at www.ICGtesting.com
Printed in the USA
LVOW12s0035190816
500949LV00002B/129/P